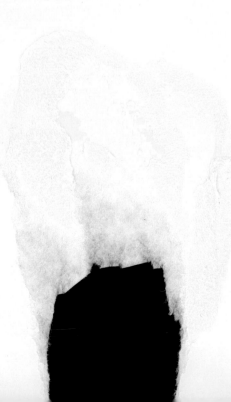

LIBRARY OF LATIN AMERICAN
HISTORY AND CULTURE

GENERAL EDITOR:
DR. A. CURTIS WILGUS

THE LIFE OF MIRANDA

General Francisco de Miranda. Portrait by an unknown artist. In the Suárez-Costa-Miranda Collection. Villa Selva e Guasto, Florence, Italy. Reproduced by courtesy of Signor Diego Suárez Costa y Miranda.

THE
LIFE OF MIRANDA

By WILLIAM SPENCE ROBERTSON, Ph.D.

Professor of History, University of Illinois

IN TWO VOLUMES
WITH THIRTY-EIGHT ILLUSTRATIONS
VOLUME II

COOPER SQUARE PUBLISHERS, INC.
NEW YORK
1969

Originally Published 1929
Published by Cooper Square Publishers, Inc.
59 Fourth Avenue, New York, N. Y. 10003
Standard Book Number 8154-0291-0
Library of Congress Catalog Card No. 77-79203

Printed in the United States of America

TABLE OF CONTENTS

VOLUME II

LIST OF ILLUSTRATIONS
VOLUME II

Chapter XV

A CLIMAX IN ENGLISH POLICY

AFTER THE decisive defeat of the French and Spanish fleets by the dear-bought glories of Trafalgar's day, England was in a position effectively to turn her efforts toward America whenever it might appear politic for her thus to check French ambitions. During Miranda's Caribbean cruise English publicists had ruminated about the policy which they should adopt toward the Spanish heritage overseas. French émigrés had directed the thoughts of Englishmen to the advantages which they would gain by Spanish-American emancipation. As Napoleonic arms on the Continent won success after success, English merchants were forced to pay increasing attention to the acquisition of markets in the New World. After the victory of the French eagles at the battle of Jena, Viscount Castlereagh, a political leader who had been a member of Pitt's last cabinet, had visions of the conquest of Mexico.

Yet English statesmen were still irresolute. On November 20, 1806, Turnbull wrote to Miranda that in a conversation with Lord Grenville the Premier had candidly explained that the cabinet felt toward Miranda as the French felt toward the Irish. "The Irish applied to the French to come and assist them, and they would all rise to coöperate with them—but the French said, 'Rise up first, and then we will come and assist you.' So Mr. Grenville said, that Ministers waited till the Americans should show their disposition to come forward." [1]

Obviously Miranda expected to probe the sentiments of English statesmen through the mission of his trusted agent Colonel de Rouvray, who arrived in London in December. Secretary Vansittart soon accompanied him to Downing Street where they conversed with the Prime Minister, Lord Grenville, and with William Windham, secretary for

---

[1] Mir. MSS., vol. 52.

war and the colonies.[2] On December 31, 1806, De Rouvray
submitted to Secretary Windham a memoir embodying his
master's sanguine views concerning the disaffection existing
among Spanish Americans and asserting that a force of four
thousand infantry could make considerable headway in South
America.[3] Though the emissary knew it not, a promising sign
was an interest in the Spanish colonies that had been awakened
in a member of the Anglo-Irish nobility named Sir Arthur
Wellesley, a prudent and capable military commander who
had won an enviable distinction in India. In February, 1807,
Sir Arthur sketched a project for an attack on Miranda's native province. He judged that after Venezuela had been cut
adrift from Spain, it would be wise for England to establish
an independent government at Caracas in order to check the
development of French interests.[4]

However, when the project of emancipating South America
seemed to have reached fruition, a serious difference arose between George III and his cabinet about the admission of
Roman Catholic officers into the English army. The outcome
was that the King dismissed Lord Grenville. Resulting changes
in the cabinet further delayed a consideration of Miranda's
designs. A new ministry came into power. The Duke of Portland became premier, while Lord Hawkesbury, George Canning, and Lord Castlereagh became respectively secretaries
of state for home, foreign, and colonial affairs.

Meantime John Turnbull urged the revolutionizing of the
Spanish Indies upon Lord Bathurst, president of the Board
of Trade; he also endeavored to have officials of the English
Treasury restore Miranda's allowance.[5] In May Castlereagh
laid before the cabinet a memorandum in which he presented
the alternative that England might either conquer or emancipate South America.[6] In a booklet entitled *South American
Independence* a writer on foreign affairs named William

---

[2] De Rouvray to Miranda, Dec. 18, 1806, Mir. MSS., vol. 53.
[3] Copy, *ibid.*   [4] Wellington, *Supplementary Despatches*, VI, 56-61.
[5] Turnbull to De Rouvray, April 14, 1807, Mir. MSS., vol. 53.
[6] Castlereagh, *Memoirs and Correspondence*, VII, 314-24.

Burke pleaded that Spanish America should be liberated by England not only through large naval forces dispatched to La Plata, Chile, Peru, and Mexico, but also by succor sent to Miranda.

That thwarted revolutionist now aspired to secure direct encouragement from Downing Street. On April 7, 1807, he addressed an epistle to Captain Popham to express the hope that this officer would soon be able to join him and "to coöperate in those wise and liberal plans which we maturely formed in England for the happiness, liberty, and independence of my native land, as well as for the prosperity, glory, and safety of your country." [7] On June 4 Miranda inscribed a letter to Admiral Cochrane to assert that a force sufficient to have opened all the ports of South America to English commerce was now paralyzed on the banks of La Plata River. With regard to the trial of Popham, who had been court-martialled for disobedience, he expressed a wish that this officer had made plain that the plans concerted with English statesmen contemplated not the conquest of South America but the establishment of its independence "for the Benefits of Trade and Commerce." [8] On June 10 Miranda sent a letter to Castlereagh to assert that a delay in the execution of his plans would subject South America to "the influence and domineering ambition of France" and to declare that his own efforts were at an end if he did not soon receive "the promised support" from England.[9] On the same day Miranda also wrote to Lord Melville, who had become a member of the Privy Council, to express the hope that this nobleman would aid in the immediate execution of plans "which had been so judiciously arranged." [10]

In his asylum in Trinidad Miranda received word through English sympathizers that Lord Castlereagh could not authorize him "to appear in any way, as an Agent of the British Government." The encouraging observation was, however, added that his "Lordship did not at all seem to have his mind

---

[7] Mir. MSS., vol. 53.   [8] *Ibid.*   [9] Robertson, *Miranda*, p. 403.
[10] Mel. MSS., f. 48.

made up against General Miranda; on the Contrary he said
that he wished much to see you and to converse with you fully
on the Subject; he appeared to be highly sensible of the Importance of preventing South America to fall into the Grasp
of the French, which can only be done by procuring for them
independence, and to be effected, but by the means of General
Miranda." [11]

That agitator now took his final resolution. Accompanied
by his secretary and a trusted captain named Downie, on October 24, 1807, Miranda sailed from Trinidad on the *British
Queen* bound for Tortola. De Rouvray, who opportunely met
his master there, assured him that his decision to proceed to
England was "a most important and decisive step in the present crisis of affairs." [12] On November 16 Miranda left Tortola
on board the frigate *Alexandria*, the flagship of the English
convoy. The voyage across the Atlantic was stormy and long.
More than a month elapsed before the voyager caught sight
of the Isle of Wight.[13] When he landed at Portsmouth on December 21 the ringers of the parish church welcomed him by
"a Peal on the Bells." [14] On the same day he secured a passport
for London that mistakenly described him as a "General in
the Army." [15]

Soon after his arrival in Grafton Street, with the aid of
Molini who continued to act as his secretary, Miranda undertook to pick up again the broken threads of his negotiations.
One of his first steps was to approach Secretary George Canning, an able publicist of the younger generation. On January
3, 1808, Canning sent a note to Miranda expressing a desire
to receive him on the following day at his residence in Stanhope Street,—an invitation which was promptly accepted.[16]
On the same day the revolutionary wrote to Lord Castlereagh
to inclose letters of recommendation, to ask for an audience,

---

[11] Turnbull to Vansittart, Sept. 25, 1807 (copy), Mir. MSS., vol. 56.
[12] Miranda to Vansittart, Nov. 16, 1807, *ibid.*
[13] Molini's Journal, *ibid;* Castlereagh, VII, 403, 404.
[14] The "Ringers" to Miranda, Dec. 31, 1807, Mir. MSS., vol. 56.
[15] Passport signed by W. Goldson, *ibid.*   [16] *Ibid.*

and to declare that he wished to make "some important communications." [17] On January 4 that Minister wrote as follows: "Lord Castlereagh presents his Compts. to General Miranda, and will be happy to receive him tomorrow in Downing St. at one o'clock, if that hour should not be Inconvenient." [18] Meantime the general wrote to Alexander Davison to explain that "Business of high importance" had prevented him from calling on his friends.[19] To this Davison made reply: "So soon as you shall have had your audience with the Great Folks, and at leisure, I shall be Happy to see you." [20]

Miranda soon met Canning and began to unfold his designs.[21] In a letter to Lord Melville on January 4 Miranda declared that he had already interviewed one of the ministers about South America. He asked Melville to recommend his projects to the cabinet; he declared that Venezuela and New Granada were "as well disposed now for emancipation as they ever were, and that a Force of 4 or 5,000 English Troops is quite sufficient to ensure the operation at this moment.—If a delay takes place I apprehend that in a very short time, we shall hear those Provinces proclaimed to belong to France— these at least were the rumors generally circulating in the Country, when I quitted the West Indies." [22] To this appeal Melville made an encouraging response.[23] In a letter to Governor Hislop the Venezuelan said that His Majesty's ministers had received him "with friendship and attention," and that they had listened to his plea "with interest and concern." [24] So certain did Miranda feel that a definite decision by the English Government was impending that he asked Hislop secretly to forward to a fellow conspirator named Francisco Febles the following letter conveying news of his negotiations:

"We have seen His Majesty's ministers who have charged

---

[17] Castlereagh, VII, 403.   [18] Mir. MSS., vol. 56.   [19] Jan. 3, 1808, *ibid.*
[20] Jan. 4, 1808, *ibid.*   [21] Miranda to Canning, Jan. 11, 1808, *ibid.*   [22] *Ibid.*
[23] Melville to Miranda, April 6, 1808, *ibid.,* vol. 57.
[24] Jan. 7, 1808, *ibid.,* vol. 56.

me in truth and sincerity to assure interested compatriots that
the matter is actually being considered and that without fail
in the next packet boat they will have positive information,
if not a formal decision, about the important business that
brought me to this capital. Transmit this news, without delay, to the Continent so that the friends of independence may
not become discouraged, and that, on the contrary, they may
resist French and Spanish influence until the receipt of my
later advice which will follow in the next mail. During the
interval proceed with circumspection, caution, and activity;
as the time is critical and very interesting for us. It would be
a misfortune not to use the occasion properly and to have that
recorded for future centuries. Consult and prepare what is
necessary with Governor Hislop to whom I have written at
length about the affair." [25]

While awaiting a decision by the ministers, Miranda conferred with Davison about the equipment of the proposed expedition. The contractor expressed his willingness to furnish
supplies on condition that he could "transact the business with
such a Character" as he esteemed Mr. Vansittart to be.[26] Despite Miranda's efforts to keep his activities secret, alert
journalists became aware of the negotiations. On January 9,
1808, the *Times* said that, as "past defeat is but a poor pledge
of future success," there were obstacles in the path to the
liberation of the Spanish Indies. It declared that General Miranda had no title to the confidence of Englishmen or Spanish
Americans. Yet it maintained that, because of Napoleon's designs, Miranda's object was desirable. That journal spoke
thus of those colonies that Miranda considered ripe for falling from the parent stem: "as all Europe is now enslaved, it
may be better for us to have free States, than dependent ones,
in the rest of the world: it diversifies interests and abates jealousy."

Shortly afterwards, with material that seems to have been
partly drawn from Miranda, Burke published a booklet en-

[25] Jan. 8, 1808, Mir. MSS., vol. 56.
[26] Davison to Vansittart, Jan. 8, 1808, *ibid.*

titled *Additional Reasons for our Immediately Emancipating Spanish America*. In this plea he again argued for the separation of the Indies from the Motherland. He maintained that Spain was now only a province of France, and that Miranda should be aided by a force of from six to eight thousand men to revolutionize Venezuela. Then troops could be sent to liberate the rest of the Spanish Indies. "A great colonial revolution," said Burke, "appears to me to be on the eve of taking place." [27]

On January 10, 1808, Miranda sent to Castlereagh a memoir concerning which he had received suggestions from Vansittart.[28] He declared that the people of New Granada and Venezuela still had a favorable disposition toward independence. Their apprehensions had been much increased, however, by rumors that Cuba and Puerto Rico had been secretly ceded to France. He intimated that the province of Caracas might be transferred to France by Spain in return for Portugal. In this distressing situation, as Miranda conceived it, he had proceeded to London to claim from English ministers "that assistance so long ago and so repeatedly promised, of supporting" the independence of Spanish America.

He now took the view that four separate governments should be established on the "Colombian Continent." The first independent state should include Mexico and Central America; the second should be made up of Venezuela, New Granada, and Quito; the third should be composed of Peru and Chile; while the fourth should include the Viceroyalty of la Plata. He expressed the opinion that the Spanish Americans had not shown a decided preference for any particular form of government. Their ambitions had been largely devoted to the achievement of independence from Europe and to the establishment of civil liberty. Identity of language, religion, and administration, he maintained, would much decrease the difficulty of changing the form of government "without convulsions."

Miranda also outlined a plan for military operations. He suggested that the attack should begin in northern South

---

[27] p. 87.   [28] Vansittart to Miranda, "Sunday," Mir. MSS., vol. 56.

America. If that section were revolutionized, and if the régime
established there were "wise and acceptable to the people,"
he expected soon to see the movement spread into Mexico from
Central America, into Peru from Quito, and into La Plata
from Peru and Chile. He estimated that an army of ten thousand men with a coöperating naval force would be sufficient
to carry out his project. The revolutionist used this opportunity to repel certain "illiberal insinuations" which he ap-
prehended had been made concerning his character. He declared that when he saw his fellow countrymen in the enjoyment of a "rational civil liberty" under a permanent form of
government that would "preserve it and promise them happiness," his "personal views and interest" would be "highly
gratified" and his labors "perfectly rewarded." The most significant difference between this scheme and Miranda's earlier
politico-military plans is the suggestion that instead of one
vast Spanish-American empire four distinct and independent
states should be created.[29] One of these nations should be
formed in the region that was later called "Great Colombia."

According to annotations preserved on the author's copy of
this memoir, it was submitted by Lord Castlereagh to the cabinet. A suggestion that Miranda had been authorized by English ministers to transmit to Trinidad the news that their government was about to carry out his plans provoked objections
from Castlereagh. In the words of Miranda, this Secretary
took the view that as he was not a prime minister "he could not
take upon himself (as Mr. Pitt did before), to transmit it to
the Provinces of South America, where in fact it had already
been sent; though he agreed that the communication was correct and desirable; but ought to be taken upon myself and
omitted in this Memoir." [30] In consequence the promoter had
an interview with Sir Charles Stewart, a half-brother of Castlereagh who was serving as under secretary of war. Stewart
pointed out specific passages in the memoir that ought to be
modified. Miranda accordingly made the required corrections.

---

[29] Castlereagh, VII, 405-12.   [30] Mir. MSS., vol. 56.

He sent word to Governor Hislop to suppress the letter that he had transmitted on January 7, 1808; he asked that Febles should be informed that he could not pledge the faith of English ministers to revolutionize Spanish America.[31]

On January 16 Miranda again addressed Lord Castlereagh to state that he had declined offers of pecuniary assistance to fit out an expedition to South America until he could hear from him. At the same time he submitted a project of military operations. In this sketch he proposed that the soldiers intended for the attack on northern South America should embark at Portsmouth or Plymouth and proceed under convoy to Grenada. After being strengthened by forces from Barbadoes and Trinidad, the expedition should rendezvous at the island of Tortuga on the Venezuelan coast. A landing should be made near La Guaira; then the invaders should march against the city of Caracas. After the fall of that city, La Guaira and Puerto Cabello were to be invested, with the aid of a naval squadron. When La Guaira was captured, a detachment of native recruits commanded by English officers should move against Angostura, Cumaná, and Barinas. Then Mérida, Coro, and Maracaibo should be attacked. After Venezuela had been overrun by Anglo-Venezuelan soldiers, they should next march against Santa Marta in New Granada. While English warships were blockading Cartagena, a land and naval force should proceed to the Isthmus to seize Chagres and the city of Panama. The possession of the Isthmus of Panama would facilitate English commercial intercourse with Spanish Americans; and it would furnish a naval base for operations against Spanish colonies on the shores of the Pacific. The city of Mexico could be most easily approached from Acapulco. The Bay of Panama would afford a convenient rendezvous for warships which were to proceed against important cities on the Pacific coast of South America.

Miranda made an estimate of the force required for the operations between La Guaira and Panama. His figures included

---

[31] Miranda to Hislop, Jan. 22, 1808, W. O., mis. series, 3/1118.

6,000 infantry, 2,000 light cavalry, 2,000 negro soldiers, and 300 artillerymen, besides flying artillery and engineers. He asked for 30,000 muskets, 50,000 iron heads for pikes, 2,000 pair of pistols, 4,000 swords for cavalry, clothing for a regiment of light cavalry and for 10,000 infantry, besides saddles, cannon, and ammunition. In commenting upon his project for the military operations, Miranda sanguinely remarked that this force might appear inadequate for the purpose and operations which had been discussed, but the ministers should "consider that the Country may immediately afford a body of 20,000 Men of good Militia that will join us with alacrity and that the disposition of the Inhabitants in favor of Independence is such, that we may expect, their cordial support and coöperation." [32]

Though Miranda's new pleas in regard to Spanish-American emancipation were for the time being in vain, yet his complaints about straitened finances were not without effect. On January 19, 1808, Davison sent a brief letter to convey the welcome information that he inclosed five hundred pounds to prevent him from being harassed by private or domestic inconveniences while his mind was occupied with matters of such importance to himself and the State.[33] Through this friend Miranda succeeded in getting some desired information from his former coadjutor, Sir Home Popham, who had been reprimanded for leading English squadrons against Buenos Aires.[34]

From 1806 to 1808 Miranda thus renewed his relations with English statesmen. Though William Pitt had passed away, yet upon Miranda's return to London he found other ministers who were ready to consider the revolutionary projects that he had freshly formulated. Prominent among those English publicists whose interest in the Spanish Indies was now stimulated were George Canning, Lord Castlereagh, and Sir Arthur Wellesley. At this epoch it seemed to become more

---

[32] "London, 16th January, 1808, Military Memoir," Mir. MSS., vol. 56.
[33] *Ibid.*   [34] Davison to Miranda, Jan. 29, 1808, *ibid.*

*Sir Arthur Wellesley. Painting by John Hoppner, R. A.,
in the National Gallery, London. Mezzotint by W. W.
Barney. In the collection of the British Museum.*

and more evident to thoughtful Englishmen that definite steps should soon be taken to keep the magnificent Spanish heritage in America from falling into the hands of the conquering Napoleon. More than ever on the alert for favorable circumstances, Miranda may be likened to a watcher who was waiting for the morning.

During January, 1808, Miranda became acquainted with Sir Arthur Wellesley, who had been made lieutenant general. In a collection of visiting cards that the revolutionary preserved are various billets of Sir Arthur. These curt epistles do not yield much information, however, about his attitude toward Miranda's designs. As an illustration read the following note which the Englishman sent the promoter from Harley Street on January 31: "Sir Arthur Wellesley presents his Compliments to General Miranda and will be much obliged to him, if he will call upon Sir Arthur at any hour which may be most convenient to the General in the course of today." [35] The conversation on that occasion pertained to South America; for on February 1 Miranda sent to the English commander certain topographic maps that he had mentioned on the previous evening. Three days later he forwarded to Wellesley documents concerning Gual's activity in Venezuela which he begged him "to peruse with attention," and to add to those which he had "left with him on Sunday last." [36]

The Tory commander, however, was evidently loath to consider the liberation of the Spanish colonists. "I always had a horror," he admitted afterwards, "of revolutionizing any country for a political object. I always said, if they rise of themselves, well and good, but do not stir them up; it is a fearful responsibility." [37]

A memoir that Sir Arthur Wellesley composed on February 8 was evidently framed by the aid of data obtained from Miranda. Wellesley expressed the opinion that the only mode of separating the Viceroyalty of la Plata from Spain was by an

---

[35] Mir. MSS., vol. 56.   [36] *Ibid.*
[37] Stanhope, *Notes of Conversations with the Duke of Wellington*, p. 69.

insurrection which would establish an independent government. He was not convinced that the failure of Miranda's attempt to revolutionize Venezuela in 1806 proved that her people were any less favorable to a revolution than they had been in 1797. Sagaciously did he declare, however, that he had not seen any proof from Miranda that the Venezuelans showed a disposition to revolt. In his judgment the most suitable regions for operations in the Spanish Indies were Mexico and Venezuela. Personally he favored an attack on Venezuela in December with a land and naval force. With regard to the political régime, he proposed to establish in each Viceroyalty a monarchical system of government with a representative legislature. In a supplementary memoir Wellesley outlined a plan of operations that might be pursued against northern South America. The Englishman proposed that the island of Grenada should be made the rendezvous for an expedition of ten thousand soldiers that should first attack Venezuela and then "should proceed to the further conquest of the country towards Santa Fé de Bogotá." [38] It would seem that at this time Wellesley was contemplating the annexation of the liberated regions to the British Empire.

As he found General Wellesley receptive to his plans, Miranda continued to press the advantage. On February 20 he wrote to that general to explain that, because of illness, he had not been able to call upon him for some days. "He will do himself the honor to call on Sir Arthur tomorrow morning about 11 o'clock in hopes of finding him at Home, and having a few minutes Conversation on an important subject.—If that hour is not convenient, he begs Sir Arthur will appoint any other time that may suit him." [39] Evidently Miranda's health was precarious; for on March 3 he addressed a note to Wellesley to state that as soon as he was "able to move out," he would "take a Coach and call at Harley Street." [40] In a letter to Wellesley ten days later Miranda explained his apparent neglect:

---

[38] Wellington, *Supplementary Despatches,* VI, 68.
[39] Mir. MSS., vol. 56.   [40] *Ibid.,* vol. 57.

"My convalescence is proceeding much more slowly than I had imagined last Sunday when I believed that in three or four days I should be able to call upon you, and that we could converse about documents which we have mentioned regarding the events that have transpired at Buenos Aires and so forth. But although my body is free from fever or any other malady, I feel so weak on my legs that it is impossible for me to walk outside my house. Meantime I am employed in securing all the necessary information from the Peruvian named Padilla, who appears to me a person of integrity and well informed concerning all that has been done or thought in regard to the Hispanic-American people as well as in regard to the heads of the governments in the Spanish Indies during these disastrous events.

"I am always at your orders, my general, and very impatient to see you and to do something to promote the important object with which we are occupied. It is my hope that in the course of next week, I shall be able to have the pleasure of visiting you, unless you judge it convenient that I should call sooner." [41]

On March 16, 1808, Miranda wrote to Sir Arthur to congratulate him on a triumph that his brother, Marquis Wellesley, had scored in the House of Commons. He stated that Lord Melville, who had just arrived from Scotland, was "a true friend of the great project," and declared that existing conditions seemed to make the time opportune to bring "our affairs to a definite conclusion." He expressed the hope that he might have an interview with General Wellesley in the course of that week.[42] In a letter addressed to Admiral Cochrane two days later Miranda stated that he had "every reason" to believe that the majority of the ministers were "as well disposed for the measure as yourself and I could wish." He averred that Lord Melville would soon be appointed first lord of the admiralty and that Marquis Wellesley would supersede the Duke of Portland as prime minister. In a postscript he asserted that certain soldiers who were preparing to embark

---

[41] *Ibid.*   [42] *Ibid.*

from England would probably never go to Sweden.[43] On
March 26 Miranda addressed another note to General Wellesley. "I find myself," he wrote, "almost completely recovered
from my fever. I shall have the honor of visiting you tomorrow about noon in order that we may converse for a few moments about the matter in question. I hope that this time will
not inconvenience you: I shall bring with me Mr. Padilla so
that I may present him to you and get some information from
him, if you judge this proper." [44] The following reply was
sent on Sunday morning: "Sir Arthur Wellesley presents his
Compliments to General Miranda: Sir Arthur has received
the General's note and will be happy to see him in Harley
Street about 12 o'clock today." [45]

In the spring of 1808 a measure by which England might
promote the separation of the Spanish colonies from the
Motherland was indeed growing in favor in London. Early in
April, Wellesley conversed with Padilla about the sentiments
of the people of La Plata toward the English as well as their
attitude toward independence.[46] On April 23 the *Courier* expressed the view that England should direct her main efforts "towards the dominions of Spain in America, and
India. * * * Independence and alliance should be held out
to them. * * * Let us see one great Expedition going forth,
four times as strong as is supposed to be necessary, thereby
insuring success, and passing from place to place, emancipating countries from the yoke of our enemies, thus raising up a
new world of friends to supply the place of the one we have
lost."

In the same month Miranda addressed a suggestive epistle
to a leader of the malcontents of La Plata named Saturnino
Rodríguez Peña of whom he had presumably learned through
compatriots. The incendiary expressed the conviction that at
this crisis the South Americans should prepare those steps
which were necessary and convenient for "the absolute emancipation" of their country. He declared that England would

---

[43] Mir. MSS., vol. 57.   [44] *Ibid.*   [45] *Ibid.*
[46] Padilla to Wellesley, April 8, 1808 (copy), *ibid.*

soon furnish "the aid that was necessary to carry out a design which was as magnificent as it was useful and necessary,— especially as the last events in Madrid and Aranjuez have made the world see that decrepit Spain is neither able to manage her own affairs nor to govern the Colombian Continent which is twice as extensive as all Europe and has twice its population. * * * Never has there been discussed on earth a more holy cause,—a cause more just or more necessary for humankind,—than that which our duty and right oblige us to defend! In their defense and in the repulse of the invader the people of Buenos Aires have given a beautiful and noble example:—let Colombia follow and let her friends say to each other: *'Patriae infelici fidelis!'* " [47]

Events that transpired in Spain afforded fresh hope to the friends of Spanish-American emancipation. On March 19, 1808, after a tumult at Aranjuez had forced the chief Minister of Spain, Godoy, the Prince of the Peace, to renounce his ministry, King Charles IV abdicated the Spanish throne in favor of his eldest son and heir, Ferdinand, Prince of Asturias. On the pretext that his health would no longer permit him to act as sovereign, Charles IV declared that Ferdinand should be recognized and obeyed as the monarch of all his kingdoms and dominions. To Joachim Murat, who had entered Madrid with a French army on March 23, Ferdinand announced that he had received from his father the crown of Spain and the Indies. These startling events attracted the attention of Miranda who appreciated their significance. His well-wisher Captain Popham felt that the promoter was distracted by the Spanish dissensions. A letter from Popham dated April 20 conveyed the advice that he should be more attentive to Davison "and dont let the disturbances in Spain so occupy your mind, as to divert your attention from the proper point. I wish you always success in all your operations. * * * If I had not more real sense in my little finger about the principle

---

[47] Navarro y Lamarca, *Compendio de la historia general de América*, II, 552-53.

and policy of expeditions than many of your office friends, I would cut it off and give it to a Dutchman for a Tobacco Stopper." [48]

On May 5, 1808, Miranda wrote a *"most secret"* letter to his friend Admiral Cochrane. His view of the international situation was thus expressed in the opening passage: "With much pleasure I received your favor of the 20th. Feby. last— and hope you have prepared in your mind all that is necessary on your side for the execution of our dear and grand object.— On this subject I will only tell you now, that the thing is ultimately decided, according to our own wishes, and that I shall very soon have the satisfaction of taking you by the Hand. (Keep this to yourself.)" [49] On May 8 the French Emperor induced the ex-King to renounce by treaty all his rights to the Spanish throne. Napoleon also forced the reluctant Ferdinand VII to endorse his father's abdication in favor of Napoleon, and to renounce his rights as heir to the crown of Spain and the Indies. On May 16 Miranda took advantage of these Napoleonic usurpations to present his views to Lord Castlereagh. He reasoned that the "late eventful occurrences in Spain" were closely related to their plans concerning the Spanish Indies and that, if they did not avail themselves of "this grand and providential opportunity," they might afterwards lament their neglect forever. He argued that, if the English appeared before the Spanish Americans offering them aid for "emancipation, rational liberty, and independence," everything would favor them but that, if the French arrived first with some plausible scheme and suitable intrigues, the project of liberation might be thwarted or defeated. [50]

Napoleonic usurpations in Spain naturally incited English ministers to consider immediate action in regard to the Indies. Castlereagh soon enunciated the view that the cabinet should make every effort to prevent the Spanish colonies "from falling into the hands of the French. * * * " [51] Miranda con-

---

[48] Mir. MSS., vol. 57.   [49] *Ibid.*   [50] Castlereagh, VII, 441-42.
[51] *Ibid.*, VI, 365.

tinued to have conferences with Arthur Wellesley; he brought to that officer's attention the uprising of the Spanish patriots against the French, as well as a project that had been formed by Eustace in 1790 for an English attack on the province of Caracas.[52] On May 26 Miranda wrote to Spencer Perceval, who was now chancellor of the exchequer, not only to remind him of a promised interview but also to mention "the late awful Events in Spain" as pregnant with "the most alarming consequences for the future state" of the Spanish colonies. He expressed the view that the present juncture was "so important for the purpcse of carrying into execution any measures towards their emancipation and Independency, that any further delay might be materially injurious both to the interests of Great Britain, as well as to the preservation of South America." [53]

About this time Miranda made another attempt to have an interview with Canning; for he wrote to him to mention the "late awful events in Spain" that were decisive in Europe and "of the most alarming consequences" for the Spanish Indies. "He conceives in fact the present moment to be so important for the purpose of carrying into execution any measures relative to their Emancipation and Independence, that any further delay might be materially injurious both to the interests of Great Britain, as to the preservation of South America.— In this conviction he would deem himself highly blameable, if he was to omit now every effort in his power, toward insuring the success of so desirable and most important Object." [54] After considerable delay the Minister replied in the third person: "The pressure of public business has alone prevented Mr. Canning from sooner acknowledging the honour of General Miranda's notes; and from appointing a time for the honour of seeing Gen. Miranda which however he the less regrets as he has had the satisfaction of learning that General Miranda was in communication with that Department to

---

[52] Miranda to Wellesley, May 25, 1808, Mir. MSS., vol. 57.
[53] *Ibid.*   [54] May 26, 1808, *ibid.*

which this Business referred in his notes properly belongs." [55]
In fact, on May 27 Perceval had sent a brief note to Miranda
stating that he would "be happy to see him on Saturday next
at one o'clock." [56]

In the early summer of 1808, the English Government was
contemplating decisive measures in respect to the Spanish
Indies. On June 4 the Duke of Manchester, who was governor
of Jamaica, was instructed to communicate with the Captain
General of Cuba in order to defeat any designs that Napoleon
might entertain upon the Spanish colonies. If the Captain
General was willing to enter into relations with the English,
Lord Manchester was to concert military measures that would
prevent the introduction of French soldiers into Cuba. Publications were transmitted to Manchester and to the commander
of the English soldiers in the Leeward Islands that described
the conduct of Spain toward France in such terms as would
tend to promote the separation of the Spanish colonies from
the Motherland. Manchester was informed that, if the Spanish governors of Cuba and Florida were disposed to act in concert with him, he might even advance money to them.[57]

Further, the ministers were arranging for the dispatch of
a corps of some 8,000 soldiers from Ireland to join General
Spencer on the Spanish coast. If circumstances did not promise success in Spain, the government intended that these soldiers, reënforced by General Spencer's army of some 5,000
men, either should sail to the West Indies to attack the Spanish colonies near the Gulf of Mexico or should be divided into
two expeditions which were respectively to attack Venezuela
and La Plata.[58] Sir Arthur Wellesley prepared a detailed
memorandum of the arms and munitions required for these
projects. In the specifications regarding the attack on Venezuela the English officer proposed that 18,000 muskets with
bayonets, 18,000 pikes, 75,000 musket flints, and 3,000,000
ball cartridges should be at once sent to the West Indies with

[55] June 18, 1808, Mir. MSS., vol. 57.   [56] Ibid.
[57] Robertson, Miranda, pp. 408-10.   [58] Wellington, VI, 68-72.

the soldiers from Spain. A generous amount of additional supplies, including intrenching tools for 16,000 men, were later to be sent from England. As soon as further communication could be had with Miranda, there was to be presented to the ministers a "list of ordnance and stores required for the use of the native government expected to be established in South America." [59] At last the English Government had actually decided upon the revolutionizing of the Spanish Indies.

The weight of Sir Arthur's influence was evidently cast in favor of Miranda's propositions. General Wellesley was selected by Castlereagh for the command of an expedition against the Spanish colonies. In a memorandum dated June 6 this officer expressed the conviction that operations ought to start in South America rather than in Mexico, for the military difficulties were not so great in Venezuela, and in that country England had the means of communicating with the people through Miranda. Further, operations there could begin sooner, success there would pave the way to operations elsewhere, and it would be easier to withdraw from that region in case of failure. [60] Transports should be prepared to convey soldiers and supplies for six months. In addition colored battalions should be gathered in the West Indies. Wellesley proposed that a field train accompanied by artillerymen with six months' provisions and a large amount of ordnance and military stores should be prepared to leave Falmouth or Cork on July 1. [61] Among the articles mentioned by Miranda as necessary for the armament of soldiers to be recruited in Spanish America, were 20,000 muskets, 10,000 iron pike heads, 2,000 swords for cavalry, and clothing for 8,000 infantry. Besides he included an estimate for sufficient ammunition for the specified firearms, 100 life preservers, and 3 printing presses. [62]

In supplementary memoranda the promoter requested that

---

[59] *Ibid.*, p. 70.   [60] *Ibid.*, p. 74.   [61] *Ibid.*, pp. 78–79.
[62] "Articles indispensables pour l'Armament des Troupes Nationales et qui'il faut emporter avec nous," May 6, 1808, Mir. MSS., vol. 57.

these articles should "be embarked with the Expedition and delivered to G. M. on the arrival upon the Coasts of South America." He asked that "the instructions for Sir A. W." should direct him "to afford the necessary assistance to Genl. Miranda" to establish "the civil government of the Country" and its independence "on a solid basis." He proposed that a frigate should be sent to the West Indies to transmit proper instructions to the English naval and military commanders at Barbadoes and Trinidad. He suggested that an agreement should be reached about his position in the attacking forces with relation "to the English Commander." He maintained that a proclamation should be framed in the name of the English King inviting the South Americans "to establish their independence" and offering them the protection of Great Britain which had been proposed as early as 1797.[63]

Nor did he forget the need of an agreement about the commercial relations that should exist between England and the liberated colonies. A memorandum found in his papers proposed that until a treaty was negotiated the produce of those Spanish colonies which declared their independence should "be received in England on the same terms as that of Brazil. Goods in English ships to pay 10 per cent less duty than in other foreign ships." [64]

Miranda was as much absorbed in the evolution of his plans as an artist in painting a picture. He did not flinch as the full size of his canvas was being unrolled. He was, however, much perturbed about the reward which he might expect from the government that was at last ready to undertake the colossal task of liberating the Spanish colonists. Early in June he committed his thoughts to paper in the following proposals that he evidently planned to make the basis of a petition to the English ministers:

"1. To propose an advance of £5,000, or whatever sum Sir Arthur Wellesley may think reasonable, for the expence of

[63] "Memorandum on Publick affairs," June 6, 1808, Mir. MSS., vol. 57.
[64] Undated, *ibid.*

equipment, suite, and military charges—

"2. A separate provision for the General's household in England—to be left at the charge of the R.H.Nic. Vansittart; or any other person that the government may think proper—

"3. An assurance that, in case of misfortune, Genl. M's pension shall be settled on the same footing as in Mr. Addington's administration; and some provision for Molini his private Secrety. in any of the public offices in London.

"4. A public dinner, or some other means of introducing Genl. M. in a becoming manner." [65]

The long-discredited and much-buffeted general now had visions of profiting to the utmost by favoring circumstances. Miranda not only expected ample financial rehabilitation but also wished distinguished public recognition. In his mind's eye he pictured himself as emerging from his inconspicuousness to don the glittering uniform of an English military commander, to become the cynosure of admiring throngs, and to be acclaimed as the future Redeemer of the South American Continent.

The national uprising of the Spaniards against Napoleon's usurpations, however, put a new face on European politics. In the principality of the Asturias a spirit of opposition to the French soon became manifest. A junta or local council which assembled at the capital city of Oviedo promptly announced that the Asturias had declared war against France. In the very region where resistance against the Moslem invaders had been organized several centuries earlier, the movement for the liberation of Spain began. On May 25, 1808, the Asturian junta decided to solicit aid from the English Government. A petition to George III asking for succor in the struggle with Napoleon was intrusted to Andrés de la Vega and Viscount Matarrosa. These emissaries ventured to sea in an open boat, embarked on an English privateer near Gijón, landed at Falmouth on June 6, and proceeded to London, ac-

---

[65] "Memorandum on *Private* Affairs," June 6, 1808, *ibid.*

companied by an English naval officer. Early on the morning
of June 8 they met George Canning and Wellesley Pole, secretary of the admiralty. On the next day the agents sent a
letter to Canning formally requesting that an English war-
ship should protect the coast of the Asturias, that the Asturian patriots should be supplied with arms and ammunition, and that munitions should be sent to the interior provinces of Spain.

The *Times* said on June 10: "Of the precise manner in
which the British Government will act on this important occasion, we are as yet able to say nothing: we have, however,
heard that the expedition from Cork under Sir Arthur Wellesley, is now directed to proceed to Gibraltar instead of South
America." Two days later Canning assured the Asturian commissioners that England was disposed to assist with military
and naval forces all parts of the Spanish dominions that might
be animated by the same spirit as the principality of the
Asturias.

The Asturian mission naturally attracted the attention of
Francisco de Miranda. Among his papers there is preserved
a copy of a song written by one Courtney entitled "The Spanish Patriots" which was dedicated to the agents from "the
Spanish Nation to the Court of Great Britain." [66] The opening stanzas ran as follows:

> Raise the song of the Warriors of Spain,
> Who, scorning the Tyrant's alarms,
> Call their King, with the Cortes, to reign
> And indignantly cry out—To Arms!

> Raise the Song to Spain's proud Volunteers,
> The sword of their Country they wield;
> 'Midst their ranks dauntless Freedom appears,
> And leads them with joy to the field.

In view of the Spanish uprising the English ministers altered their long-meditated plans. The political balance was

---

[66] Mir. MSS., vol. 58.

now so inclined that they tentatively decided to send the soldiers who had been camping on the Irish coast to the Iberian Peninsula instead of to the Spanish Indies. If Miranda's later allegation were true, the English Government actually offered him a military position in the expedition commanded by Sir Arthur Wellesley. Early in June Miranda sent to Castlereagh a copy of his note to Pitt dated June 28, 1791, which asked that services should not be required of him for any other purpose than the emancipation of Spanish America.[67] The onerous task of announcing to the confirmed revolutionary the startling change in England's plans devolved upon Sir Arthur Wellesley. Twenty-seven years later the Duke of Wellington thus described the ensuing scene:

"I think I never had a more difficult business than when the Government bade me tell Miranda that we would have nothing to do with his plan. I thought it best to walk out in the streets with him and tell him there, to prevent his bursting out. But even there he was so loud and angry, that I told him I would walk on first a little that we might not attract the notice of everybody passing. When I joined him again he was cooler. He said: 'You are going over into Spain (this was before Vimiera)—you will be lost—nothing can save you; that, however, is your affair; but what grieves me is that there never was such an opportunity thrown away!' "[68]

On June 10 Miranda sent a note by his secretary to inquire of General Wellesley when it would be convenient for him to get "the Papers and other things agreed in yesterday's conversation." Incidentally he wished "Sir Arthur every sort of prosperity and success."[69] Soon afterwards Wellesley left London to take charge of the battalions at Cork of which he had been appointed commander. On June 20 the Duke of Manchester was directed to inform the Captain General of Cuba that, hoping for Cuban support, England had decided to coöperate with the provinces of Spain "in rescuing their

---

[67] Antepara, *South American Emancipation*, p. 221.
[68] Stanhope, p. 69.   [69] Mir. MSS., vol. 57.

Country from the tyranny of the French." [70]

In a generous fashion on July 4, 1808, England published a formal proclamation of peace with Spain. Among other stipulations this proclamation provided that any goods belonging to Spanish colonists which might henceforth be detained by English cruisers should be carefully preserved until it was ascertained whether or not the Spanish colonies "shall have made common cause with Spain against the power of France." [71] In the King's speech to Parliament on the same day, the announcement was made that, because of the resistance of Spain to the usurpations of France, the Spanish nation could "no longer be considered as the enemy of Great Britain," but was considered by His Majesty as "a natural friend and ally." It was expressly declared that King George III had "no other object than that of preserving unimpaired the integrity and independence of the Spanish monarchy." [72]

Other detachments of soldiers were meantime added to the forces which had been bivouacking on the Irish coast; and on July 12, 1808, the expedition commanded by Wellesley sailed from Cork toward the Iberian Peninsula.[73] With a touch of prophecy Gillray the caricaturist depicted this turn in Napoleon's fortunes in a cartoon which portrayed the Corsican Matador being savagely tossed by a Spanish bull. The spirited uprising in the Asturian principality was indeed fraught with much significance. Instead of becoming the leader of an expedition that would have radically altered the status of the Spanish Indies, Sir Arthur Wellesley began those military exploits that were destined to thwart the ambitions of Napoleon the Great. Francisco de Miranda was not compelled to determine exactly what his relation would be to an English expeditionary commander.

Miranda was soon notified that his future communications with the English Government should be carried on through Sir Charles Stewart. While the negotiations for revolutioniz-

---

[70] Robertson, *Miranda*, p. 412.   [71] *London Gazette*, July 2—July 5, 1808.
[72] Hansard, *Parliamentary Debates*, XI, 1140-41.
[73] *Times*, June 22, and July 19, 1808.

"The Spanish Bull Fight, or the Corsican Matador in Danger." Cartoon by James Gillray. From Wright, "The Works of James Gillray."

ing Spanish America had been going on, Miranda had not forgotten to initiate steps for the readjustment of his fiscal relations with the English Government. His financial condition was far from enviable; for Davison was now urging the reimbursement of funds amounting with interest to fifteen hundred pounds that he had advanced to Miranda between June 28, 1804, and April 12, 1808.[74] On May 13, 1808, the bankrupt promoter addressed a letter to Cooke in regard to his finances; he asked to be given "any part of the sum mentioned some days ago." [75] Early in June the question of Miranda's fiscal relations with the English Government was seriously taken up. Among his papers is a copy of a letter to Cooke, dated June 7, 1808, that mentions "the inclosed receipt of One Thousand Pounds by the desire of Sir Arthur Wellesley—begs Mr. Cooke to have the goodness to send the same by his Secretary Mr. Molini the bearer of this Note." [76]

About this time the disappointed revolutionist brought his distressed finances to the attention of Sir Charles Stewart. A diarial note of Miranda stated that this official received him in an honest fashion and promised him a prompt decision about "the pension and an arrangement in favor of Molini." [77] The topic of "General Miranda's allowances" was also the subject of correspondence between him and Perceval's private secretary, John C. Herries, to whose attention the matter had been brought by Miranda's constant friend Vansittart.[78] On October 15, 1808, Miranda wrote to this friend to declare that he had discussed the matter with Sir Arthur Wellesley.[79] It was near the end of November, however, before Miranda received a letter from Vansittart to the effect that Cooke had informed him that "everything was arranged according to the memorandum" which he had given to Lord Castlereagh." [80]

This transaction is made clear by a letter from Vansittart

---

[74] Davison to Miranda, June 20, 1808, Mir. MSS., vol. 57.
[75] *Ibid.* [76] *Ibid.* [77] "June, 1808," *ibid.*
[78] Herries to Miranda, Sept. 12, 1808, *ibid.*, vol. 58. [79] *Ibid.*
[80] Nov. 22, 1808, *ibid.*

dated November 29, 1808, that reposes among Miranda's manuscripts and which gives the substance of the missing memorandum. "General Miranda received in all £700 a year made up by an allowance of £500 on the Emigrant Fund paid by Ramus and another of £200 paid privately by me. He requests that these allowances, or an equivalent, may be restored to him from the date of his arrival in England, and that Mr. Molini who went abroad with him as secretary may be provided for in some public office for which employment he is perfectly qualified by his fidelity and knowledge of business, and that till an opportunity may occur an allowance of £200 a year may be made to him from the same date: and the General is the more anxious for this as Mr. M. has necessarily become acquainted with the private details of this expedition and correspondence." [81]

This epistle indicates how Miranda's finances were undoubtedly adjusted in the end of 1808. Though his obligations to Davison were not all liquidated, yet arrangements were made for the reimbursement of considerable sums which had been advanced by that contractor to prepare the revolutionary expedition.

To suggest the results that would have flowed from the execution of Miranda's plans by the aid of English squadrons is to discuss one of the might-have-beens of history. Chance or design or compulsion might have induced a commander trained in struggles against the freebooters of India to plant garrisons at strategic points in Spanish America. Miranda, who wished to accompany General Wellesley in an advisory capacity and as the prospective commander of hosts of his fellow countrymen that were expected to rise against their Spanish oppressors, might have been forced to behold his native land transformed into a dependency of Great Britain. Instead of conjuring into existence a family of independent nations in the vast domain stretching between the Mississippi River and Cape Horn, he might have been largely responsible

---

[81] Copy, unaddressed, Mir. MSS., vol. 58.

for the addition of a new group of colonies to that empire
upon which the sun never set. Guided by English administra-
tors and transformed by British immigrants, those colonies
might have become tranquil, happy, and prosperous depend-
encies of an Anglo-Saxon type. Whatever might have been the
ultimate destiny of those possessions, there is little doubt that
the apostle of Spanish-American independence would have
been bitterly reviled by some of his compatriots. To imagine
the rôle that he would have essayed under such circumstances
is to indulge in speculations. Let it suffice to suggest that his
long and confidential attachment to Downing Street might
have attracted him in one direction, while his ardent desire
for the independence of the Spanish Indies would inevitably
have impelled him in another direction.

In fact the spirited uprising in the principality of the Asturias caused English publicists to change their plans with
regard to the Spanish Indies. Although, as the sequel will
show, there still were Englishmen who thought of separating
the Spanish colonies from the Motherland, yet English ministers shortly realized that they could no longer view Spain
as the actual or potential ally of France. The military and
naval aid furnished to the Asturians signalized the beginning
of a *rapprochement* between England and Spain that proved
to be an insuperable bar to the execution of any project for
the emancipation of the Spanish Indies by the aid of scarlet
clad soldiers. This radical change of policy eventually dis-
pelled the rainbow of promise that Miranda had so often
beheld above the English horizon.

Chapter XVI

ACTIVITIES AS A PROPAGANDIST

THE PERIOD following the departure of Wellesley's soldiers for the Iberian Peninsula forms an interlude in Miranda's life. While patriotic juntas that assumed governmental functions were being formed throughout Spain, he lived quietly in London in the enjoyment of a regular allowance from the English Government. His literary interests revived. He frequently expressed the hope that the Continent might be delivered from the French. He spent much time meditating about the fate of the Spanish dominions in the Old World and the New.

Steps that Napoleon took to insure his brother the allegiance of the Spanish colonies had meantime exerted a significant influence upon South America. An agent conveying reports of the accession of Joseph Bonaparte to the throne of Spain and the Indies reached the capital of Venezuela on July 15, 1808. This emissary made the people, as well as the Captain General, acquainted with the downfall of the Spanish Bourbons. To paraphrase the words of Captain Beaver, who brought news of the Spanish uprising against the French, the people proclaimed Ferdinand VII by heralds throughout the city of Caracas and placed his portrait in the hall of the *cabildo*. On July 28 that council in vain presented an address to Captain General Casas praying for the creation of a junta at the capital. Some time afterwards Colonel Cochrane Johnstone invited Miranda "to eat a Mutton Chop with him" in order to meet Captain Hope. Under date of September 28 Miranda recorded in a diarial note that this captain had informed him of the tumult caused in Caracas by news of the Napoleonic usurpations in Spain. "If this story is true," concluded Miranda, "it appears to me a favorable augury for the independence of our America." [1]

---

[1] Mir. MSS., vol. 58.

His relations with Castlereagh and Wellesley were not completely severed. On August 19, 1808, Miranda wrote to Castlereagh to state that he had received communications from Trinidad and from the city of Caracas in regard to the condition of Venezuela. As he had been unable to discuss the matter with Sir Charles Stewart, Miranda declared that he had advised his correspondents to communicate directly with the English Government in order to agree upon "such measures as circumstances might require." He had further suggested that the South Americans should not wait for advice from the juntas that had arisen in Spain, but that the *cabildos* should assume the government of the country.[2]

On July 20, 1808, Miranda had sent a significant letter to the Marquis of Toro and the *cabildo* of Caracas. In it he maintained that the existing circumstances were "most critical and dangerous" for the Spanish Indies. The most probable result of the conquest of Spain by France, he declared, would be the subjection of "the Colombian Continent" to the same misfortunes as the Iberian Peninsula. In consequence he urged that the *cabildo* of Caracas should assume the government of that province, and that it should send agents to London to negotiate directly with English ministers about the destiny of the New World. He asserted that the interests of the Spanish juntas were incompatible with the "interests and rights" of the Spanish-American provinces and asked the *cabildo* to forward copies of his letter to Bogotá and Quito.[3]

Miranda planned to transmit this epistle to South America through Admiral Cochrane. In a letter in English addressed to the admiral on July 21 he complained that "our Expedition is again retarded on account of the late Events in Spain— which result will bring forward the accomplishment of my views on South America." He asked Cochrane to forward his missive by English cruisers to La Guaira, and urged that the

---

[2] Castlereagh, *Memoirs and Correspondence,* VII, 448-51.
[3] Martínez, "Miranda," *El Cojo Ilustrado,* V, 509; *cf.* Antepara, *South American Emancipation,* pp. 270-71.

Venezuelans should dispatch agents to Downing Street at once. "We are all," said Miranda, "in expectation of the result of a great conflict in Spain, which must bring matters to an issue in a very short time." [4] On September 10 he addressed a letter to the *cabildos* of Habana and the city of Mexico to suggest that although England had altered her plans in respect to the Spanish dominions, yet her views remained the same. Annexed to this communication were documents that illustrated the policy of France toward Spanish America in 1792 as well as a copy of his note that explained why he did not accompany Wellesley to the Spanish Peninsula.[5]

On October 6, 1808, Miranda sent an important letter to the Marquis of Toro and the *cabildo* of Caracas. In this communication he expressed grave fear that a conflict would soon be precipitated between peninsular officials and Spanish colonists. He argued that because of the absence of a representative system the Spanish patriots had been compelled to form an imperfect scheme of government, and that subsequently they scarcely had time to concert a plan of defense and a general organization before their country was overrun by French troops. In order that his countrymen might be prepared for impending changes, he inclosed plans of government for liberated Spanish America. These were the projects submitted to the English Government in May, 1801, which he had slightly modified. Miranda took occasion bitterly to denounce the administration of Captain General Vasconcelos of Venezuela. He implored his countrymen to follow the example that had been set by Spanish patriots in reforming their system of government and claiming their "liberties and independence." The propagandist also inclosed documents illustrating his endeavors in England, France, and the United States to promote the emancipation of the Spanish Indies.[6]

On December 9, 1808, he addressed an explanatory letter to Admiral Cochrane. He declared that he was anxiously awaiting "some answer from South America to the Letters I

---

[4] Mir. MSS., vol. 58.   [5] Antepara, pp. 276-77.   [6] *Ibid.*, pp. 278-81.

had the honor of transmitting through your care. The Principal Object in sending them, was to persuade the Cabildos to send some Deputies that might explain and shew to this Government the feelings of the Continental People of South America on this momentous occasion. The time for acting is near at hand, and I hope we shall receive the above information soon so as to enable us to make a proper use of it." [7]

In the end of January, 1809, Governor Cockburn of Curaçao and Captain Fyfe, commander of the English naval forces at that island, intercepted a packet of letters that Miranda had addressed to the Marquis of Toro. After examining the letters these officials decided that to forward them to South America would not be compatible with the relations existing between England and Spain. To Spanish colonial officials Cockburn expressed the view that this correspondence was a French intrigue which was designed to shake Spain's confidence in England. Yet, upon transmitting the missives to his government, he declared that Miranda was "held in general detestation" in northern South America, and that a connection with him would tend to weaken English prestige and influence in that region.[8]

About the same time Miranda had sent other packets of letters to Habana and to the city of Mexico. Upon opening them Governor Cockburn saw that they contained revolutionary papers which had been copied from Miranda's manuscripts. One of the packets addressed to Habana contained the following documents: copies of missives that Miranda had addressed to Caracas and Buenos Aires between July and September, 1808; copies of correspondence that described the French plan of 1792 for the emancipation of the Spanish Indies; a copy of Miranda's letter in which he declined to enter the English service against Spain; and a copy of Hamilton's epistle of August 22, 1798, which expressed his views about the liberation of Spanish America. When he reported to Castlereagh his action in detaining this correspondence Cock-

---

[7] Mir. MSS., vol. 58.   [8] Robertson, *Miranda*, pp. 525-26.

burn said that he could not believe that the English Government had sanctioned "such an attempt to dismember the dominions of His Catholic Majesty in America," while it was "so nobly struggling to support His Empire in Europe." [9]

Admiral Cochrane also had scruples about forwarding such packets. Hence he wrote to Spencer Perceval to state that, in the belief that this Minister was acquainted with their contents, he had transmitted to South America certain letters which Miranda had sent under the "cover" of the Chancellor of the Exchequer. Cochrane asked for instructions about the disposal of similar packets that might subsequently reach him. The situation was indeed awkward. On January 14, 1809, the English Government and the Central Junta, which had assumed the reins of government in Spain, put the seal on their informal relations by a convention of peace, friendship, and alliance. To Miranda's hope of English coöperation in his life purpose this treaty in reality gave the coup de grâce. On February 2, 1809, inclosing an extract from Cochrane's letter, Herries asked the propagandist for an explanation of the admiral's damaging statements.[10] A copy of Miranda's retort shows that he tried to exculpate himself from the charge of carrying on a seditious correspondence under an official cover by the allegation that Cochrane had altered the sense of his letter by substituting the word "Perceval" for the word "government." [11]

Meantime the Captain General of Venezuela had not been idle. He warned the Central Junta about Miranda's transmissal of seditious papers. In March, 1809, it accordingly instructed the Spanish Minister in London, Admiral Apodaca, to protest to the English Government against intrigues directed from London by a "revolutionist who was celebrated only because of treason against his King and country." If he could do so without compromising himself, the envoy was directed to have Miranda arrested or even transported to

---

[9] Inclosures in Pole to Hammond, Aug. 31, 1809, F. O., 72/89.
[10] Mir. MSS., vol. 59.   [11] "Febrero 3," *ibid.*

Spain.[12] On May 16, 1809, Apodaca accordingly sent a letter
to Canning in which he protested against the activities of "the
traitor Francisco de Miranda," who, taking advantage of the
disturbed condition of Spain due to the French invasion, by
inflammatory documents transmitted from London was attempting to separate Venezuela from the Motherland. Canning's attention was pointedly called to the fact that, in spite
of the close relations between England and Spain, the revolutionary conspirator was being allowed to carry out "his de-
praved projects" through Admiral Cochrane.[13]

In a diarial note Miranda recorded that on the forenoon of
May 23 "with no little surprise" he had received a visit from
Under Secretary Cooke. Read Miranda's account of the ensuing interview. "With serene and friendly countenance he
said to me smiling: *You are denounced, the Spaniards say
that you keep writing to Caracas, and stirring the minds of
that Province; there are the Letters,—I'll send them to you!*'
'I am not surprised,' I responded, 'that the Spaniards should
denounce me; for that is their custom.' " According to his own
story, Miranda added that he had duly informed Wellesley,
Castlereagh, and Stewart of his correspondence with Spanish
America. Miranda thus suggestively linked this episode with
other incidents of his romantic career.

"Finally, in taking leave Cooke said to me: *Don't write
any more to the Southamericans—unless it is in answer to
their Letters.*' 'I shall not,' I responded, 'for I have resolved,
at least that if they do not declare their independence, I shall
not move from here.' This remark seemed to please him.
Then I added: 'Do you know, sir, that your allies are famous
for their denunciation of falsehoods? In my case, for example,
they accused me of being a contrabandist in company with
Cagigal and Espeleta; later they sent me a complete justification of our honorable innocence.—Lastly when I was in Paris
in the year 1800 they made accusations to Napoleon that I

---

[12] Rojas, *El general Miranda,* pp. 243-44, 246.
[13] Robertson, *Miranda,* p. 423, note f.

was a friend of England,—Anduaga being the chief ac-
cuser,—and even that, being the principal agent of Mr. Pitt,
I had directed the infernal machine which was thrown at his
coach in the Rue Nicaise shortly after my arrival in Paris!
By this infamy they merely succeeded in having me detained
in the prison of the Temple for about five days until the false-
hood was ascertained and I returned to this country!" [14]

The Under Secretary evidently thought that it was necessary to warn the propagandist again. On May 27, 1809, at
the instance of Castlereagh, Cooke sent the following note to
Miranda:

"You must be sensible that under the existing Relations
between Spain and Gt. Britain it is necessary to abstain from
any measure which can cause jealousy between them. It has
been understood that since the Pacification with Spain you
have continued a Correspondence with Persons in the Caraccas
which however justifiable previous to that Event have no
longer any claim to Support or Connivance from the British
Government. I am therefore directed by Lord Castlereagh to
make this intimation to you and at the same time to state his
Hope, that you will abstain from any Correspondence of the
Nature alluded to, that no suspicion may be cast upon His
Majesty's good faith, and trust it may not be necessary to
remove you from His Majesty's Dominions." [15]

In response Miranda spiritedly avowed that his conduct
did not warrant such a harsh judgment.[16] On June 3 Canning
sent a letter to Minister Apodaca to express his "most perfect
confidence" that Admiral Cochrane was not aware of the contents or the authorship of the seditious letters. Apodaca was
assured that Cochrane had been ordered to discover how this
correspondence had been conveyed to him. Canning emphatically declared that the Venezuelan had dispatched his communications without the cognizance of the English Govern·
ment.[17] Miranda was evidently informed that, if the ministers

---

[14] "Mr. Secretary Cooke, Mayo 23, 1809," Mir. MSS., vol. 60.   [15] *Ibid.*
[16] Miranda to Cooke, May 29, 1809, *ibid.*   [17] F. O., 72/84.

became aware of any further activity of this sort, he would be ordered to depart from English soil.[18] The allowance that he was receiving from the English Treasury must now have seemed to the agitator as a very apple of Sodom.

Near the end of June, 1809, one Captain Sanz, alias Juanico, arrived in London with tidings from the Marquis of Toro and the *cabildo* of Caracas.[19] On June 23 Miranda wrote a diarial entry to the effect that Captain Sanz had called at his house and had presented evidence to show that he was "a faithful partisan and lover of our liberty and independence." This captain declared that to kindle a revolution in South America there was needed only a *caudillo* like Miranda in whom the people had confidence.[20] Under date of July 3 the latter took note of another visit from Sanz who advised him to proceed at once to St. Thomas where compatriots would meet him.[21] Although he was warned by a Spanish-American friend named Cortés that this emissary had been in secret conclave with the Spanish Minister in London,[22] yet Miranda evidently intrusted his fellow countryman with letters for Venezuela.[23] Meantime the informer had furnished Minister Apodaca with the names of friends of Miranda at Caracas, had given him some of Miranda's incendiary literature, and had assured him that the propagandist was now directing his activities toward Brazil and La Plata.[24] Hence Apodaca sent a fresh complaint to Canning that, despising the intimations given him by the English Government, Miranda was transmitting his revolutionary propaganda to southern South America by way of Brazil.[25]

Because of this letter Lord Castlereagh asked Vansittart to discover how much truth there was in Apodaca's complaint. Castlereagh said that he would be reluctant to adopt any un-

---

[18] Draft to Cockburn, June 7, 1809, W. O., 1/102.
[19] Rojas, *El general Miranda*, p. 239.
[20] "Viernes, 23 de Junio," Mir. MSS., vol. 60.   [21] *Diario, ibid.*
[22] Cortés to Miranda, "Wednesday," *ibid.*   [23] *Diario*, July 20, *ibid.*
[24] Apodaca to Garay, July 17, 1809, A. G. S., estado, 8172.
[25] Rojas, *El general Miranda*, p. 247.

kind measures toward the exile, "but, connected as we are with Spain, the honor of the country and of the Government must not be compromised; and I think you will be able to obtain assurances from Miranda, so distinct with respect to his conduct, as to justify me in continuing to him the protection which he now receives." [26] In response to this query Vansittart expressed his confidence in Miranda's desire to be quiet.[27] Accordingly on August 15, 1809, Canning informed the Spanish Minister that, as a result of his inquiries, he was certain that Miranda's actual conduct could not justify the least disquietude or lack of confidence on the part of Spain.[28] Six days later Vansittart wrote a letter to Miranda to inform him about Castlereagh's inquiry "respecting some supposed correspondence" through Brazil. "I answered his letter," said Vansittart, "and I believe satisfied him that the complaint was without foundation; but it shows how closely your actions are watched and how much they are misrepresented." [29]

The seditious communications from Grafton Street did not reach their destination without the knowledge of Spanish colonial officials. Upon receipt of Miranda's letter of July 20, 1808, the Marquis of Toro transmitted it to Captain General Casas. The Marquis alleged that in the same sealed packet he had received the instructions of a spy for the English King. Toro denounced his correspondent as an "outlawed Traitor"; he charged that "the perfidious Miranda" was assiduously attempting to undermine the loyalty of Venezuelans to Ferdinand VII. With a show of indignation, he asked that these underhand activities should be brought to the attention of the Spanish Government in order that the traitor might be punished for the atrocious affront that he had offered to the honor of a nobleman.[30] It is to be presumed that the Marquis of Toro thus brushed the stigma of treason from his own name.

Miranda also strove to initiate a correspondence with col-

[26] Castlereagh, VII, 454. [27] Ibid., p. 456.
[28] Rojas, El general Miranda, p. 248. [29] Mir. MSS., vol. 60.
[30] Oct. 25, 1808 (translation), Ad. R., 1/4354.

onists in the Viceroyalty of la Plata. On July 24, 1808, he
sent a letter to the *cabildo* of Buenos Aires. In this communication, modifying his arguments to suit a different audience,
he praised the citizen soldiers of Buenos Aires for their ex-
pulsion of the English invaders who had attempted "to subjugate our America." As illustrative of the intentions of England, he mentioned the instructions to Generals Crawford and
Whitelocke and the King's speech to Parliament on July 4,
1808. In a postscript he asked that his missive should be forwarded to Chile, Peru, and Quito.[31]

Soon afterwards he got into touch with dissatisfied creoles
of La Plata. From Rio de Janeiro on July 28, 1808, Saturnino
Rodríguez Peña, who had been dispatched as an emissary to
Brazil, had sent an instructive letter to the agitator. Rodríguez Peña asserted that the mere report that Miranda was
to be "the principal agent" of South America emancipation
would stimulate his compatriots more than "all the might of
England." With a proclamation conceived like that which he
had circulated at Coro, said Rodríguez Peña, all the provinces of La Plata might easily have been emancipated.[32] On
July 25, 1809, Miranda sent Rodríguez Peña and the *cabildo*
of Buenos Aires plans for the government of the liberated
Spanish colonies and papers indicative of England's attitude
toward Spanish America.[33] Three days later he addressed
another packet to Rodríguez Peña with the request that it
should be transmitted to Buenos Aires with promptness and
security.[34] His letter to the *cabildo* of that city, however, fell
into the hands of Santiago de Liniers, the new viceroy of La
Plata, who submitted it to the audiencia of Buenos Aires
which decided to make the incident known to Spanish officials
at Lima.[35]

On November 2, 1808, Miranda addressed another epistle

---

[31] Antepara, pp. 273-74.
[32] Mir. MSS., vol. 60. On Saturnino Rodríguez Peña and his mission to Rio de
Janeiro, see Levene, *Ensayo histórico sobre la revolución de Mayo y
Mariano Moreno*, I, especially pp. 312-24, 341-44.
[33] Mitre, *Historia de Belgrano*, I, 481.
[34] Mir. MSS., vol. 58.   [35] Mitre, I, 480.

to Rodríguez Peña and inclosed a copy of the circular letter
that he had transmitted to Venezuela. He expressed his dis-
gust at "the dishonest and infamous conduct" of Padilla for
whom he had secured a pension and "gratifications" from
the English Government.[36] Through this correspondence Miranda came into touch with a mysterious character named
Felipe Contucci who had evidently acted at Rio de Janeiro as
the agent of "a powerful junta of Americans that had been
secretly formed in Buenos Aires." [37] Two days later that emissary sent Miranda the following explanatory missive:

"I should like to send you an exact account of the actual
condition of the provinces of the Río de la Plata; but as
Rodríguez Peña has done so, I shall only say that we are
laboring to calm those domestic disorders which agitate the
colonists and which occasioned my agency near Her Royal
Highness, Princess Carlota. Although this mission has not
had the best results, yet fortunately it has enabled us to follow with due caution the steps of Your Excellency which lead
to the most just and useful road for my beloved Americans.
Everything has been well arranged, and I believe that the only
obstacle which we can foresee will be easily surmounted. First,
it will be necessary for us to invite Viceroy Liniers to join our
party. When this slight difficulty is overcome, we shall accomplish our desires and enjoy the felicity for which you, more
than any other man, have labored with much ardor. There is
nothing that we need. If we should await the succor that England could give us, the most opportune occasion would be lost;
and we would subsequently encounter new obstacles to be surmounted. Oh, if the South Americans could only have the satisfaction of seeing you by their side, what would be their
glory! You ought to decide to leave England in order better
to regulate the affairs of the vast and rich Argentine provinces. Their inhabitants would doubtless receive you with the
love and tenderness of which they are capable and to which
you are so much entitled." [38]

---

[36] Mir. MSS., vol. 58.
[37] Rodríguez Peña to Miranda, Jan. 24, 1809, *ibid.*, vol. 60.
[38] Antepara, pp. 285-86.

In his reply to Contucci, on May 1, 1809, Miranda inclosed a copy of his latest communication to English ministers about the emancipation of the Spanish Indies. "I am," wrote Miranda, "and ever will be the vigorous defender of the rights, liberties, and independence of our America, whose honorable cause I have defended and will defend all my life, not only because this attitude is just and necessary for the salvation of its unfortunate inhabitants, but also because at present that region is interesting to all mankind! Count on me, therefore, until the end!" [39] On the same day he addressed Rodríguez Peña in similar terms: "Follow in the meantime your prudent plan with determination and good judgment; you may count upon me to defend the rights and liberties of our beloved Motherland unto death!" With regard to Felipe Contucci the promoter said that he appeared to be a capable person "and very suitable for the affair." Miranda expressed a wish that Contucci were by his side at that moment: "I am here alone to champion the rights of America in this capital which swarms with an incredible number of Saracens and enemies of our independence." [40]

Meantime Rodríguez Peña had become dissatisfied with the proceedings of Padilla whom he had authorized to act as his agent. On August 21, 1809, he wrote to ask Miranda to serve as his representative in London and to complain that, because of Padilla's negligence, he had been left "without honor and without a pension" from the English Government. [41] In consequence Miranda made a plea to English ministers on behalf of Rodríguez Peña. Then Padilla undertook to defend himself. He affirmed that Miranda had "begun his imposture by passing himself off as a representative of the people of S. America";[42] he denied "*having received any letters*" from Rodríguez Peña for "*many months past.*" [43]

On March 13, 1810, Miranda sent to Sir Arthur Wellesley

---

[39] Mir. MSS., vol. 60. [40] *Ibid.* [41] *Ibid.*, vol. 62.
[42] Padilla's undated memorandum, W. O., misc. series 3, vol. 1121.
[43] Curtis to Miranda, March 2, 1810, Mir. MSS., vol. 62 .

a résumé of the fiscal relations of Padilla and Rodríguez Peña
with the English Government. This exposé showed that pen-
sions had been granted by the English Government to both
these men because of their services to English commanders
at the time of the invasion of La Plata, but that Padilla had
not transmitted Rodríguez Peña's quota to South America.
According to an undated memorandum preserved in the
archives of the English Government, it had assigned to Padilla
an annual pension of four hundred pounds and to Rodríguez
Peña one of three hundred pounds.[44] As Miranda's pleas were
reënforced by the arguments of a merchant from Rio de
Janeiro named Curtis, the English ministers became convinced of Padilla's duplicity. Arrangements were accordingly
made for the payment of his correspondent's pension through
a banker. In April, 1810, Lord Strangford, the English ambassador in Rio de Janeiro, was informed of Rodríguez Peña's
needy circumstances and directed to furnish him with six hundred pounds.[45] Thus Miranda's intercession secured just
treatment for an Argentine compatriot.

Through Francisco Febles, who had remained in Trinidad,
Miranda had meantime been receiving reports of conditions
in his homeland. On October 8, 1808, Febles acknowledged receipt of letters which the propagandist had addressed to the
city of Caracas. He expressed the opinion that, if the French
succeeded in dominating Spain, the people of Venezuela would
struggle to establish their independence under English protection.[46] In imaginative words on January 15, 1809, Febles
assured Miranda that the Venezuelans adored his standard as
though it were an idol of worship,—even as the Jews adored
the Messiah. "I hope that divine Providence and the Creator
of the world will guard such an important life as that of Your
Excellency," continued Febles, "in order that we may accom-

---

[44] W. O., misc. series 3, vol. 1121.

[45] "C. J." to Strangford, April 13, 1810, *ibid.*, vol. 1122. In a postscript to a
letter of Apr. 3, 1810, to Rodríguez Peña, Miranda declared that he had recently learned that "el dicho P—," evidently meaning Padilla, had been acting
as an "Agente ó Espia de Apodaca," Mir. MSS., vol. 48.

[46] Mir. MSS., vol. 48.

plish our desires; for the present juncture furnishes a most opportune occasion to gain our ends. The people of Caracas have made some movements but they have lacked force, valor, and a star like Your Excellency to direct so great an enterprise." [47] On June 21, after mentioning the arrival in Venezuela of the new Captain General, Vicente Emparán, Febles avowed: "The province of Caracas is in a more suitable condition for independence than ever before, but a leader is lacking." He asserted that a fifth or a sixth part of the forces sent by England to the Iberian Peninsula would have been "sufficient for our independence, an achievement desired by all, and one which would endure for centuries." [48]

On December 8 Febles wrote to Miranda to declare that if any European nation should desire to separate the Spanish colonies from Spain, that juncture would be the appointed time, as the South Americans were favorably disposed. Yet he added that the "sons of America are not capable of raising their heads and of maintaining a movement of such consequence. At least, unless you or some person of equal importance should lead them; for among them not only is there much ignorance but also much fear of the subordination in which the Spanish Government has kept them all their lives." [49] About the same time another Spanish-American revolutionary named Casanares wrote from Trinidad to Miranda to inform him about the varying opinions of Venezuelans concerning their political status. He declared that some of his compatriots were opposed to the rule of King Joseph, others desired no other ruler than Ferdinand VII, but that certain influential persons cherished Miranda's views. The sentiments of Casanares are epitomized in two sentences: "Our native land needs a man who is capable and intelligent,—a man endowed with your virtues. Only a spirit like yours can bring our compatriots out of this servile captivity into the sunlight!" [50]

Though the expedition that had been designed for the lib-

---

[47] *Ibid.*, vol. 60. [48] *Ibid.*, vol. 61. [49] *Ibid.*, vol. 63. [50] Dec. 1, 1809, *ibid.*

eration of Spanish America had been sent to fight French troops in the Iberian Peninsula, yet Miranda did not altogether relinquish hope of English aid in the execution of his projects. His expectations naturally rose in proportion as the prospect of English victory over Napoleon seemed to wane. In the end of 1808, when Wellesley paid a visit to London, after the defeat of Spaniards upon the Ebro by Napoleonic soldiers, Miranda addressed a letter to him. "You see clearly, Sir Arthur," said he, "that I am not surprised about the occurrences in Spain and their disastrous results." [51] On January 26, 1809, after Napoleon had triumphantly entered the gates of Madrid, in the course of "a long conference" with Wellesley, Miranda submitted English translations of his recent correspondence with Spanish Americans. The English commander read these epistles with much care. Miranda's account of the interview proceeds:

"When he had finished, he said to me calmly: 'I can only say to you in friendship and confidence that at present the ministry does not direct its views toward South America, and hence it appears to me better that we should drop the matter until the Spanish affair has terminated.' 'How then,' I responded, 'do you not judge that England's attempt to secure the independence of the Iberian Peninsula is already frustrated?' 'Yes,' he replied, 'but we cannot,—without failing the Spaniards and dishonoring ourselves,—treat with agents who come from the Spanish colonies; for the Spaniards always say to us that if we should protect the independence of their Americas it would be better for them to treat with France.' 'Then to deal with me,' I responded, 'will be even more incompatible than to treat with anyone else.' 'No,' he replied, 'for I have an express order from the ministers to renew whatever communications you may judge convenient in these affairs but neither to communicate with nor to receive any other person.' In the supposition that Spain would declare for Joseph Bonaparte, he proceeded immediately to ask my opinion about the public spirit of the continental Spanish-Ameri-

[51] Dec. 12, 1808, Mir. MSS., vol. 58.

can colonies. Upon learning that I believed that the majority of the people would favor absolute independence, he promptly said: 'Thus it is as we desire, and in regard to government, England should not intermeddle. The political system will be attended to in America.' " [52]

To judge by Miranda's diarial note, after he had shown Wellesley letters that he had received from the West Indies and South America, the English general declared that when the Spanish affair had ended, which he did not believe would last long, "we would direct all our attention to America!" From this conference Miranda thought that he could divine the intentions of the English Government in regard to the Spanish Indies. His inaccurate hypothesis was as follows: that, if the Spaniards should propose an alliance against France, the English would abandon the Spanish Americans "without the slightest remorse"; that as the English had discerned that the Spanish Americans desired to be independent of the French, so they now affected to be indifferent in order that they might sell their friendship or protection as dearly as possible; that, having perceived that Spanish America would not follow their guidance in regard to government and commerce, the English wished to display indifference about the form of government which the Spanish colonists might wish to adopt, "as it would not be that of Ferdinand VII, their worthy ally." [53]

On March 24, 1809, Miranda again brought the problem of the Spanish Indies to Castlereagh's attention. He stated that he had always been zealous "in promoting the Liberties and independence of the Colombian Continent" and "in preventing its subjugation by the new pretended King of the Indies, Joseph Bonaparte." He expressed the opinion that the "best informed" Spanish Americans detested the idea of "becoming subjects to the French or to any other foreign nation" and much desired "emancipation and a better form of Government framed by themselves." He declared that, if the

---

[52] *Diario,* "Enero 26, 1809," *ibid.,* vol. 59.   [53] *Ibid.*

colonists did not take an attitude, the Spanish officials in America would ultimately decide in favor of King Joseph. Miranda thus described to Castlereagh the interview which he had recently had with Sir Arthur Wellesley:

"I offered my services to Great Britain for the purpose of proceeding without delay to Mexico or Habana in company of one or two English Commissioners that might explain to the constituted authorities of the Country the favorable dispositions of Great Britain * * * and after hearing and debating, in presence of the English Representatives, the interests on both sides, to come to a decision agreeable to their Instructions upon which we could frame a solid and general Plan to act upon in the future operations and measures to be taken hereafter for the independency of that Continent. His answer was 'that his Majesty's Ministers could not for the present enter into any further discussion upon the subject, while the Spanish attempt was pending; but as soon as that subject should be over, the business he presumed would be resumed and the promised answer transmitted to me':—we agreed, however, that my communication should be imparted without delay to your Lordship. * * * Weighing all these circumstances—and seeing the Squadrons of France and Ferrol ready for sea, and one of them already sailing in the direction of S. America, my anxiety is certainly increased to an alarming degree!" [54]

Glimpses of Miranda's thoughts about the condition of the Spanish Indies may also be had from other papers. On May 3, 1809, Vansittart wrote to him and stated that he had shown to Castlereagh a letter from Contucci but that the Minister had declared that England was bound by treaty to Spain.[55] In the comment which Miranda made about this episode he recorded that Vansittart had informed him that Castlereagh had appeared surprised and embarrassed at Contucci's letter. Evidently this friend also read to the Minister the propagandist's replies to the letters of Contucci, Rodríguez Peña,

---

[54] W. O. I., misc. series 3, vol. 1119.   [55] Mir. MSS., vol. 60.

Febles, and Hislop.[56] On November 18, 1809, Miranda declared to his confidant that he no longer had any doubt of the
fatal result of English expeditions to the European Continent. "If we allow the Colombian Continent to be lost also," he
continued, "one may then well doubt whether the enemies of
England are in France or here in this island!" [57]

In the spring of 1809 Miranda made new acquaintances in
London. He met a student of English politics named Gould
F. Leckie with whom he corresponded about Spanish America.
Among other books Miranda loaned to Lord Sheffield, De
Pons' *Voyage à la partie orientale de la Terre-Firme* which
that nobleman found so instructive that he sought to procure
a copy for his own library.[58] The Duke of Gloucester also became interested in Miranda's designs. At the instance of the
Duke,—so wrote Miranda in a note,—on April 24 they called
on Lord Grenville. There they met Lord Grey; and a conversation sprang up among these noblemen about the Spanish
colonies. They also discussed the means by which Venezuela
might be revolutionized without the inconveniences that had
been experienced in France. This long discussion about "the
independence of the Colombian Continent," said Miranda,
greatly pleased the Duke of Gloucester who felt convinced
that Grey and Grenville would favor Spanish-American emancipation.[59]

When he accidentally met Castlereagh the South American
reminded him that he desired to have his precious papers returned. In response the Englishman said that the ministers
were dissatisfied with him because he was maintaining a correspondence with the Spanish-American provinces while "at
the same time receiving a considerable income from this government." In exculpatory phrases Miranda evidently replied
to the Minister that he had made known his intercourse with
Spanish Americans to Wellesley and Stewart, and that he had

---

[56] *Diario,* "May 4," *ibid.*   [57] *Ibid.,* vol. 61.
[58] Sheffield to Miranda, April 2, 1809, *ibid.,* vol. 60.
[59] *Diario,* April 22—April 28, 1809, *ibid.*

never been anything else than "the principal agent of his compatriots near the British Government." Whereupon, wrote Miranda, Castlereagh's countenance became serene, and he advised him to write no more letters about the affair. As a result of this interview Miranda felt that he had offset the unfavorable influence of Cooke and had advanced his plans for the liberty and independence of the Spanish Indies. Through Vansittart the promoter seems also to have taken steps to make known his ideas to Lord Sidmouth with the hope of thus influencing the ministers.

During the period which followed the arrival of the Asturian envoys in London the promoter of Spanish-American independence thus became the director of a propaganda of rebellion. In this new rôle his activities took on various forms. By means of letters addressed to correspondents in Spanish and Portuguese America, he strove to spread a knowledge of his carefully devised projects for the liberation of the Spanish Indies. Further, he tried to make his countrymen acquainted with the kaleidoscopic changes that were taking place in Europe. Above all, he aimed to instill in their minds the thought of independence from the Old World. Though Englishmen had not altogether relinquished the idea of separating the Spanish colonies from the Motherland, yet upon becoming fully aware of Miranda's attempts to spread the doctrine of revolution in the American dominions of their new ally, English ministers took energetic steps to force him to cease what to them had become a pernicious activity. On at least one occasion a minister insinuated to the propagandist that he was biting the hand that fed him.

Chapter XVII

ESSAYS IN JOURNALISM

DURING THE interlude that followed the beginning of the war of the peoples against Napoleon, Miranda not only carried on a revolutionary propaganda by letters to his compatriots but also through the printed page. Accordingly we shall now consider a phase of his activity that may be styled journalistic.

In divers ways Miranda sought to influence public opinion in England. In the end of November, 1808, Dr. William Thompson wrote to him and pointed out that the description in the *Annual Register* for 1806 of his attack on Venezuela was a calumny. Thompson expressed his intention to correct the misrepresentation in the next number of that annual; "the Sting shall be pulled out and as much balm as possible poured into the wound." To him Miranda declared that the account of his expedition published in the *Register* was such as "any infernal imposter could ever devise"; he sent documents to Thompson that would aid him "to make the refutation complete." Further, he declared that "the cure of the Disease, *Calumny,* can be obtained only from its contrary, *Truth.*" [1] After the *Annual Register* for 1807 had issued from the press, Miranda wrote Vansittart to inform him that in it he would find narratives of his expedition against Venezuela in 1806 and of Popham's attack on Buenos Aires, "which were truly interesting and authentic!! *Sed magna est vis veritatis, et prevalebit.*" [2]

Perhaps this attempt at justification led Thompson to bring to Miranda's attention a proposal by one John Murray to prepare his biography. Murray's plan was to publish "a complete narrative of the whole of the General's transactions not only in regard to his grand object of emancipation but

---

[1] Both letters dated Nov. 23, 1808, Mir. MSS., vol. 58.
[2] Nov. 18, 1809, *ibid.,* vol. 61. A revised account of Miranda's attack on Venezuela is found in *An. Reg.,* 1807, pp. 206-9.

during the time that he served in France and respecting all of which he has probably retained official documents and notes—in this way it would prove very interesting to the public and highly creditable to the character of General Miranda of the actual grandeur of which the millions are little aware.— I think that I would venture upon a Volume in Quarto for which extent I conceive there will be facts sufficient to produce a genuine, interesting, and valuable work." [3] Though nothing came of this proposition, yet it may have suggested to Miranda the idea that bore fruit during the next year in a volume about the liberation of Spanish America.

In conjunction with Vansittart the South American became much interested in a project to publish an English version of the *Diccionario geográfico-histórico de las Indias Occidentales ó América* by a learned Spaniard named Antonio de Alcedo. As a fit person to undertake the large task of translation Vansittart recommended the son of an intimate friend, "an excellent young man" named George A. Thompson who had been well trained in languages.[4] Upon becoming acquainted with this youth, Miranda was favorably impressed, and soon intrusted to him a volume of Alcedo's monumental work.[5] By the midsummer of 1810 the young man had begun the task of translating the Spanish encyclopedia into English. It was not until 1812, however, that the results of this literary enterprise began to appear in "Thompson's Alcedo."

During this period of apparent retirement Miranda also aimed to disseminate a knowledge of Viscardo's *Lettre aux Espagnols-Américains*. In the end of 1808 he undertook to have a notice of that tract printed in an English journal. As the magazine in which to publish this article he selected the *Edinburgh Review*. The ostensible author of this essay, who in reality worked in conjunction with Miranda, was a philosopher and journalist named James Mill, the father of John

---

[3] Inclosure in Thompson to Miranda, March 21, 1809, Mir. MSS., vol. 59.
[4] Vansittart to Miranda, Oct. 19, 1809, *ibid.*, vol. 61.
[5] Miranda to Vansittart, Dec. 16, 1809, *ibid.*

Stuart Mill, the classical economist.

On January 4, 1809, this philosopher sent the general for examination the first part of the manuscript, and asked for data from Miranda's books to fill certain gaps. Mill was of opinion that the liberation of Spanish America was too extensive a subject for "an article in a *Review.* * * * It is hardly possible to place all the important points in the light which they would require. What we can do, will, however, I think, produce a strong impression." [6]

Three days later he wrote to Miranda that he had finished the essay and would call on him that evening in order that they might "discuss every point together." Then he proceeded to explain his object: "You will perceive that my great aim, in the part of the review you now receive, has been to present the subject, as strongly as I was able, in that particular aspect which would most fall in with the prejudices of this nation, and at the same time give instructions which might, as far as possible, prevent those who are to decide from adopting any erroneous and pernicious plan of action." [7] In another letter of the same date Mill said: "I received a letter on Tuesday from the Editor of the *Edinburgh Review* in which he states his great satisfaction with the description I had previously given him of the plan and purport of our Article and expressed his longing desire to see it." Soon afterwards the collaborator wrote to Miranda, however, to state that he had just received a note showing that the omniscient editor, Francis Jeffrey, was not altogether satisfied with the essay: You will see, by reading the letter, said Mill, "that he is a little startled at several things but at last gives up every particular, except the appearance of harboring a design to emancipate the Spanish colonies, even if the Spaniards should succeed in expelling the French. As the present news puts that out of the question, I think there will be no great difficulty in solving that knot too." [8]

This correspondence reveals that the author of the essay

---

[6] Mir. MSS., vol. 59.   [7] *Ibid.*   [8] Undated, *ibid.*

about Viscardo's *Lettre aux Espagnols-Américains,* which was published in the *Edinburgh Review* for January, 1809, drew his information and his inspiration alike from the self-styled agent of the Spanish-American colonies. That interesting article was appropriately entitled the "Emancipation of Spanish America." In its pages Mill paid a tribute to the learned Jesuit exile who had written this tract as an appeal to his compatriots to shake off the galling yoke of their Spanish masters. Then he took occasion to consider "the brilliant prospects" that, in view of the titanic struggle between England and France, seemed to be dawning for mankind in the New World. In outlining "the mighty benefits to be expected from a just and wise arrangement of the affairs of Spanish America," he cited the United States as an example, and laid emphasis upon the advantages that would flow to English merchants from the liberation of the Spanish Indies.

Mill descanted at length about the persistent efforts of Miranda to free his native country from Spanish rule. Appropriately did he declare that in the Venezuelan's "breast the scheme of emancipation, if not first conceived, seems at least to have been first matured." Mill included in the article excerpts from significant, inedited documents concerning Miranda's career. Here and there the essayist conveyed hints about the ramifications of the promoter's activities. As an illustration let us notice what was said about the policy of the English Government in 1808. "After various delays, a force was at last assembled; and it has been oftener than once publicly stated, we believe with perfect accuracy, that the expedition which was prepared at Cork last summer, and which was to be commanded by Sir Arthur Wellesley, was intended to coöperate with Miranda in the long projected measure of emancipating South America, and, had not the extraordinary revolution which broke out in Spain given to those forces a different destination, it is probable that, by this time, that important measure would at length have been accomplished." [9]

---

[9] *Ed. Rev.,* XIII, 297.

As these phrases suggest, the people of England were thus informed of negotiations concerning a matter that had for years been "almost exclusively the nurseling of ministers." [10]

In one of the letters written to Miranda by a sympathizer named Edward Fryer the latter declared that he was pleased at the graceful policy suggested by this article in regard to the Spanish Americans, "of receiving them, like honest men and not grasping at them like ruffians." [11] During the following month Miranda wrote to Governor Hislop of Trinidad to declare that the disposition of the people of Spanish America was to reject King Joseph while their officials wished to accept him. Then follows a commentary:

"This conduct is so natural that I have never expected anything else. And for this reason I have advised my compatriots that they should assume absolute governmental authority and dispatch capable, authorized persons to this capital in order that we may treat with England concerning the most certain manner of saving Spanish America by separating it in time from Spain. To me there never was any doubt about the subjugation of the Motherland. You, my friend, have been deceived by vulgar fables and yarns that the gazettes have been constantly disseminating among the people in spite of my precautions. * * * My friend, America is the only asylum left to us, the only part of the Spanish dominions that can now be saved!" [12]

A Spanish American called José María Antepara stated that upon arriving in England his attention was directed to the article in the *Edinburgh Review*. He judged that it contained "highly interesting statements and speculations" about his native country. In regard to Miranda he went on to say: "Among these important materials were many facts relating to a fellow countryman, of whom I had indeed heard much, but vaguely. It became a natural object of my ambition to obtain his acquaintance, which, through the intervention of

[10] *Ibid.*, p. 311.
[11] "March 30," Mir. MSS., vol. 59.
[12] April 21, 1809, *ibid.*, vol. 60.

common friends, I accomplished." [13] Señor Antepara seems
to have lived in Mexico: more than once Miranda described
him as his "Mexican friend"; and memoranda found among
Miranda's manuscripts indicate that this crony was acquainted with Mexican leaders who were discontented with the
Spanish régime.[14] There is a possibility that Antepara, who
declared himself to be "a native of Guayaquil," was a Jesuit
who had been banished from the Spanish Indies.[15]

Though we are not certain when this mysterious character
first met Miranda, yet it is clear that they had become acquainted before the close of the year 1809; for at that time
they were having printed a work ascribed to Antepara. On
January 24, 1810, a printer named Juigné, who had an office
at 17 Margaret Street, wrote to Miranda and informed him
that he had seen Antepara that very morning, had given him
"his book," and had quoted him a price on an edition of seven
hundred copies bound in a blue paper cover. "Mr. Antepara
told me," added the printer, "that he would talk with you
about this matter." [16] One of Miranda's significant efforts
as an editor was accordingly made by the aid of a Spanish-
American sympathizer. Early in 1810 there was published in
London under Antepara's name a book entitled *South American Emancipation: Documents historical and explanatory
showing the designs which have been in progress and the exertions made by General Miranda for the attainment of that
object during the last twenty-five years.* The first item in the
volume was the article from the *Edinburgh Review* entitled
the "Emancipation of Spanish America." This treatise also
contained a number of inedited documents respecting Miranda. Among these was a letter of commendation that Catherine II had addressed to her ambassadors, correspondence
concerning Miranda's career in France, papers pertaining to
his attempt to revolutionize Venezuela in 1806, and selections

---

[13] Antepara, preface, p. iii. In a letter to Miranda endorsed "Agosto 23,
1809," Cortés wrote that he had talked with Antepara who contemplated meeting him, Mir. MSS., vol. 60.   [14] *Ibid.,* vol. 62.   [15] Antepara, title-page.
[16] Mir. MSS., vol. 62.

from his recent correspondence with Spanish Americans. It also printed diverse inedited papers that illustrated other phases of his propagandism.

As Antepara stated in his preface, this illustrative material had been selected from "a treasure of upwards of sixty volumes of private and other papers" that Miranda preserved in his library. Miranda's guiding hand can be detected in the choice of these documents that were obviously selected to throw light upon various phases of his romantic career, to rehabilitate him in the eyes of the world, and to furnish the English public with detailed information about the true object of his insurrectionary designs. As some of these papers were intended for perusal by South Americans, they were presented "in a purely Spanish dress." By translation into English they were made more available to "European eyes." [17]

To forge another instrument for his campaign of propaganda, Miranda formed the design of publishing a pamphlet for circulation in the New World. This tract he obviously intended should convey to American subjects of Ferdinand VII information that would enlighten them about the critical state of European affairs.[18] His design resulted in the founding of a new journal. That periodical he placed under the direct charge of Antepara who was to be assisted by other "Mexicans" sojourning in London. In an undated note signed "Alerta," which was ascribed to Antepara, the writer said that his compatriots wished to start the periodical, and that he had informed them of a conference which he had held concerning it with Miranda.[19]

The first number of this periodical was printed in London on March 15, 1810. It was a small two-columned journal in Spanish named *El Colombiano*. Across the top of the title page was printed a motto from Cicero's *De Finibus: Nec magis vituperandum est proditor patriae, quam communis utilitatis*

---

[17] Antepara, preface, pp. iv-vii.

[18] Circular letter, March 24, 1810, Mir. MSS., vol. 62.

[19] *Ibid.*, vol. 63. On March 12, 1810, Juigné sent Miranda an estimate of the cost of publishing two hundred and fifty copies of a tract, *ibid.*

aut salutis desertor, propter suam utilitatem, aut salutem.
The first article began in these words: "The critical circum
stances in which the Spanish possessions in America are placed
in consequence of the disgraceful events that have just taken
place in the Iberian Peninsula which will probably be followed
by the entire subjugation of Old Spain, the necessity that the
inhabitants of the New World should know the condition of
affairs in Spain so that in accordance with events they can
take the decision which they may judge suitable in so perilous
a crisis, the desire that we have of being useful to those countries and of contributing to their felicity,—all these have incited us to communicate to the inhabitants of the Colombian
Continent the news that we believe interesting for their guidance in so intricate a complication of affairs. This information
will put them in a position to judge with rectitude and to work
with certainty in a matter that so much interests them. It
ought to prove the origin of their future felicity."

The editor criticized the organizations that had successively
undertaken to exercise national governmental functions for
the Spanish patriots. The eminent Spanish publicist Jovellanos was cited in regard to the illegal status of the Supreme
Junta. A quotation was made from one of its decrees to show
its "insanity and ambition." A decree of the Regency dated
February 14, 1810, which conceded delegates in the Cortes to
Spanish America, was denounced because it did not give the
colonists proportionate representation. An extract was quoted
from a recent exposition of the French Minister of the Interior
in which he announced that his government would not favor
Spanish-American independence. In a prophetic vein the article declared that the "independence of the Colombian Continent is an event that has been foreseen for a long time. All
the nations have fixed their eyes upon the New World in order
to see what decision it will take in the actual crisis that con-
fronts the Spanish monarchy."

The second number of this periodical dealt with the French
invasion of Spain. It contained translations of documents
illustrating the policy of France. Then under the rubric, "In-

crease of the Monstrous Power of Napoleon," the statement
was made that his marriage to Princess Louise of Austria had
"given to France and to the Confederation of the Rhine such
a great accession of force, that every effort to diminish the
ascendancy of Napoleon will be useless at present, and highly
dangerous in the future." He was ironically characterized as
the regenerator of the human race. The allegation was made
that opposition to him developed in the same ratio as that in
which his colossal power increased. After a discussion of
French decrees concerning state prisons and the press, the
editor asked Spanish Americans to judge "from these terrible
and notorious facts, what lot those nations must expect who,
being subjected to the influence of France, are obliged to live
under such laws! The most oppressive system that could ever
affect mankind! May Providence that has separated you from
Europe by the vast ocean also preserve you from an influence
so pestilential and so fatal!" [20]

On April 3 Miranda sent copies of the first and second numbers of the *Colombiano* to Mr. Herries and stated that, if this
official noticed anything in it "worth correcting," he could
prevail upon its owner, a "Gentleman from South America,"
to make any alterations that might be desired.[21] Two days
later the sponsor of the journal wrote to Arthur Wellesley,
who had been made Lord Wellington after defeating the soldiers of Marshal Victor and King Joseph at Talavera. Miranda expressed the hope that the Duke would terminate his
campaign in a manner which would be as useful and glorious
for his country as satisfying to his military and personal reputation. In reference to his own darling project he proceeded
to say:

"The affairs of South America are still in the suspense in
which they were placed by your departure. It is only a short
time ago that I wrote to Mr. Perceval with his consent about

---

[20] *El Colombiano*, April 1, 1810. Copies of this rare periodical were found by
the writer in the Mir. MSS., vol. 63.
[21] Mir. MSS., vol. 63.

that important subject. At this moment we have in London
certain natives of Mexico and Peru who have made strong appeals to me in regard to the affairs of their countries but we
have not made great progress. I send you the two numbers of
El Colombiano which they have had printed here at their own
expense in order to transmit news of the most important events
in Europe to their compatriots of the Colombian Continent." [22]

A translation of the second number of the journal was soon
submitted by its founder to a trusted official in Downing
Street to indicate "the complexion" which he would try to
give that paper if he were "permitted to influence it." [23] This
literary enterprise, however, did not favorably impress Vansittart. When he wrote to Miranda from Torquay to acknowledge the receipt of two numbers of the *Colombiano*, he said:
"I think that if I had been in town I should have advised
against such a publication; as it will require extraordinary
caution to avoid exciting jealousies and giving a handle to
your enemies. At any rate I hope it will be conducted with the
greatest vigilance and care." [24]

As early as March 27 Señor Abella informed the Spanish
Minister that this journal was not designed for sale but for
circulation in the Spanish Indies. The informant was convinced that the *Colombiano* was "an incendiary paper, sub-
versive of the good order, tranquillity, and union that ought
to reign in the Americas." He declared that he had "immediately undertaken to refute it. This action did not completely
satisfy my zeal and good intentions; hence I have attempted
with the keenest diligence to learn who was its author. Finally
I discovered in the very printing office of Juigné where it was
published that its author is General Miranda." [25]

On the following day Apodaca informed his government
that the *Colombiano* misrepresented events in the Peninsula
and attacked its authority in those American provinces that
had furnished many proofs of fidelity to Spain. "In conse-

[22] Mir. MSS., vol. 63.   [23] Robertson, *Miranda*, p. 427, and note b.
[24] April 20, 1810, Mir. MSS., vol. 63.
[25] Abella to Apodaca, A. G. S., estado, 8173.

quence," he continued, "as Miranda is a subject against whom by order of my government I had previously addressed formal complaints to the English ministers, I shall not lose an instant in asking that they should take some steps which will make it impossible for him to continue such revolutionary machinations." [26] The Spanish Minister subsequently informed his government that the incendiary journal was being edited by Miranda with the aid of a Spaniard called Cortés and of an American named Antepara. Yet Apodaca's complaint to Downing Street about this new activity of "the traitor" was fruitless; for the envoy was soon informed that the laws of England allowed the publication of such a periodical.[27] Miranda's inedited correspondence shows that he promptly sent the *Colombiano* to Rodríguez Peña for transmittal to Buenos Aires.

Meantime other numbers of the journal had been printed. The third issue published a decree of the Spanish Regency dated February 14, 1810, and declared that it made an illegal claim to the possession of sovereign authority. This number also contained extracts from letters of Sir John Moore discussing the government of Spain. It likewise printed a speech that Marquis Wellesley had made in Parliament touching the evil conduct of the Supreme Junta. A supplement printed a manifesto of Carlota Joaquina, consort of the Prince Regent of Portugal, dated Rio de Janeiro, August 19, 1808, and an extract from an American newspaper concerning French agents who were supposed to be en route to the Spanish Indies. In an appeal to Spanish Americans against such machinations, the *Colombiano* declared that the enemy was "not idle; as it is impossible to subjugate you by force, he aims to subjugate you by astuteness. Be vigilant against his emissaries who beyond doubt are going to sow discord among you in order that they may dominate you. Remain united and you will be invincible." [28]

The fourth number of *El Colombiano* translated from an

---

[26] *Ibid.*   [27] Apodaca to Bardaxi, May 15, 1810, *ibid.*   [28] April 15, 1810.

English periodical comments about South American affairs which suggested that the Spanish Americans should form a new government. This number also printed items concerning conditions in Spain that were taken from *El Español*, a Spanish periodical of London which was edited by a journalist styled Blanco White, who utilized information that was transmitted to him by English officials. The fifth number of the *Colombiano* reprinted other material from the same periodicals. In connection with the excerpts from *El Español* the comment was made that a real revolution was necessary to liberate Spain. The Spaniards were entreated to get rid of all vestiges of their former government: "If the heat of a revolution terrifies you, if preoccupations make you fear even the thought of liberty, you should realize that you are destined perpetually to remain slaves!" [29]

On May 19 the vigilant Spanish Minister wrote to the Captain General of Galicia to warn him that copies of *El Español*, a magazine intended to discredit Spanish operations in the Peninsula, and *El Colombiano*, a journal designed to revolutionize Spanish America, were being distributed from London.[30] The editor in chief, however, soon decided that it was wise to cease publishing his periodical. On June 2, 1810, he addressed a letter marked "private" to Vansittart to state that he need not be disquieted about the *Colombiano* any longer: "one has taken every possible precaution; and number five will be the last for the present." [31] Yet Miranda's purpose had been in part accomplished; for before the end of this year extracts from his journal were published in such secessionist organs as the *Gaceta de Caracas* and the *Gaceta de Buenos Aires*.[32]

From 1808 to 1810 Miranda's home in Grafton Street was undoubtedly a rendezvous for those discontented Spanish Americans who found their way to London. In addition to Antepara and Sanz, at this time Miranda became acquainted with

---

[29] May 15, 1810.   [30] A. G. S., estado, 8173.   [31] Mir. MSS., vol. 63.
[32] *Gaceta de Buenos Aires*, Oct. 4, 1810; *Gaceta de Caracas*, Nov. 9, 1810.

a Spaniard named Cortés who had served under the French flag in the Antilles. After becoming interested in revolutionary projects, he had proceeded to Europe in order to sound the intentions of England in regard to Spanish America. Shortly after his arrival in London he sent a letter to Miranda to assert that the French aimed to absorb the Spanish colonies in America and to offer his services to prevent that calamity.[33] Early in 1809 another mysterious conspirator who went by the name of Toledo sought the society of Cortés and also made approaches to Miranda.[34] He was promptly informed by Cortés of the arrival in London of disaffected Mexicans.

The leading advocate of Spanish American independence also became acquainted with patriots from Portugal who had sought an asylum in England. A Portuguese who had friends in Brazil afforded him an opportunity to transmit letters to Rio de Janeiro. As early as October, 1808, Miranda was in touch with another Portuguese named Hippolyto José da Costa who vainly endeavored to publish in the *Times* an article about events at Caracas. Further, to paraphrase the words of an Edinburgh periodical, one of the Portuguese journals published in England was induced to favor the schemes and to "exaggerate the merits of Miranda, as one who was to be the Washington of the southern continent." [35]

This journal was probably the *Correio Braziliense ou Armazem Literario* that was founded in London in 1808. In number XI of this periodical, which bore the date of April, 1809, its editor began to publish in Portuguese a synopsis of the article on the "Emancipation of Spanish America" that had just appeared in the *Edinburgh Review*.[36] Six months later Da Costa, who was the founder and editor of the *Correio Braziliense*, wrote to Miranda to inform him that a certain essay concerning Spanish-American affairs had been printed in Portuguese, to ask for suggestions about an article respect-

[33] Jan. 26, 1809, Mir. MSS., vol. 59. [34] Toledo to Miranda, Feb. 12, 1809, *ibid.*
[35] *Edinburgh Annual Register,* vol. IV, pt. I, p. 387.
[36] *Correio Braziliense,* II, 349-59.

ing Venezuela, and to inquire regarding the date of a certain number of the *Gaceta de Caracas* that had evidently been loaned to him by the Venezuelan.[37] In the midsummer of 1810 the *Correio Braziliense* published Portuguese translations of some of the seditious letters that Miranda had been dispatching to capital cities in the Spanish Indies.[38] Da Costa was undoubtedly a channel through which information regarding the separatist movements in Spanish America found its way from Miranda into the pages of Portuguese-American journals.

Miranda kept watch upon articles concerning his native land that appeared in English newspapers. An intermediary through whom he presented his views to the English people was a Spanish American styled Dr. Constancio who seems to have been a Mexican.[39] Notes inscribed upon newspaper clippings that Miranda carefully preserved among his papers show that articles printed in London dailies above the pseudonym of "Las Casas" were in reality written by Dr. Constancio. In a communication published by the *Statesman* on September 13, 1809, "Las Casas" criticized English policy toward Spain. In what seems like an adaptation of Miranda's views, he asked the following questions:

"Why, shall we ask, was there any stipulation made concerning America, with the Spanish patriots? Why did we pledge ourselves for the continuance of the slavery of our natural friends? Why not allow *them* the same liberty of choosing a government which the Spaniards claimed? Had the self-elected Juntas acquired, or inherited, any rights over America? * * * If we were determined to support the Spanish insurrection, we ought to have done it without binding ourselves to keep the colonies united with the mother-country. * * * Unless then we again address ourselves frankly to the Americans, laying aside our Spanish connections, it is impossible for us to succeed, while by our fruitless attempts we shall only increase the influence of Bonaparte, when he is master of Spain,

---

[37] Oct. 20, 1809, Mir. MSS., 61.   [38] *Correio Braziliense*, V, 204-12.
[39] Wilberforce, *Life of William Wilberforce*, III, 434.

over the rich continent of America. * * * *Let the natives alone frame their own government.*"

On November 1, 1809, "Las Casas" contributed an essay to the *Statesman* entitled the "Emancipation of Spanish America." In this article Constancio argued that Napoleon was now "the sole Lord of the whole Continent," that the liberation of Spanish America would furnish new and profitable markets for English goods, and that "a new power in America" would also serve to counterbalance the prestige of Napoleon in Europe. In the following month Constancio informed Miranda of his prospective departure from England. After expressing pleasure at having become acquainted with Miranda's merit, loyalty, and talent, Constancio continued: "It is with regret that I have resolved to abandon your beautiful and sublime project, but the condition of my finances does not permit me long to remain without any employment." [40]

The essayist in chief did not altogether escape public criticism. On April 5, 1810, the *Times* published an anonymous letter, apparently written by a Spaniard, which deliberately conveyed the impression that the people of South America were not generally desirous of achieving their independence. An intimation was also conveyed in this communication that a South American who had striven to promote that independence did not possess a reputable lineage. Miranda's secretary soon tried to have the editor of the *Times* insert a refutation to what was considered a "disreputable charge." [41] When that attempt failed Miranda endeavored to clear his escutcheon by articles in other London newspapers. [42] In a letter about "South America" signed by "A Peruvian" that was published in both the *Statesman* and the *Morning Chronicle*, a reply was made to the reflections upon the general's ances-

---

[40] Dec. 7, 1809, Mir. MSS., vol. 61. On May 30, 1811, Dr. Constancio, who was then in Paris, sent a letter to Bassano, French minister of foreign affairs, to propose that he should be sent to sound Miranda and other Venezuelan patriots concerning close relations with France, A. A. E., Portugal et Brésil, 127. [41] Courteney to Miranda, "Friday 6 o'clock," Mir. MSS., vol. 63. [42] "To the Editor of the *Morning Chronicle*," *ibid.*

try. The Peruvian,—if such indeed he was,—declared that
"General Miranda was received into the armies of the King
of Spain at the age of seventeen, at the rank of Captain, which
he could not have been without proving titles of nobility."
The polemist further declared that authentic documents at-
testing his assertions had been deposited with a bookseller
named Dulau in Soho Square, "where any person on whom
the assertion of the anonymous Spaniard has made an impression, may receive satisfaction." [43]

Though Miranda's time was largely absorbed by journalistic labors, yet he did not become a recluse. On December 25,
1808, Lady Townshend asked him to dinner to meet the Duke
of Cumberland.[44] A card found in General Miranda's papers
dated "St. James 6th Jany. 1809," bears an invitation to him
to dine with the Duke at the palace.[45] Shortly afterwards the
general was invited to dine with Admiral Nugent.[46] In May,
1809, he brought to the attention of Francis Jeffrey, who was
visiting London, the posthumous works of his friend "the
illustrious artist" Barry as a publication worthy of attention
in the *Edinburgh Review*.[47] A letter from an old English
friend named Benjamin Waddington dated July 5, 1809, inviting Miranda to pay his family a visit of a week or a month
at Hanover House, near Abergavenny, shows that he was still
popular in other circles. With this invitation Waddington inclosed a billet in which his wife and daughter expressed an
anxious desire "to form an acquaintance with a person whose
virtues and talents" had long excited their admiration. They
expressed the hope that the general would grant "from gal-
lantry to *two women*, the request that motives of convenience
might induce him to refuse to a *man*." [48] It is to be regretted
that Miranda did not explain in the letter announcing his intention to obey "their amiable commands" what he promised
to expound verbally to Waddington, namely, the motives

---

[43] *Statesman,* April 9, 1810; *Morning Chronicle,* April 16, 1810.
[44] Mir. MSS., vol. 58.   [45] *Ibid.*   [46] "Saturday, March 25th," *ibid.*
[47] Miranda to Jeffrey, May 8 and May 27, 1809, *ibid.*, vol. 60.   [48] *Ibid.*

which induced him "to decline accompanying Sir A. Wellesley into Portugal and Spain, etc." [49] During his excursion to Monmouthshire the Venezuelan visited Abergavenny, Cheltenham, Gloucester, and Oxford University.

In 1809 Miranda became well acquainted with the curious dwarf, the philosopher Jeremy Bentham, to whom he loaned books and maps relating to Spanish America. On his part, Miranda borrowed from Bentham a treatise of the Spanish publicist Jovellanos.[50] In August, 1809, the utilitarian philosopher directed their mutual friend James Mill to invite Miranda to visit the farm house in Surrey where he was sojourning. "May you," wrote Bentham to Miranda, "by God's grace live a thousand years." [51] It was probably under Miranda's influence that Bentham's interest turned from Mexico to South America.

With the philanthropist William Wilberforce, who was a member of Parliament, the exile formed a deep attachment. After dining with Wilberforce at Kensington Gore early in May, 1809, Miranda wrote in a diarial entry that his host had treated him with much "friendship and tenderness." There Miranda met a director of the East India Company, who discussed "with great pleasure and approval" his plans concerning South America. Miranda was now convinced that news of the rout of the Austrians by Napoleon had caused Englishmen to look with fresh interest to the Spanish Indies. In consequence he believed that they wished to be informed about its "climate, population, and productions. I also perceived," he said, "some sentiments of liberty in the conversation of Wilberforce and of horror for the Inquisition. Hence I have sent him the works of De Pons about Venezuela and the *Archives Littéraires* about the Inquisition." [52] In the letter to the reformer Miranda stated that in this periodical under the rubric Spain the philanthropist would find discussed "some of the nefarious proceedings of the Holy Tribunal as late as

[49] July 31, 1809, *ibid.*   [50] Bentham to Miranda, April 1, 1809, *ibid.*
[51] Aug. 25, 1809, *ibid.*   [52] "Mayo 6," *ibid.*

the year 1804; where by its unremitting efforts to degrade human understanding [it] has at last so perfectly succeeded as to bring the Nation, and the Monarchy that supported it," to its absolute subversion.[53]

In the company of Dr. Constancio, in January, 1810, the South American dined with Wilberforce. In his *Diary* the publicist wrote that Miranda talked until half past eleven, "and still untired—very entertaining and instructive, but used God's name lightly, else all his sentiments and positions just, humane, and even delicate; as his refusing to bear arms against Spain." [54] On his part the reformer hoped to interest Miranda in the abolition of negro slavery. So deep a concern in Spanish America did Wilberforce show that Miranda submitted to his inspection confidential papers concerning his negotiations with English and French ministers from 1790 to 1808.[55] As a result, said Miranda, the philanthropist "was filled with zeal for our independence and desired to see the plans originally drawn up with his friend Mr. Pitt carried out by the present government." [56] It is evident that the promoter hoped through Wilberforce and Nepean to influence the English Government to favor his long-meditated projects.[57] A letter written in the third person displays the propagandist at work:

"General Miranda has the honour to send to Mr. Wilberforce the few extracts from the late classic authors about the Spanish Colonies of South America, which he promised the other day.

"He sends also the copy of Cap^n. Beaver's letter about the occurrences that took place in the City of Caracas, when they learnt the invasion of the French, etc. (and which paper, if he should not absolutely want, he begs him to return after perusal).

"Two printed copies of Viscardo's *Lettre aux Espagnols-*

---

[53] May 8, 1809, Mir. MSS., vol. 60.　　　[54] Wilberforce, III, 434.
[55] Miranda to Wilberforce, Jan. 13, 1810, Mir. MSS., vol. 62.
[56] Miranda to Vansittart, Jan. 19, 1810, *ibid.*
[57] Miranda to Wilberforce, April 26, 1810, *ibid.*, vol. 63.

Américains, where he will find the solid grounds of our contention with the Spanish oppressors, and their abominable old government. There is more truth, justice, and solid reasoning in this small Pamphlet, than in all the speeches and assertions about Spain and South America, that he has yet seen or heard of from the noble Lord H———d." [58]

At the invitation of Captain James Stanhope, who declared that his sister was "very anxious" to make his acquaintance, Miranda also met the eccentric Lady Hester Stanhope, who had managed the household affairs of her uncle, William Pitt.[59] Captain Stanhope had recently returned to London from Coruña where he had witnessed the tragic death of Sir John Moore, an intimate friend and correspondent of Lady Hester. On April 29, 1809, the South American thus recorded his impressions of Lady Hester in a disjected jotting scrawled on the back of a note from her brother:

"I have dined with Lady Hester Stanhope (niece of Mr. Pitt) who enchanted me by her amiability, erudition, and liberal conversation. At one time she talked about Rome and Italy, which she had visited; at another time she talked about Greece, which she wished to visit and which she was not able to see when she was in Naples. She also talked about Venezuela whose independence she wished to see established upon a basis of rational liberty. In this connection she said to me that her uncle Mr. Pitt had upon various occasions talked to her with interest and warmth about this affair, and had particularly lauded my patriotic ideas. With this motive he had shortly before my embarkation for New York proposed that we should dine together at Walmer Castle. Ever since, Lady Hester had wished to become acquainted with me, and had also wished to visit my interesting country. She said further that if I needed a recruit of her species, she was ready to follow me there though it should be to do nothing else than to manage schools and hospitals. All this she descanted upon with the greatest jocularity and grace until midnight when I retired

---

[58] June 4, 1810, *ibid.*
[59] J. Stanhope to Miranda April 19, 1809, *ibid.,* vol. 60.

most highly impressed by her conversation, good judgment, amiability, and interesting person. She is one of the most delightful women I have ever known,—and, if her behaviour accords with my first impressions,—she is certainly a rarity among her sex." [60]

In a letter dated July 31, inviting Miranda to visit at a farm house near Bath where she was sojourning, Lady Hester expressed her delight at the prospect of seeing him "in this part of the world." She hoped that, whether he should lodge at an inn or at a neat house in town she should have the pleasure of seeing him every day to dinner "and that you will spend as much *more* of yr time here as you can spare from yr *books*, a certain number of which I suppose travel with you." [61] There is no doubt that Miranda discussed his grand passion with her at length. On January 21, 1810, he wrote to her that "the interview on Wednesday last, with Mr. W——, was long, interesting, and satisfactory; and I had another the next day (by his own request) with the Duke of G——, on the same subject whom I am to see again tomorrow and shall not forget your message. They seem both earnest and hopeful; I wished you was near to communicate, and to give advice—things appear certainly promising now, and in a short time we must perceive the reality." [62] About this time, with an acknowledgment of his solicitous inquiries about her health, Lady Hester sent Miranda a book and wrote thus: "May I be allowed to flatter myself that the pages which contain an account of the brilliant political career of Lord Chatham, will not be rendered less valuable, from being presented to you by his Granddaughter. * * * " [63] Untoward events were perhaps what saved the revolutionary from an *affaire de coeur*.

Miranda's notions regarding the Spanish Indies at this juncture are expressed in his correspondence with Vansittart and with Spencer Perceval, who had become prime minister

[60] *Diario,* "April 29," Mir. MSS., vol. 60. See further, Bentham, *Works,* X, 458.   [61] Mir. MSS., vol. 60.
[62] Miranda to Lady Stanhope, Jan. 21, 1810, *ibid.,* vol. 62.
[63] "Tuesday night," *ibid.*

in October, 1809. In a letter addressed to Vansittart under date of January 1, 1810, Miranda declared that the news from South America about revolutionary discontent and commotions was "satisfactory in every point of View." [64] In a letter to the same friend about two months later he said: "I have seen Mr. Wilberforce and the Duke of Gloucester who displayed a great interest in my affairs. * * * Mr. Wilberforce has promised to speak to Mr. P—— upon the subject, but I believe that the government is at present in a most unfavorable position to act." [65] A month later Miranda addressed a letter to the Prime Minister to ask that he would appoint some trusty person or persons with whom he might confer about the policy that England should adopt toward the Spanish colonies. "This mode," commented Miranda, "might perhaps be most efficacious for bringing this affair to a final decision; and to rescue, if possible, those Colonies from the imminent danger of falling under the baneful influence of France:—which circumstance would be attended in all probability, with the ruin of its innocent inhabitants, and an immense detriment to the commerce and interests of Great Britain." He added that the means necessary to emancipate Spanish America would be nothing "in comparison of what was formerly required, and Great Britain had agreed to afford." [66] However, as he admitted in a letter addressed to Lord Wellington, Miranda did not feel that he was now making much progress toward the execution of his long-cherished designs.[67]

Evidence that will help us to divine the state of Miranda's mind can also be gleaned from letters which he addressed at this juncture to persons in America. In October, 1809, in a letter to a North American friend named Loudon the promoter expressed the opinion that in proportion as the French gained control of the Iberian Peninsula, South America seemed "to fly away from Old Spain." [68] In an epistle to Con-

---

[64] *Ibid.*   [65] February 26, 1810, *ibid.*
[66] Miranda to Perceval, March 31, 1810, *ibid.*
[67] Miranda to Wellington, April 3, 1810, *ibid.,* vol. 63.
[68] Oct. 3, 1809, *ibid.,* vol. 61.

tucci on January 17, 1810, he declared that Spain was now entirely evacuated by English soldiers and that almost all of her provinces had been either completely subjugated by the French or had submitted to King Joseph. He expressed the hope that in a short time the intention of the English Government in regard to the Spanish-American cause would become as favorable as it had hitherto been "vacillating and contradictory." [69]

In a letter addressed to his old friend Colonel Smith on February 7, Miranda declared that a change of administration was expected in London every day. "The course of events," he avowed, "are however, in favor of our Patriotic and just Views for the Independency of the Colombian Continent, and even for its *Liberties*, that is a much more important object. The late accounts I have received relative to *Quito, Peru,* and *Buenos aires* promise freedom, under a representative form of government." He expressed the hope that these blessings would soon be extended to all the Spanish colonies in spite of "Spanish imbecility" and English nonsense.[70] In a letter to Febles on February 8, Miranda declared that there were in London certain creoles from the Spanish Indies who thought and felt as he did but with more vehemence and severity. "You will see this," he continued, "by the brief addition to the tract of Viscardo which they have reprinted here and which you will soon receive for distribution to interested persons in Terra Firma. Colonists in southern South America have much solicited me to join them, but I shall watch with caution and vigilance without forgetting my old friends and compatriots." [71] Obviously the plotter thought that England would soon be forced to give up her struggle against Napoleon on the European Continent and that she would then undertake the execution of his plans. At least, he wished to encourage this belief among his diverse correspondents.

During the years when Miranda was busying himself as an essayist and propagandist he was again harrassed by finan-

---

[69] Mir. MSS., vol. 62.   [70] *Ibid.*   [71] *Ibid.*

cial difficulties. On November 18, 1809, he wrote to Nicholas Vansittart to explain that he had called on Under Secretary Herries in regard to his finances. "He promised me," said Miranda, "to speak to Mr. Jenkinson, successor of the detestable Cooke, about the payment of the three-fourths of my allowance that is due me. If you know this new secretary I wish that you would write him a line on this subject * * * in order that he may use it suitably. This would counteract the perfidious insinuations of Mr. Cooke whom I believe capable of anything." [72] On November 30 Herries wrote to Miranda to inform him that Jenkinson would "be glad to see him at his office in Downing Street between 12 and 2 o'clock tomorrow,— when, if General Miranda will bring with him some document to show to what period his allowance was last paid by Mr. Cooke, Mr. Jenkinson will pay him what is due upon it. [73] On December 4 Miranda informed Herries that he had "received the total amount of his allowance to this day" but that Molini's allowance had not yet been paid. [74]

In the middle of December, Davison who was in financial straits because of disreputable practices as a government contractor turned over a promissory note of Miranda for one thousand pounds to a banking firm in Pall Mall that demanded immediate payment. Not being able to do so, Miranda was forced to appeal to Nicholas Vansittart. In response that friend sent him a note on December 23 declaring that the contractor had played him a very villainous trick. [75] On the next day Vansittart wrote thus: "Davison has acted infamously but there is no remedy but to pay him off. You must pay as much as you can without distressing yourself and I have written to Messrs. Boehm and Tayler, one of the most reputable mercantile houses in London who have acted as bankers to my father and mother and since to me, to assist you with whatever may be necessary to complete Davison's demand." [76] Mr. Tayler accordingly took over the promissory note to Davi-

---

[72] Mir. MSS., vol. 61.   [73] *Ibid.*   [74] *Ibid.*   [75] *Ibid.*   [76] *Ibid.*

son; and Miranda wrote to his constant friend: "I feel quite relieved indeed, by being out of any connexion with that odious and despicable *Being*, and thank you very much for it." [77] Vansittart replied in a sympathetic strain: "I am very glad you have had a satisfactory interview with Mr. Tayler. * * * I congratulate you on having put an end to your connection with Davison." [78] It was in this wise that Miranda incurred a not inconsiderable obligation to John Tayler which was not liquidated at the time of his death.

The change in the policy of Downing Street caused by the Spanish uprising did not altogether prevent Miranda from following developments in South America. Neither did it hinder him from enlarging his acquaintance with discontented Mexicans and South Americans who continued to visit England. During this period the chief spokesman of dissatisfied Spanish-American colonists deliberately undertook to use the press as a vehicle of propaganda. By spicy articles in newspapers and journals and by the publication of the unique volume entitled *South American Emancipation*, Miranda disseminated a knowledge of conditions in Spanish America and of his own designs more widely than ever. His most distinctive literary achievement was perhaps the founding of *El Colombiano* that was designed to spread in the Spanish Indies news of the distracted condition of Spain. Thus the seeds of revolution were to be widely scattered.

Aside from these activities, his sojourn in London had served to stimulate an interest in the cause of Spanish-American emancipation not only on the part of certain English publicists but also among literati, merchants, philosophers, and social leaders of the English metropolis. It is scarcely an exaggeration to say that Miranda thus helped to lay foundations for the sympathetic yet interested outlook on American affairs that reached fruition many years later in Canning's decision to acknowledge the independence of the emancipated Spanish colonies in the New World.

---

[77] Jan. 1, 1810, Mir. MSS., vol. 62.   [78] Jan. 3, 1810, *ibid.*, vol. 61.

Chapter XVIII

THE RETURN OF THE EXILE

THOUGH IN 1808 manifestations of loyalty to the Mother-land had been made in the Spanish Indies, yet here and there provisional juntas had been formed. Separatist tendencies were soon manifested. Miranda judged that the quasi-insur-rectionary commotions which took place in 1809 in various quarters of South America were important and satisfactory from every point of view. In a letter addressed to Governor Hislop on February 8, 1810, the revolutionary thus expressed his views on the international situation:

"You can scarcely form a correct idea of the vacillating and disgusting state of this country. The trouble is that neither do we have a competent administration nor can we form the kind of administration that is necessary. Whatever plans have been formed here during the past two years seem to have been so absurd or so badly executed that the enemy has gained incalculable successes and advantages. * * *

"Commercial and political attention is now being turned toward Spanish America at a time which to me seems some-what tardy. According to the latest advices, Quito, Charcas, Arequipa, Chuquisaca, and perhaps even Lima and Buenos Aires, have already formed a popular administration that is independent of the cursed Central Junta. Persons of standing and influence in those provinces have recently written to me in regard to these movements, but, after consulting with my friends here I have decided not to change my situation until the favorable moment arrives. Perhaps that time is not far distant." [1]

The transfer of political authority in Spain from the Cen-tral Junta to a Regency convinced Miranda that the juncture was auspicious for a change in English policy toward the In-dies. He accordingly designed to urge his views upon Van-sittart but that Minister was unfortunately absent from Lon-

---

[1] Mir. MSS., vol. 62.

don. Miranda then called upon Sir Evan Nepean, but found
that he was in the country looking after a new estate. Hence
the disappointed Venezuelan described the situation to Wilberforce in the hope that they might be able "to devise some
other mode of pressing a decision from the Government at
this critical moment." [2]

The distracted condition of Spain soon stimulated movements in America that formed the prelude to the protracted
struggle for independence. In Venezuela a supposition that
Captain General Emparán was in the French interest encouraged those colonists who dreamed of altering their political régime. The spirit of dissent did not decrease when prominent Venezuleans became aware of the irruption of French
soldiers into Andalusia and the dissolution of the Central
Junta. On April 18 Spanish agents arrived in the city of Caracas with the announcement that the newly established Regency
should be recognized. This order convinced disgruntled creoles
that the proper time for action had arrived.

Upon the following day, which was Holy Thursday, the
cabildo of Caracas assembled in an extraordinary session that
Emparán was invited to attend. Deputies of the clergy and
the people eventually proposed that a junta of government
should be formed for Venezuela. A persuasive canon named
José Cortés de Madariaga, who was a native of Chile, urged
that the Captain General should be excluded from this junta.
Emparán evidently appealed to the people from the balcony
of the town hall to retain him in supreme command. When
they refused to do so, he relinquished his office. Accordingly,
by what seemed like a preconcerted movement, on April 19,
1810, the governmental authority of the Captaincy General
was assumed by the extraordinary *cabildo* of the capital city.
In reality, this dramatic change signalized the beginning of
a disguised revolution.

On April 20 the *cabildo* issued a manifesto that announced
the change of government, avowed its fidelity to Ferdinand

---

[2] Miranda to Wilberforce, April 26, 1810, Mir. MSS., vol. 63.

VII, and invited the people of Venezuela to join this movement. On the same day it framed an address to Spanish Americans declaring that the Venezuelans were resolved to assume "the political independence which the order of events" had restored to them. The town council even avowed that Venezuela had entered the ranks of "the free nations of America!"[3] It also enacted some reform decrees. The *alcabala* or tax upon the sale or exchange of certain articles of consumption was swept away. The tribute or poll-tax exacted from the aborigines was abolished. Provision was made that the soldiers who had effectively supported the revolutionary changes should be rewarded by double pay. A subscription was started to raise funds to pay the expenses of the provisional government. Agents were selected who were to be dispatched to adjacent provinces to solicit support for the new régime.

Twenty-three prominent citizens were soon selected to act as a governmental junta. Secretaries of war and the navy, finance, justice, and foreign affairs were appointed. On April 27 "the Supreme Junta" issued a proclamation to the *cabildos* of capital cities in Spanish America inviting them to imitate the political transformation that had taken place at Caracas. It also suggested that a Spanish-American federation should be formed.

On the following day the junta appointed Juan V. Bolívar, an elder brother of Simón Bolívar, and Telésforo de Orea as agents to the United States. Their credentials stated that the governmental junta, which wished to preserve the rights of Ferdinand VII in Venezuela, desired to improve the relations of amity and commerce with friendly or neutral nations. Early in May the junta framed an address declaring that the Venezuelans would not recognize the Spanish Regency but that they would gladly obey a government in the Motherland which was founded upon legitimate and equitable principles. In August it abolished the slave trade. In September it made a commercial agreement with the secretary of the governor

---

[3] *Times*, July 2, 1810.

of Curaçao to the effect that goods imported into or exported from Venezuela by English subjects should be allowed to pass on the payment of three-quarters of the duties that were levied upon other foreigners.[4]

Let us now pass quickly over the rest of Spanish America of 1810 and take a rapid bird's-eye view. In May an extraordinary *cabildo* at Buenos Aires replaced Viceroy Cisneros by a provisional junta which announced that it would preserve the King's authority. In July a *cabildo* at Bogotá formed a semi-independent junta for the Viceroyalty of New Granada. In September the Captain General of Chile was replaced by a governmental junta that avowed allegiance to Ferdinand VII. About the same time a daring curate named Hidalgo started an insurrection against Spanish rule in Mexico. It seemed indeed as though a seismic convulsion had passed through the Spanish Indies. Although the distracted Spanish Americans loudly proclaimed fidelity to their captive King, yet it appears that some audacious creoles had visions of secession from Spain. Eager for news from dissentient Spanish America, in a confidential letter written in English to Colonel Smith on June 18, 1810, Miranda thus gave voice to his sentiments:

"I have already received applications, even from opposite parties in S. A., inviting me to join them; with offers of the most Pre-eminent situations, honours, etc., but I think that prudence requires I should defer it, until the abominable Spanish Agents shall be expelled from the Country; and then it would be the proper time for me to appear, and to take an active part in ascertaining the Independencies of those Provinces, under the solid basis of a permanent, rational, and free government.—*Then*, all our anxiety and suspence will cease, and better prospects and satisfaction will dawn for us—May Divine Providence protect our patriotic and virtuous de-

---

[4] Ponte, *Bolívar y otros ensayos,* pp. 332-35. However, this arrangement was disapproved by Lord Liverpool, who in a dispatch to Governor Layard, Jan. 19, 1811, informed that governor that commerce with the Spanish colonists would have to be carried on in accordance with Orders in Council, C. O., 66/3.

signs, for the welfare and protection of mankind in the most awful and threatening period of its subjugation!" [5]

Near the end of June reports of the events of April 19 at Caracas reached England. Suggestive commentaries upon the kaleidoscopic changes in Venezuela soon appeared in London newspapers. Blanco White published some "Political Reflections" in which he asserted that "the standard of independence had been raised in South America." [6] On June 23 the *Courier* declared that the important news was not unexpected. "It will be more a matter of astonishment that that vast territory should have preserved its dependence upon the Mother Country so long, considering the total want of energy on the part of the Spanish Government, and its subserviency to the councils and commands of France, than that it should at last have disclosed a spirit of independence, and expressed a determination to exist as a separate State."

Ever on the alert for favoring circumstances Miranda promptly learned of the formation of a junta in Venezuela. In a note to the Duke of Gloucester written at half-past two on a Monday morning he declared: "The late News from Caracas are confirmed by various letters received from the contiguous Islands, by Merchants in this City." [7] An article in the *Examiner* on July 1, which noticed Miranda's plans, naturally attracted his attention. It avowed that a decisive revolt against the miserable Government of Spain had long been expected. Distracted Europe now turned an eager eye to the New World. Reports about an insurrection in Venezuela should excite strong sympathy in every Englishman as suggesting "the dawn of a new era in history." Its editor declared that if the Spanish colonies should choose to declare their independence, "they have at least a full claim to our forbearance against them, and should be left to work out their deliverance on every ground of policy and natural right." Then he added: "Whatever we may do, will be done rather against

[5] Mir. MSS., vol. 63.   [6] *El Español*, IV, 42.   [7] Mir. MSS., vol. 63.

Bonaparte than for them,—rather against the overturner of old systems whom we have helped to make a powerful despot, than in favor of the overturners of old systems whom we may help to make friends and freemen." Upon the manifesto issued by the junta of Caracas the *Examiner* made the comment that it approached "a complete declaration of independence" and that Ferdinand VII was "now a mere name." When Miranda sent a copy of the *Examiner* to the Duke of Gloucester, he declared that its description of "the late revolution at Caracas" was more accurately stated "with the exception of the too flattering account of himself" than any other he had read in the London newspapers.[8]

Miranda soon took measures to transmit his sentiments to friends in the West Indies. In a letter to Francisco Febles on July 7, he declared that the steps which had been taken at Caracas seemed very favorable to him and that they appeared to be in accordance with instructions that he had sent from London "a year ago by a person who came for that purpose." He requested Febles to dispatch certain Spanish Americans from Trinidad to Venezuela in order that they might succor their compatriots. He enclosed a copy of the *Examiner* with the comment that it described the affairs of Venezuela and her "relations with England very well, although what it says about me personally is very extravagant." [9] On the same day in a letter of similar tenor addressed to Governor Hislop of Trinidad with whom he maintained a correspondence, the revolutionary suggested that perhaps the governor might wish to print extracts from the *Examiner* in the Trinidad *Gazette*. He declared that the news of the events of April 19 at Caracas had "excited very general interest for the emancipation and freedom of South America at this most critical period. * * * God grant to the new Governors of Caracas wisdom and moderation, as everything depends on their conduct to win the affections and good will" of all Europe or to lose them.[10] Miranda also undertook to disseminate the news of the Venezue-

---

[8] July 2, 1810, Mir. MSS., vol. 63.   [9] *Ibid.*   [10] *Ibid.*

lan uprising in other parts of South America. On August 2 he addressed a letter to Felipe Contucci, and, after expressing astonishment at views which his correspondent had expressed in favor of the founding of a monarchy in La Plata under Carlota Joaquina, he said:

"The Captaincy General of Venezuela has just furnished you, it appears to me, with a grand example of patriotism, prudence, and policy. If you follow that example, with the limitations and reserve which are necessary under the conditions existing in your country, I believe that you will do much better than if you embark in perilous projects for the purpose of introducing foreigners and new sovereigns into your provinces. In number XXVI of the *Correio Braziliense* you will find authentic documents and details about the memorable events which happened on April 19 in the province of Caracas. The annexed numbers of the *Colombiano* will furnish you with the news of Europe that should most interest our Americas. Read these with care and draw from them the benefit that I sincerely and cordially desire shall accrue to those beautiful and hitherto mistreated regions." [11]

About this time Miranda became acquainted with Matías de Irigoyen, an agent of the junta of Buenos Aires. Irigoyen had arrived in London with instructions to negotiate with the English Government for permission to procure military supplies. We extract the following from a discerning letter addressed by Miranda to Saturnino Rodríguez Peña, after learning from Irigoyen and his colleague Larrea about the establishment of a governmental junta at Buenos Aires in May, 1810:

"From their reports it appears to me that the events at Buenos Aires do not promise any less success than those at Caracas. It is a remarkable thing that those two cities, so distant from one another, at an interval of only thirty days, without the slightest communication, have followed throughout the same steps and have taken the political measures which are adapted to carry out their glorious revolutions! Take care,

---

[11] *Ibid.*

my friend, to support this policy; for every retrograde step that is now taken will involve the most fatal consequences for the happiness of those countries. * * * Liberty is nothing else than justice wisely administered; and where atrocious crimes are committed with impunity, true liberty cannot have an abode!

"From what Señor Larrea tells me I am convinced that you have gone to join your worthy brother in Buenos Aires. You should then labor with zeal and activity to lay the bases of civil and representative government, allowing time to mature progressively these institutions. Thus you will give your country the greatest benefit that men can confer upon their fellow-beings,—that is, to redeem them from slavery and to make them free and independent. May Providence grant you complete success in such a noble enterprise and give them the enjoyment of such great felicity!" [12]

Miranda soon received letters from Venezuela regarding the April revolution. Two citizens of Caracas wrote to their compatriot to declare their esteem for his character and to express the hope that he would by his knowledge and ability contribute "to the perfection of the portentous work which had been begun." [13] In reply Miranda characterized April 19 as "a celebrated and glorious day for Caracas. An ever memorable epoch, if its results are as favorable as its good beginnings promise, and as the patriotism of her citizens should expect." He ventured the opinion that the "great task has only been started and that the most difficult and arduous work is necessary for its perfection. Still, if everyone coöperates with unselfishness and good will to the same end, the consummation of the work appears to me not merely probable but easy. 'With concord,' says a great writer, 'small states become great, while discord destroys even the greatest state.' " The enthusiast expressed hope that he might soon proceed to his native province where he would behold "those people free and happy" whom he had "left servile and oppressed." [14]

[12] Aug. 15, 1810, Mir. MSS., vol. 63.
[13] J. E. Sizo and F. A. Miranda to Francisco de Miranda, June 6, 1810, *ibid.*
[14] Miranda to Sizo and F. A. Miranda, Aug. 3, 1810, *ibid.*

J. M. Fernández of Caracas, who seems to have been a relative of Miranda, also sent him a laudatory letter. This correspondent stated that he had celebrated the events of April 19 with a group of Miranda's friends which included members of the Bolívar family and the Marquis of Toro. He declared that there were other patriots in Caracas who esteemed Miranda "as the first patriot of the country, and the champion upon whom we count. The influence of his eloquence should secure the support and protection of England, and thus bring to these provinces the greatest degree of felicity." [15] In his reply Miranda said that "Messrs. Bolívar and Méndez, who have corroborated the information which you sent me, will doubtless tell our friends in that city how much I am pleased by their estimable favors. Oblige me by offering my regards to the Toros, the Bolívars, and the other persons who have wished to be remembered to me, until Providence grants me the pleasure of giving them an embrace and of felicitating them personally on the glorious events with which they have immortalized themselves and rendered their fellow beings free and happy." [16]

At this critical juncture Miranda was again harassed by delays in the payment of his financial allowance. In the end of June he sent Molini to a trusted official of the English Government with a request that the half-year quotas of the allowances due to himself and his secretary should be paid. A form of receipt found among his papers indicates that the amount then due him was three hundred and fifty pounds. [17] The youthful Robert Peel, however, referred Miranda to Mr. Jenkinson, an under secretary in the war department, and declared that the account from which the "allowance" had previously been paid had not yet been transferred to him. [18] Not being able to obtain satisfaction from Peel, Miranda next applied to Herries who informed him that the difficulty was due to "a delay in

---

[15] June 4, 1810, *ibid.*   [16] Aug. 3, 1810, *ibid.*
[17] Miranda to Peel, June 29, 1810, *ibid.*
[18] Peel to Miranda, June 29, 1810, *ibid.*

the issue of a sum of money to the Secretary of State" out of which his allowance was to be paid.[19] In spite of assurances that his monetary affairs would be settled by the payment of the six months' quota due him, a letter addressed by Miranda to Herries shows that in the end of July, 1810, the arrears were still unpaid.[20]

English publicists meantime realized the import of the changes that were taking place in America. As early as June 29, 1810, Lord Liverpool sent careful instructions on this matter to Governor Layard of Curaçao. After stating that England's object hitherto had been to assist the Spaniards to maintain the "independence of the Spanish Monarchy in all parts of the World," and to discourage any proceeding that would have "the Effect of separating the Spanish Provinces in America from the parent State in Europe," he wrote that if "the Spanish Dominions in Europe should be doomed to submit to the Yoke of the common Enemy," the King would be bound by the same principles which had "influenced his Conduct for the last two years in the Cause of the Spanish Nation, to afford every Assistance to the Provinces in America which may render them independent of French Spain." His Majesty expressly disclaimed any design of territorial acquisition.[21] In secret and confidential instructions to Layard of the same date Liverpool declared that nevertheless it was not the King's intention to become involved in hostilities with the Venezuelans if they should determine to maintain their independence. Any measure that could be construed as involving a formal recognition of the new government at Caracas should be scrupulously avoided.[22]

A knowledge of the deep interest that England had often shown in the fortunes of Spanish America had meantime impelled the junta of Caracas to select agents to lay Venezuela's case before English ministers. Early in June it appointed

---

[19] Herries to Miranda, July 3, 1810, Mir. MSS., vol. 63.
[20] July 28, 1810, *ibid.*
[21] W. O., 1/103. This dispatch is printed, with modifications, in *Ed. An. Reg.*, vol. IV, pt. I, pp. 381-82.   [22] W. O., 1/103.

Simón Bolívar, a scion of a distinguished family, and an influential creole named Luis López Méndez as commissioners to England. Andrés Bello, a young Venezuelan scholar, was made the secretary of this mission. Bolívar and Méndez brought with them an address from the junta of Caracas to the English King. This communication suggested that England was destined "to complete the grand work of confederating the scattered sections of America, and to cause order, concord, and rational liberty to reign therein." [23] The credentials of the agents declared that they were to inform the English Government of the political changes in Venezuela, that they should claim the protection of George III, and that they should offer to negotiate a treaty of alliance.

Their instructions directed the agents to justify the political transformation in Venezuela because of the arbitrary administration of colonial justice and the illegitimate character of the Central Junta. The fact that Spanish provinces had established governmental juntas was to be adduced as an additional justification for the acts of April 19. With regard to the new government at Caracas the statement was made that it intended to consult the people through an assembly of delegates from the Venezuelan provinces. Explicitly did the instructions declare that there was a universal sentiment in Venezuela for "adhesion to the metropolis," if the patriot cause prevailed in Spain, but for the establishment of independence, if French soldiers should be victorious. A wish was expressed that the enormous burdens which restricted colonial agriculture and commerce should be decreased and that the administration of justice should be improved. A desire was manifested for the formation of a Spanish-American federation. The allegation was made, however, that Venezuela still viewed herself as "an integral part of Spain." Bolívar and Méndez were instructed to ask the English Government to facilitate the purchase of arms for the Venezuelans, to protect

---

[23] Walton, *An Exposé on the Dissentions of Spanish America,* Appendix, p. xxv.

their commerce, and to see that English officials in the West Indies favored the new régime. They were also to solicit the English ministers to adjust any differences that might arise among the Venezuelans or between them and the adjacent Spanish colonies.

Between the lines of this clever document one can read the desire of the Venezuelan junta to reap whatever advantage might be afforded by changing circumstances. Its anomalous position was aptly illustrated by the clauses of the instructions that aimed to guide the conduct of the agents toward their long-exiled compatriot. Though those clauses stated that Miranda should be viewed as a person who had rebelled against Ferdinand VII,—whose rights this junta professed to support,—yet the suggestion was made that if his influence might in any way promote the success of the mission, he ought not to be slighted.[24]

The Venezuelan agents arrived at Portsmouth in the English brig *Wellington* on July 10.[25] Within a few days after their arrival in the English capital Bolívar and Méndez had met their famous compatriot. On July 19 Miranda wrote to the Duke of Gloucester as follows:

"Envoys of Caracas have finally arrived on a mission to this government to offer their friendship and a free commerce in all ports of the extensive territory of Venezuela. Their independence applies only to the authorities established in Spain on behalf of Ferdinand VII under the name of Junta or Regency which they do not recognize, and whose agents have been expelled from the country without bloodshed or mistreatment. The envoys consider themselves as the true representatives of that portion of the Spanish-American people who while recognizing Ferdinand VII, yet propose to treat with him upon this important matter, if he ever secures his liberty. They have been politely received by ministers of His Majesty to whom they have delivered their dispatches in spite of Apo-

---

[24] "Instructions from their Highnesses the Supreme Junta of Venezuela to their Commissioners going to the Court of London," June 2, 1810, W. O., 1/104. [25] Rojas, *Simón Bolívar,* pp. 13, 14.

Simón Bolívar in 1810. Portrait by Charles Gill. From Mancini, "Bolívar et l'émancipation des colonies espagnoles." Reproduced by courtesy of Perrin et Cie., Paris.

daca and his associates who wished absolutely to prevent this. * * *They brought me flattering recommendations from my relatives and from other actors in the memorable April revolution. Those communications display amity and esteem toward me because of the services I have rendered that noble cause and not only urge in the name of leading personages of the country that I should vigorously second the negotiations with England but also that I should come to join them." [26]

At this time the English Secretary for Foreign Affairs was Marquis Wellesley, the elder brother of Lord Wellington. At the first interview that Bolívar and Méndez had with the Marquis they were evidently informed that the English Government could enter into no official relations with them because of its alliance with Spain. There is a tradition that, acting upon impulse, Bolívar made an eloquent plea for the acknowledgment of the independence of Venezuela. Wellesley doubtless divined that the Venezuelans aimed to secure an alliance with England: he pointed out the dangers to which Spain and her allies were alike exposed by the separation of a colony from the patriot government in Spain, and urged that a conciliatory policy should be adopted which would reunite Venezuela to the Motherland. Bolívar and Méndez argued, however, that their provisional government was the only organization by which they could hope to preserve the rights of Ferdinand VII against French usurpations. In an unofficial manner Wellesley then offered to promote an amicable adjustment between Venezuela and Spain. He assured the agents that England would furnish naval protection to Venezuela to enable her to defend the rights of Ferdinand VII and to resist France.[27]

The rôle of England was indeed a difficult one. As was sug-

---

[26] Mir. MSS., vol. 63. On the interest of the Duke of Gloucester in the cause of Venezuela, see further, Glenbervie, *The Diaries of Sylvester Douglas*, II, 129.

[27] Robertson, "The Beginnings of Spanish-American Diplomacy," *Turner Essays in American History*, pp. 242-46.

gested in an official English memorandum, she wished to prevent Venezuela's separation from the Mother Country, to induce Spain to alter her exclusive commercial policy, and to preserve the Spanish-American colonies from the influence of France.[28] Still, in spite of the cautious attitude of the English Minister, Spain took umbrage at the countenance given to the Venezuelan agents which she feared would encourage her colonies to declare their independence.[29] An English sympathizer now intimated to Miranda that Marquis Wellesley might decide to send Wellington to Venezuela sword in hand "to form a royal regency" and to arrange an alliance with England.[30]

While the Foreign Secretary was formulating the policy of neutrality and mediation in the differences between Spain and her continental colonies in America that England was destined to follow for several years, Bolívar and Méndez were making acquaintances in London. Their exiled compatriot soon undertook to introduce them to both his English and his Spanish-American friends. On July 19, 1810, Miranda asked a South American named José de Tovar to a tea in Grafton Street where Bolívar and Méndez were expected to be present.[31] On the next day he invited Richard Wellesley, a son of the English Secretary, to his home to meet "the South American friends." [32] A few days later he asked Wilberforce when he would be "in Town, and at leisure to receive a visit from the Deputies of Caracas, his Countrymen, who wish to pay their respects to the protector of oppressed humanity." [33] On August 17 the philanthropist wrote to Miranda as follows: "It will give me very sincere pleasure to see you and your friends from South America on Tuesday and I beg you will assure them that I account myself fortunate in being in this part of England when they are in London." [34]

---

[28] Robertson, "The Beginnings of Spanish-American Diplomacy," *Turner Essays in American History*, p. 247.
[29] H. Wellesley to Marquis Wellesley, Aug. 29, 1810, Add. MSS., 37, 292.
[30] Courteney to Miranda, "10 O'Clock, Wednesday," Mir. MSS., vol. 63.
[31] Miranda to Tovar, July 19, 1810, *ibid.*
[32] *Ibid.*   [33] July 26, 1810, *ibid.*   [34] *Ibid.*

An entry in Wilberforce's *Diary* informs us that upon one occasion Miranda and two Venezuelan agents appeared on the veranda of the reformer's house when the family was engaged in morning prayers and remained there until half past twelve.[35] It seems possible that on another occasion both Bello and Irigoyen were members of the party that visited the reformer; for Miranda wrote to Wilberforce to state that he would in a few days accompany five agents from Caracas and Buenos Aires to his residence.[36] In August, 1810, Miranda also made an appointment for a visit by Bolívar and Méndez to the royal observatory.[37] As he was interested in the system of mutual instruction for poor children that had been introduced by an educational reformer named Joseph Lancaster, accompanied by these deputies, Miranda paid a visit to a training school for teachers established by that educator. It seems that the South Americans decided to send to England two Venezuelan youths in order that they might be educated in the principles of the Lancasterian system.[38]

The exile undoubtedly took the impressionable Bolívar to the top of a high mountain and showed him the promised land. Miranda's enthusiasm for the cause of Spanish-American independence must have influenced the ardent and volatile Venezuelan, who while abroad on an earlier occasion had been impressed by the military glory of Napoleon and by the free institutions of the United States. By virtue of his knowledge of European conditions and of English policy Miranda was admirably fitted to give hints to Bolívar and Méndez for the management of their delicate negotiations with Marquis Wellesley. Evidently they consulted their compatriot about ways and means to accomplish the object of their mission. On July 27 in a letter to John Turnbull that explained his delay in declining an invitation to dinner, Miranda said: "The sole motive has been a constant and pressing attention on the

---

[35] Wilberforce, *Life of William Wilberforce*, II, 459.
[36] Aug. 21, 1810, Mir. MSS., vol. 63.
[37] Enderby to Miranda, Aug. 7, 1810, *ibid.*   [38] *Ed. Rev.*, XIX, 20.

Business that has brought a Deputation from Caracas to this Country." [39] In a letter to Governor Hislop a week later Miranda said that he was much occupied with the affairs of the Venezuelan agents and that he soon expected to leave England in their company.[40] The dramatic story that Bolívar and his companion had to tell about the political changes at Caracas must indeed have stimulated the exile's desire to return to his native land.

A luminous account of this meeting is found in the memoirs of General O'Leary who long served as the aide-de-camp of the Liberator. That general avowed that in reality one of the chief objects of Bolívar's mission to London was to induce General Miranda "to aid the cause of America with his military talents and experience by returning to Venezuela. For Bolívar had for some time recognized in Miranda great military genius"; and he believed that he had discovered in him "the man whose happy destiny included the glory of realizing the splendid project of emancipating South America." Although some of his compatriots viewed Miranda as a dangerous man, yet Bolívar "who would not forget the interest of his native land for any consideration, took the course that his judgment indicated as being the best in an affair of so much importance. He used his warmest arguments to insure that Miranda would continue to coöperate in the cause for which he had suffered so much. Although age had weakened a constitution that was worn by the fatigues of a life full of misfortunes, this proposal coincided with Miranda's desires, and Bolívar urged it with such enthusiasm that the old man accepted with pleasure and without hesitation." [41]

A few days after Bolívar and Méndez had held their first interview with Marquis Wellesley, Miranda wrote the following letter to that Secretary:

"The Events that have taken place in the Province of Venezuela, in April last, which have most essentially altered the

---

[39] Aug. 4, 1810, Mir. MSS., vol. 63.
[40] Ibid.   [41] O'Leary, *Memorias*, XXVII, 33-34.

connexions between that People and the old Spanish Government—together with the arrival of their Deputies in this Metropolis, rendering my presence in England totally unnecessary;—form the motive of this application to Your Lordship.

"In the course of those remarkable changes, I observe with satisfaction, that a spirit of Justice, Moderation, and Wisdom, guides those illustrious Patriots, in the pursuit of a reform, worthy in my opinion of admiration, and if consolidated, pregnant with all the progressive happiness I could wish—therefore meeting with my most hearty approbation.

"These circumstances, united to the most pressing solicitations for my immediate return to that Province, from my relations and other distinguished friends in the City of Caracas, induce me to request from H. M. Ministers the due permission for carrying these wishes into execution. It is in fact not only the inclination of acquiescing with my Countrymen's invitation; but the great desire I naturally feel of returning in a private situation, to the bosom of my family, and to the Country that gave me birth and education; after more than thirty years absence and anxiety, for its welfare and happiness.

"Permit me, My Lord, at the same time, to testify here my most sincere thanks to the British Government, not only for the friendship and generosity, with which they have supported me for the space of more than twenty years of an intimate connexion, in affairs of the greatest importance, and in the most eventful times—but for the Hospitality and approbation shewn to me, by the various administrations, that have governed Great Britain during such a length of time.—The continuation of their good will, in granting me now a definite arrangement, in the pecuniary allowance settled upon me—with a safe passage, in one of H. M's Ships of War to any of the Ports in the Province of Venezuela; will perfectly gratify and enable me to return to my beloved country, with sentiments of the highest respect, friendship, and gratitude, for the British Nation,—whose prosperity and happiness I sincerely desire; and whose friendship, and mutual intercourse between both Countries, it shall be my constant study to promote.

"If H. M. Ministers should deem it proper to entrust me with any Message, or Despatches, for the present Government of Venezuela—or should afford me the opportunity of accompanying any agent from this Country to that Province, it will afford me both gratification and pleasure." [42]

To reënforce this request Miranda soon addressed a letter to Richard Wellesley that was couched in these words: "I understand that a frigate is being prepared to convey the agents of Venezuela to La Guayra, and, as a return to my native land in the company of my relatives and friends is of the utmost importance to me, I beseech you to procure from Marquis Wellesley a favorable response to the respectful petition that you had the kindness to send him in my name." [43] Nor did Miranda fail to indicate his intentions to his compatriots. On August 3, 1810, he wrote to the Venezuelan junta. He sent his felicitations on the events of April 19: he declared that this date marked "the most celebrated epoch in the history of Caracas and in the annals of the New World. You will be forever lauded as illustrious men who accomplished a work so holy and immortal." Miranda then praised the selection of Bolívar and Méndez as commissioners to London; he stated that he had informed them of the steps which he had taken in respect to Spanish America, and declared that in their first conferences with the English ministers they had conducted themselves creditably. He stated that in view of information received from them and from his "relatives and other friends at Caracas," he had informed the English Government of his desire to terminate the long negotiations that he had carried on with it for Spanish-American independence. "I do not doubt," declared Miranda, "that the English ministry will concede to me so just and equitable a request,—and I hope that Your Highness will also approve these desires, which are dictated by my zeal and by sentiments that are natural and patriotic." [44]

As he had received no response from Marquis Wellesley, on August 29, after consulting Simón Bolívar, Miranda sent

[42] July 25, 1810, F. O., 72/103.
[43] Aug. 11, 1810, Mir. MSS., vol. 63.   [44] *Gaceta de Caracas*, Nov. 20, 1810.

another letter to that Minister about "his desire and intention" of leaving England for the New World. He declared that he had received "new intimations" from Caracas and "very pressing solicitations" from Bolívar urging him to proceed to his native land, "which circumstance leaves him no alternative in the possibility of remaining by choice, any longer in this Country." He even expressed a willingness, if his pecuniary proposals were inconvenient at that moment, to postpone or to relinquish them "though with no small inconvenience to his private concerns," in order that he might promote the welfare and salvation of South America. To Vansittart, who had so often given him friendly personal advice, Miranda made this appeal:

"Here is a copy of the letter which I have just sent to Lord Wellesley and which seemed suitable to Bolívar and Richard Wellesley. The latter promised me a reply from his father without delay. The only objection which he could foresee to my request was the fact that the Spaniards might take in bad part the fact that I would accompany the agents from Caracas on their return at a time when England is about to offer her mediation to Spain. My response was that the agreement between the English Government and myself was of a much earlier date, and implied the absolute condition that I should be allowed to depart at the moment when my country had need of my services or whenever I might wish to return there. It would be more incompatible with the good faith of the English Government to retain me here at this moment against my will than to infringe the treaties made with the defunct Central Junta." [45]

To this appeal Vansittart replied on August 30 to assure the expatriated Venezuelan that he fully approved of his letter to Lord Wellesley and hoped that he would receive a favorable answer. "Perhaps it might be in some degree more satisfactory to the Spaniards if you were not to go out in the *same ship* with the Deputies," he continued, "and that would

---

[45] Aug. 29, 1810, Mir. MSS., vol. 63.

be of no consequence provided you had passage in another ship of war at the same time. With regard to the mediation offered by England, you ought to take the opportunity of explaining that you are so far from being adverse to it that you are willing to give every assistance in your power in carrying it into effect, having no other object than to bring about a good understanding between the Colonies and Spain (provided she is able to maintain her own independence) on terms calculated to secure the liberties and happiness of both." [46]

Marquis Wellesley, however, evidently felt that he confronted a dilemma. Because of the alliance of England with Spain, because of a desire to support in every way the struggle of his brother Arthur in Spain, and because of England's declaration that she would support the integrity of the Spanish dominions in both hemispheres, he was loath to grant Miranda's request. Obviously the Minister was apprehensive of the revolutionist's influence in his native land. Like Vansittart, he was doubtless averse to the departure of the exile in company with Bolívar. On September 9 Wellesley asked him to delay his departure "for eight or ten days only." [47] In vain did the Spanish Ambassador try to secure a pledge from the Marquis that Miranda would be prevented from returning to his native land.[48]

In the meantime the Venezuelan mission was making arrangements for departure. Its members reached the decision that Méndez should remain in London to represent Venezuela, while Bolívar should return to Caracas. On September 19 the luggage of a party of Spanish Americans and also voluminous papers of Miranda were received on board His Majesty's brig *Sapphire;* at noon on the following day, by order of the Admiralty, five members of this group were allowed to embark on the frigate. Besides the names of Simón Bolívar and José Antepara, the muster of that frigate for September 20 and

---

[46] Mir. MSS., vol. 63.   [47] F. O., 72/104.
[48] Apodaca to Bardaxi, Nov. 26, 1810, A. G. S., estado, 8173.

25 contains the name of Antonio Leleux, an obscure person
who thus projects himself into our story. Shortly afterwards
the *Sapphire* made sail for the West Indies without the long-
exiled son of Caracas.[49]

Miranda had meanwhile been urgently pressing his case
upon the English Foreign Minister. On September 24 he
asked for Wellesley's "kind decision and commands," for
Venezuela. He avowed that the object which he had "most at
heart," next to "the preservation" of his native country, was
"the welfare and prosperity of Great Britain." On the next
day he sent to Wellesley a memorandum about "his pecuniary
concerns" stating that he wished the government either "to
continue the payment of his Pension of £700 a year and his
Secretary Mr. Molini of £200; in the hands of his friend the
Right Honorable Nicholas Vansittart or to give three or four
years purchase once paid, as it is customary; which he should
prefer." Then he presented to the consideration of the ministers if the losses he had "sustained in the late fire at the Island
of Trinidad, by the circumstance of retaining there, various
articles of Clothing, Arms, and Ammunition, through the
recommendation of Sir Arthur Wellesley (now Lord Wellington) for the purpose of being used in the Expedition prepared
for the Coasts of Caracas in the year 1808; should not be entitled to a compensation.—The estimate of the various articles
consumed, he computes to be from Eight hundred to One thousand Pounds Sterling." [50]

Influenced presumably by representations of the Spanish
Minister, who naturally feared the results that might flow
from the return of Miranda to his native land, Marquis Wellesley still hesitated about reaching a definitive decision. Doubtless Miranda had already realized that the English Minister
desired to detain him in England or at least to delay his departure for South America. In any case his final and irre-
vocable decision was soon taken. On October 3 he addressed a

[49] S. L., 1245; Ad. M., series 2, vol. 3169.
[50] F. O., 72/105; Robertson, *Miranda*, pp. 433-34.

farewell letter to Wellesley to announce that he was about to leave England. He expressed the hope that this step would not be considered precipitate and that the financial claims set forth in his memorandum of September 25 would receive proper attention from English ministers. In that affair his representative was to be his tried friend, Nicholas Vansittart.[51]

Thus did Miranda make known his determination to depart from the home that had so long served him as an asylum. At last he had decided to leave the shores of England without the express consent of her government and without any understanding about his financial status.

Just before his departure he took some preliminary measures with regard to reforms to be introduced into his native land. He took with him the draft of a law that Jeremy Bentham had framed to establish the liberty of the press in Venezuela.[52] Influenced by Bentham and Wilberforce, he evidently proceeded to South America with the intention to oppose slavery and the slave trade. The activities of Miranda as well as the political changes that were taking place in Spanish America stirred the interest of English manufacturers and merchants. "The joyful anticipation of mercantile adventurers also found their way into the newspapers," said an Edinburgh journalist, "and enthusiasts were not wanting, who, taking no lesson from experience, exclaimed with Dr. Price, 'Now, Lord, lettest thou thy servant depart in peace.' " [53]

On October 10, 1810, accompanied by Thomas Molini, Francisco de Miranda left England without his family. Possibly he again traveled under the name of Martin. After sojourning a few days at Curaçao, he left for La Guaira on December 4 in the English sloop of war the *Avon*. His compatriot Simón Bolívar had preceded him. According to a letter which he sent to Marquis Wellesley, Miranda landed at La Guaira on December 11. After the *Avon* returned to Curaçao, the governor of this island sent word to Downing Street that

---

[51] Robertson, *Miranda*, p. 434.
[52] Bentham, *Works*, X, 457-58. [53] *Ed. An. Reg.*, IV, pt. I, p. 380.

the junta of Caracas had appointed Bolívar a member of a committee to assure the returned native of its extreme pleasure at his safe arrival.[54]

On December 10 Miranda had addressed a letter to the junta of Caracas. Its secretary, Juan G. Roscio, replied that, in view of the patriotism that his negotiations in behalf of Spanish America had displayed and of the recommendations made by Bolívar and Méndez, the junta had granted him permission to proceed to the city of Caracas. The returning exile was, however, informed that a transformation had taken place in his native land: that the ancient tyranny had been replaced by a government which aimed solely to promote the happiness of the people; and that every citizen was convinced that his first duty was toward society. A suggestion was made that, as Miranda had enjoyed many more advantages than his compatriots by his residence at foreign courts, the obligations that he owed his native land were correspondingly greater. The tone of this epistle indicates that certain Venezuelans viewed the return of the famous exile with grave misgivings.[55]

On the other hand, there is no doubt that many of his fellow citizens received him with joy. An epistle from Caracas dated December 18, 1810, stated that General Miranda was given "that enthusiastic reception to which he is so justly entitled. A great number of the first citizens went down to La Guaira to escort him to his native place, which he entered about noon on Thursday last, mounted on a beautiful white charger." This letter added that Miranda was accompanied by "a numerous cavalcade of men of the first distinction; and followed by an immense crowd of citizens who greeted his return." [56]

On December 21, 1810, the *Gaceta de Caracas* stated that the people had welcomed the man who had not forgotten his native land despite the distinctions that had been showered

---

[54] Robertson, *Miranda*, p. 438, note f; *Gaceta de Caracas*, Dec. 11, 1810.
[55] Rojas, *Simón Bolívar*, pp. 32, 33.
[56] *London Packet*, March 6, 1810.

upon him in Europe. A few days later the *cabildo* of Valencia declared that incriminatory documents about his revolutionary designs which had been lodged in its archives were concerned with "the decorous, irreprehensible, and wise Patriotism" of Miranda. On January 7, 1811, the *cabildo* of San Carlos congratulated the general on his happy return; it declared that his efforts to liberate his fellow countrymen deserved their "eternal gratitude." On February 4 the *cabildo* of Caracas announced that the acclamations of a people who had carried him in triumph to the heart of his country had demonstrated the pleasure caused by his safe arrival. The junta of Bogotá sent an address to Miranda avowing that he would purify these regions, which had been "stained by the blood of so many victims, offered up at the shrine of despotism." In a letter to Bello, the secretary of the Caracas junta stated that Miranda was soon accorded the rank and pay of lieutenant general, and that papers denouncing his revolutionary activities were burned.[57]

Still, there were some Venezuelans who did not hail Miranda's return with unmixed pleasure. Reflections made by Roscio indicate that a minority of the people of Caracas soon viewed Miranda's conduct with suspicion, dislike, or even hatred.[58] In recollections of the revolution in Venezuela that were composed many years later a royalist named José Díaz stated that the most turbulent youth of Caracas viewed the illustrious exile as a man endowed with wisdom and as the only person who was capable of governing the new nation. On the other hand, Díaz asserted that those persons who entertained moderate opinions soon looked upon him as a perilous being who might overturn the State.[59] This antagonistic attitude did not improve after the patriots became aware that the returned native maintained a secret correspondence with persons in England.

[57] Robertson, *Miranda*, pp. 439-40.
[58] Amunátegui, *Vida de Don Andrés Bello*, p. 98.
[59] *Recuerdos sobre la rebelión de Caracas*, pp. 30, 31.

On the other side, a notice of his arrival in Venezuela soon found its way into the *Correio Braziliense*, which announced that he had been received by the junta "with most distinct honors." [60] On January 7, 1811, Miranda wrote thus, in part, to Marquis Wellesley:

"The Government and the people of Venezuela have received me with great applause, friendship, and affection, conferring at the same time civic and military rewards; by which means I shall be able I hope, to have the influence required for the purpose of promoting the interests of Great Britain, as perfectly compatible with the welfare and safety of these Provinces.

"On my arrival at this Capital I did not fail in communicating to the Government, what the views and wishes of the British Government were, with respect to the safety of these Provinces, and the support they were at the same time bound to give to the Spanish Cause in the Peninsula. I found their sentiments perfectly in unison with Your Lordship's views and have no doubt but that they will continue following the same moderate course; notwithstanding the provocations and harsh proceedings of the Agents of the Spanish Regency at Puerto Rico, without which, no disturbance would have occurred at Coro or Maracaibo,—nor in this Capital, where their plots obliged the government to take coercive measures, far distant from their wishes, and the conciliatory spirit they were pursuing. * * * The Right Honorable Nicholas Vansittart * * * has my Power of Attorney; and as this country has already conferred upon me Military charges and duties, incompatible, I conceive, with any foreign emoluments, I beg Your Lordship would have the goodness to order the settling of the pecuniary arrangements proceeding from my Pension agreeable to the Memorandum I left, when I quitted England * * * ." [61]

Miranda did not lose touch with his friends in London. From time to time Nicholas Vansittart sent him sage counsel

---

[60] *Correio Braziliense,* VI, 300.
[61] F. O., 72/125; in part in Robertson, *Miranda,* p. 441, note c.

in regard to Venezuelan affairs. On March 7, 1811, Vansittart wrote urging his correspondent to send Méndez "frequent and detailed accounts" of occurrences in Spanish America, as people in England were puzzled by the contradictory reports that were being received. The discerning friend added this wise advice: "I hope your influence will be sufficient to repress any violence and controul any spirit of persecution, which may appear among your countrymen." [62] After hearing reports of the execution of Spaniards at Caracas, Vansittart asked Miranda for an explanation of the attendant circumstances. "I am sure," he opined, "that nothing would more indispose both our Government and the public here to any connection with you than an appearance of severity; or so much unite opinions here in your favor as measures of mildness and conciliation to all classes of inhabitants in your country." Further, he advised Miranda that the credit of Venezuela should be placed on a firm basis in London by regular remittances.[63] Whatever responses the Venezuelan may have sent Vansittart have unfortunately not come down to us.

The adjustment of Miranda's financial relations with England formed an important topic of this correspondence. On July 3 the Englishman wrote to Miranda: "I have spoken several times to Mr. R. W. respecting your pension. He is not able to get a decided answer from his father, who seems however more inclined to reimburse the pension in the manner desired by you than to continue it. I believe it will be settled at last; but the time is uncertain, and it cannot be relied upon as an immediate resource." [64] In the same connection Vansittart wrote to Miranda on August 19: "I have had several conversations about your pension with Mr. W. who appears to have the most friendly disposition towards you, but he has not been able to get his father to determine anything, though I proposed such an arrangement as I hoped would have removed his difficulties. You who know by experience how diffi-

[62] Add. MSS., 31, 230, ff. 206-7.
[63] *Ibid.*, 31, 230, ff. 212-14.   [64] *Ibid.*, 31, 232, ff. 73-74.

cult it is in this country to get any business done out of the common course will not be surprised that I have not yet succeeded." [65]

The South American also kept in touch with Turnbull, Bentham, and Wilberforce. To Wilberforce he wrote that he found the feelings of the Venezuelans very sympathetic toward the reformer's "philanthropic sentiments." [66] Through Jeremy Bentham an attempt was now made to bring Miranda into close relations with Aaron Burr. In the autumn of 1811, when that discredited conspirator had returned to England from a trip to the Continent, Bentham wrote to him with the intention of removing any dislike that he might entertain for the Venezuelan. With some reluctance Burr yielded to Bentham's desires. [67] Hence, in January, 1812, James Mill indited a note to express the wish that the cause of Venezuela should have Burr for a friend and to suggest that Miranda should reply by a letter expressing a willingness "to enter into a reciprocation of good offices" with the American. [68] Whatever dreams of coöperation between Burr and Miranda their mutual friends in England may have entertained, however, were soon destroyed by unexpected events.

Before describing the spectacular career of Miranda in Venezuela, let us notice the explanation which the English Government made about its relations with him. On June 5, 1811, Lord Liverpool wrote in disingenuous terms to John Hodgson, who had just been made governor of Curaçao:

"In the personal Communication which I had with you previously to your departure from this Country, I acquainted you that General Miranda had left England without intimating his intention to any Member of the British Government, and without even a suspicion on its part that he had left it until his arrival at Curaçao was notified to me by Brigr. General Layard and I assured you that it was not without great surprize and dissatisfaction that I learnt from that Officer

---

[65] *Ibid.*, 31, 230, f. 216.   [66] Wilberforce, III, 434, note.
[67] Burr, *Private Journal*, II, 252, 287.   [68] *Ibid.*, p. 288.

that General Miranda had been conveyed from Curaçao to the Carraccas in a British Ship of War.

"I have determined to take the earliest opportunity of repeating officially what I then communicated to you verbally, and of acquainting you that as the British Government had not the means of preventing or discouraging the enterprise into which General Miranda embarked wholly without their concurrence, they feel on that account still more desirous that you should abstain from any engagements or correspondence with him personally which might induce a suspicion either on the part of the Mother Country or the Spanish South American Provinces that General Miranda had been abetted by the British Government or encouraged by its connivance.

"With regard to the general line of conduct to be pursued by you, I must refer you to the Instructions which I have given to General Layard in the course of the Events that had taken place on the Neighboring Continent and to the assurances you have already received that it is the anxious wish of the Government of this Country to conciliate the differences between Spain and her Colonies to render available the common resources of both to the prosecution of that Contest which is their Common Cause." [69]

A few years later in refutation of the charge that England had acquiesced in the return of the exile, which was brought by the Minister of the restored Ferdinand VII, the English Ambassador at Madrid, Henry Wellesley, made this comprehensive disclaimer for his government:

"The next complaint relates to the permission which, in defiance of the repeated protests and representations of the Spanish Government, it is alleged was given to General Miranda to leave England. Don Pedro de Cevallos cannot be ignorant that the laws of Great Britain do not admit of any Individual being forcibly detained in the Country unless he shall commit an offence which shall render him answerable to those Laws. But it happens in this case that, at the instance of the Secretary of State for Foreign Affairs,

---

[69] C. O., 66/3.

General Miranda was induced to continue in England for a considerable period of time after he had made preparations for his departure, and when he did depart, so little was he encouraged by the Government to persevere in his enterprize, that upon his arrival at Caracas, he is known to have expressed his dissatisfaction at the conduct of His Majesty's Ministers, and to have publicly stated that no hopes were to be entertained by the Insurgents of assistance from Great Britain." [70]

In 1810 patriots in Spanish America caught a glimpse of the independence that Miranda had long predicted. To the Venezuelan exile the news of the formation of a governmental junta in his native city was a clarion voice that challenged him to battle for his ideals. Encouraged by reports brought to London by agents of colonists who secretly aimed at the separation of their countries from Spain, he decided to relinquish the monetary recompense that England had been paying him in return for past or potential service. He bade farewell to his comfortable home in London without any pledges from English ministers in regard to fiscal adjustments and voyaged to his native land in the wake of Simón Bolívar. The man who, for many long years, in good repute and ill repute, in both the New World and the Old, had preached a crusade for the emancipation of Spanish America with a fervor akin to that of Peter the Hermit, was now to essay to lead a band of new crusaders into the holy land of liberty.

In one way or another Miranda had transferred to his native city the bulky tomes that contained the constitutional projects which, as he fondly imagined, he had perfected for the government of the liberated Spanish-American colonies. Though he managed to keep up a correspondence with friends in England who were deeply interested in his fortunes and those of Venezuela, yet we know that the English Government instructed its agents in the West Indies not only that he should receive neither aid nor encouragement from Downing Street

---

[70] Wellesley to Cevallos (copy), Feb. 4, 1815, F. O., 72/173. The complaint to which Wellesley replied was made to him by Pedro de Cevallos, Jan. 20, 1815, *ibid.*

but also that England now desired to reconcile with Spain those very colonies which, to use words attributed to Lord Melville, she had so often planned "to insurge." Still the wind seemed to be in the sails of the revolution.

Miranda was still suspected of cherishing a design to ascend a barbaric throne in the Spanish Indies. The available evidence would indicate that in 1810, as in 1797, he viewed England and the United States as the two nations from which his compatriots could most readily expect aid in the impending struggle against their Spanish masters. His study of existing conditions had led him to the conclusion that the *cabildos* or town councils would have to take the lead in initiating the wars for liberation and that the great task would be forwarded by the convocation of regional congresses. There is little doubt that he still entertained the idea of forming an association or confederation of independent Spanish-American nations.

General Miranda had much changed in appearance and characteristics since the trying times of the French Revolution. By 1808 his hair had turned white. No longer was he animated by the unresting energy and abundant vitality of his young manhood; his iron constitution was corroding. In 1808 he suffered from at least one serious illness. At the dawning of the momentous year 1810 Miranda stood near the threshold of a distinct era of his adventurous career. Sixty summers and winters had passed over his head. By far the major portion of these years had been spent in foreign climes among peoples whose manners and customs were alien to his own people. In a European atmosphere he had received some outward marks and his personality had largely unfolded. Aggressive, ambitious, and dogmatic, scarcely as magnetic as of yore, Miranda had acquired a certain austerity of demeanor. This adventurous son of Caracas was not of a conciliatory disposition; he either attracted or repelled strongly. Harassing experiences and grievous disappointments had rather embittered his disposition than chastened his spirit. Yet, despite his years, he was still animated by a youthful and contagious enthusiasm for liberty. He dreamed that, escaping from the toils of tortuous, Machiavellian diplomacy, he might saunter in the green pastures and lie down beside the still waters of his emancipated Fatherland.

Chapter XIX

VENEZUELA'S DECLARATION OF INDEPENDENCE

THE HOROSCOPE of Venezuela had altered greatly since Miranda departed from La Guaira for Cadiz. The revolution of April, 1810, constituted a great step toward separation from Spain. Many Venezuelans, however, opposed independence. An influential factor in determining the attitude of the people was the activity of clever, persuasive, and forceful leaders. Among the most capable of those personages was that native of Caracas named Simón Bolívar. By December, 1810, his remarkable energy and iron determination were consecrated to the patriot cause. He was destined rapidly to increase in influence and prestige. There is a tradition that for some time after his arrival the returned exile resided in Bolívar's house. Miranda had almost reached the pinnacle of his fame. Yet to a large number of his countrymen he was scarcely known at all. To others he was notorious merely as a revolutionist whose attempt to liberate Venezuela in 1806 had failed miserably. An occasional Venezuelan had heard rumors about his romantic adventures in Europe. Some compatriots viewed him as a soldier of fortune who had drawn his sword in divers causes. Certain leaders were aware that while they had been groaning under the Spanish yoke, he had been living comfortably on English gold. Miranda was soon forced to realize that not all of the Venezuelans considered him a gift of favoring Providence.

Yet such was his military experience and political knowledge that he soon became the focus of public attention. His rôle was peculiarly difficult not only because he was a stranger to South America but also because his native land was in many respects strange to him. Imperfectly acquainted with conditions in Venezuela and with fixed notions about what her political future should be, he suddenly appeared on the stage in the midst of a stirring drama. Supremely confident that among

Francisco de Miranda. A lithograph. In Marqués de Rojas, "El Général Miranda." Reproduced by courtesy of Garnier Frères, Paris.

his precious papers he had the prescription for certain ills of his country, he was destined to influence her fortunes profoundly. To describe Miranda's career in South America is almost to write the early history of independent Venezuela.

In spite of declarations by Venezuelan leaders that they were faithful to their captive King, the Spanish patriots mistrusted them. The Minister of State of the Regency said that they had been so audacious as to declare themselves independent and to create a junta to exercise a pretended authority. On August 1, 1810, the Regency announced that a blockade would be laid against the province of Caracas.[1] It authorized Antonio Ignacio de Cortabarria to proceed to that province as a commissioner clothed with royal authority who was to recall the people to their allegiance.[2] In October, 1810, an Extraordinary Cortes which had assembled at Cadiz declared that the Spanish dominions in both hemispheres formed the same nation and that Spain's subjects residing in the Spanish Indies should have the same rights as her citizens.[3] When he learned that the Venezuelans were arming to support their new government, from Puerto Rico on December 7, 1810, the royal commissioner directed a letter to the junta of Caracas to request that those Venezuelans who had rebelled should quietly disarm and return to their homes.[4] Although Cortabarria's appeal probably reënforced the loyalist spirit that had appeared in certain sections, yet it did not recall the radicals to their allegiance.

In October, 1810, Robert K. Lowry, who had been sent from the United States to Venezuela as marine and commercial agent, wrote from La Guaira and stated that certain Venezuelan leaders were contemplating the establishment of a representative government in imitation of the United States. The desire for the rule of Ferdinand VII is fading away, declared Lowry, "and I am informed that ere long they will throw the

---

[1] Blanco, *Documentos para la historia de la vida pública del libertador*, II, 571-72.   [2] *Ibid.*, pp. 693-94.
[3] *Colección de los decretos y órdenes que han expedido las cortes generales y extraordinarias*, I, 9-10.   [4] Blanco, II, 693-96.

phantom aside." [5] In a letter from Caracas on November 30, 1810, he expressed the opinion that "a large portion of the people" in that city wished independence.[6]

On Christmas Day, 1810, the junta of Caracas complained to Cortabarria that he was seducing those subjects of Ferdinand VII who were satisfied with its measures.[7] Early in 1811 the royal commissioner announced that he would enforce the blockade against the recalcitrant Venezuelans. On February 5, 1811, in a letter to Cortabarria the junta of Caracas severely criticized those persons who were conspiring against the new régime. An emissary from the Cortes named Montenegro who made his way to Caracas was imprisoned in Miranda's house whence he escaped to the West Indies.[8] Such incidents widened the breach that had opened between Spain and her continental colonies in the New World. A decree of the Cortes dated February 9, 1811, tardily declared that colonists were to enjoy the same rights as Spaniards, that in the future the representation from the Spanish Indies in the Cortes was to be on an equality with that from the Peninsula, that all restrictions on American industry were to be removed, and that creoles were to be as eligible to civil, ecclesiastical, and military offices as Peninsulars.[9] But by the time this conciliatory decree reached Venezuela her leaders had taken other steps that clearly showed a drift toward separatism.

Meantime the influence of the press began to be felt in Venezuelan politics. The *Gaceta de Caracas* had been issued since 1808 from the very printing press that Miranda had brought to the shores of the Caribbean in the *Leander*. In November, 1810, a journal styled the *Semanario de Caracas* was founded. In January, 1811, another periodical named the *Mercurio Venezolano* was established by an enterprising

[5] Oct. 1, I. & A., Consular Letters, La Guayra, I.   [6] *Ibid.*
[7] "Answer of their Highnesses, the Supreme Junta of Caracas, to Don Antonio Ignacio de Cortavarria," W. O., 1/107.
[8] Montenegro to Hodgson, July 2, 1811, *ibid.*, 1/108.
[9] *Colección de los decretos y órdenes que han expedido las cortes generales y extraordinarias,* I, 68-69.

creole named Francisco Isnardi.[10] In June the first number appeared of the *Patriota de Venezuela*, the organ of the Patriotic Society.[11] These journals became the vehicles through which novel political ideas were disseminated.

Beginning in November, 1810, William Burke, who had preceded Miranda to Caracas in the hope of contributing to the success of the revolutionary cause,[12] published in the *Gaceta de Caracas* a series of articles entitled the "Rights of South America and Mexico." Taking inspiration from Thomas Paine, Burke presented arguments for the absolute independence of Venezuela from Spain. He urged the Venezuelans to incorporate among their political rights not only the writ of habeas corpus and trial by jury but also the doctrine of complete religious toleration. He pleaded with them to receive foreigners who professed the Protestant faith "as sons of a same Creator and a same God." [13] To counter his arguments on February 23, 1811, the University of Caracas selected two distinguished alumni to prepare a formal refutation.[14] In a letter to Bello, Roscio alleged that Miranda tried to increase his prestige by denouncing the doctrine of religious toleration to the archbishop of Caracas.[15]

A club designated the Patriotic Society, which had been established to promote industry and commerce by a decree of the junta dated August 14, 1810, had meantime furnished Miranda an opportunity to exercise his talents as a director of the revolutionary spirit.[16] In this society, which was located at the capital city, social and political problems of moment were discussed and new policies were formulated. Some of its members entertained very liberal ideas. Discussions led by Miranda and Bolívar in this Jacobin Club stimulated a spirit of independence among Venezuelan leaders. Eventually it

---

[10] Picón-Febres, *La literatura venezolana en el siglo diez y nueve*, pp. 110-12.
[11] "Prospectus," in Hodgson to Liverpool, July 5, 1811, W. O., 1/108.
[12] Burke, *Derechos de la América del Sur y México*, p. iii.   [13] *Ibid.*, p. 81.
[14] Universidad de Caracas, *La intolerancia político-religiosa vindicada.*
[15] Amunátegui, *Vida de Don Andrés Bello*, pp. 99-100.
[16] *El Español*, II, 248.

came to exercise a radical influence upon politics. "The society," wrote José de Austria, a patriot who wrote a useful account of this period, "made itself odious to the enemies of the separatist movement; for in its meetings the tyranny of the government of the metropolis was denounced, attention was directed to the atrocities of the Welsers, to the monopoly of the Company of Guipúzcoa, to the venality of officials entrusted with the administration of justice, and to the despotism of Guevara and Emparán. To follow the example of the United States was declared to be the only remedy for these evils, the only way to prevent a repetition of such abominations." [17]

In accordance with the action of the junta of Caracas, steps had been taken in Venezuela for the election of deputies to a Congress. Early in November, 1810, six delegates for the province of Caracas were selected by an electoral assembly which had been chosen by the freemen. Fortunately for Miranda, when he arrived in Venezuela elections had not been held in all of her districts. He was chosen as delegate for the district of Pao in the province of Barcelona. Delays in the arrival of delegates compelled the junta to postpone the date when Congress was to begin its deliberations. Composed of some forty members from the provinces of Barcelona, Barinas, Caracas, Cumaná, Margarita, Mérida, and Trujillo, on March 2, 1811, this assembly opened its sessions.

The inaugural ceremonies of the first Congress of Venezuela were interestingly described in the *Gaceta de Caracas*. It stated that, after an arrangement was made for a temporary organization in the former "palace" of the Captain General, the delegates, accompanied by a guard of cavalry and infantry, proceeded to a church where members of municipal organizations had gathered. Attired in his pontifical robes, the archbishop of Caracas celebrated mass. The delegates then took oath on the Holy Scriptures that they would defend the rights of Ferdinand VII, that they would oppose any other

[17] *Bosquejo de la historia militar de Venezuela*, pp. 40-41.

ruler who might aim to exercise authority in the Venezuelan provinces, that they would maintain pure and inviolate the Roman Catholic religion, and that they would duly respect the regulations of Congress and faithfully fulfill their duties. The military commander at Caracas took a similar oath. Heralds then announced to the people that a new nation had been brought into existence.

After salvos of artillery, and the solemn chanting of *Te Deum*, the congressmen returned to the palace of government. There the members of the provisional junta took an oath to recognize the authority of Congress as a legitimate representative of Ferdinand VII and faithfully to exercise the executive power until Congress should transfer it to other hands. An oath of fidelity to the executive and legislative authorities of Venezuela was then taken by prominent military officers and by civil and ecclesiastical dignitaries. Words and phrases employed in the description of these impressive ceremonies indicate that certain Venezuelans viewed them as constituting an important step toward the attainment of nationality.[18]

With regard to the mode of voting to be used, Congress decided that each province should have one vote.[19] It soon undertook to assume the political functions of the junta by exercising governmental authority. After selecting certain persons who were to act as departmental secretaries, Congress elected three creoles, Baltazar Padrón, Cristóbal de Mendoza, and Juan Escalona to serve as the executive power of the State. Roscio declared that upon the day when this choice was made, Miranda anxiously awaited the results. "In the election he got eight votes," continued Roscio, "from thirty-one members of Congress. He received this news in his house, and veiled his regret by saying: 'I rejoice to learn that there are in my country persons more suitable than I for the exercise of supreme power.' " [20] On July 1 Congress declared that foreigners of whatever nationality would be received in the fertile

---

[18] *El Español*, III, 330-35.
[19] *El libro nacional de los Venezolanos*, pp. 11, 12.   [20] Amunátegui, p. 100.

province of Caracas, and that their persons and property would enjoy the same protection as those of citizens, provided that they recognized the country's sovereignty and independence and respected the Roman Catholic religion.

The Secretary of State soon announced that the government would allot lands to those aliens who wished to cultivate them. Further, he made known that, although the slave trade was prohibited, yet foreigners would be allowed to bring slaves into Venezuela for use in industrial pursuits.[21] Attracted perhaps by these inducements, a number of adventurous Europeans soon proceeded to Venezuela. In their number was an audacious Scotchman named Gregor McGregor, and Colonel John Robertson, who had been secretary of the English governor of Curaçao. Among the Frenchmen who had already yielded to the lure of the new land of promise was Louis Delpech, who married into the prominent family of Montilla.

Important political problems were soon considered by Congress. As a result of Miranda's exhortations, it decided that laudatory inscriptions to Captain General Vasconcelos should be removed from public monuments.[22] In June, 1811, the question was raised whether Congress represented several definitely constituted states or merely certain peoples without a constitution. This crucial problem was provoked because of a proposal to divide the province of Caracas. A consideration of that project precipitated a debate regarding the status of the Venezuelan provinces and the powers of Congress. As usual, Miranda had an opinion which he was not loath to express. On June 25 he argued that the renunciation of the crown of Spain by the Bourbon dynasty had restored to the Spanish Americans their rights. Congress, he maintained, was a sovereign body, which should decide upon the time for independence.[23]

When on July 2, 1811, letters from Telésforo de Orea containing news from the United States were read to Congress, a

---

[21] *Academia nacional de la historia; prólogo á los anales de Venezuela,* pp. 88-89.　　　[22] *El libro nacional,* p. 24.　　　[23] *Ibid.,* pp. 8, 9.

resolution was introduced which asserted that Venezuelan independence was imperative. A motion that Congress should be transferred from Caracas to an interior town where it might labor in tranquillity was opposed by Miranda and lost.[24] On July 3 Congress reached the momentous decision that the time had come to consider a declaration of independence. The ensuing debate was opened by J. L. Cabrera, a deputy from the province of Barinas, who declared that it would be necessary to formulate the reasons why the Venezuelan people considered themselves independent. Cabrera expressed himself in favor of a measure that would announce that the rights of Ferdinand VII were null and that would place the new State in a position where her independence would be acknowledged by other states.[25]

The discussion that took place in the halls of Congress on July 3 helped to crystallize the views of its members. Luis Tovar of the province of Caracas boldly argued that the Venezuelans had desired independence since April 19, 1810, but that they had postponed making the announcement because of political reasons. In a similar manner Fernando Peñalver, the delegate for Valencia, maintained that the Venezuelans had a right to declare themselves free and independent and that they should frame a republican constitution. In reply to those who feared that a declaration of independence might antagonize England, José M. Ramírez of Aragua explained that as England was allied with Spain, she had adopted a policy of mediation toward Venezuela. He alleged that the name of Ferdinand VII had been used by Venezuelan leaders to cloak their real designs so that the people would not take alarm.[26]

The opponents of an immediate declaration of independence pleaded that the time was inopportune, that a confederation of the Venezuelan provinces should first be formed, and that Congress lacked the authority to declare Venezuela independent of Spain. Manuel Vicente Maya, the delegate from La

---

[24] *Ibid.*, pp. 29, 42.   [25] *Ibid.*, pp. 43-44.   [26] *Ibid.*, pp. 44, 45, 48.

Grita in the province of Mérida, declared that his instructions did not permit him to favor an announcement of independence. Juan G. Roscio, who was a representative of the province of Caracas, stated that although he favored a declaration, yet he believed that the people of Venezuela should first unite in common action. He expressed the apprehension that an immediate declaration of independence would antagonize those people who had opposed the measures of the governmental junta.[27]

On July 3 Miranda made two speeches in favor of an immediate declaration. In regard to one speech the secretary of Congress merely stated that the orator argued in favor of independence in an "energetic and lengthy discourse." It appears, however, that he reasoned cogently that the establishment of a republican form of government would be inconsistent with an acknowledgment of Ferdinand VII, and that the Venezuelan people had for some time been in a position to proclaim their independence from Spain.[28]

Fortunately Miranda's argument in regard to the influence of a declaration of independence upon the international relations of Venezuela has been preserved. He maintained that in the ambiguous situation in which she was placed a nation that might succor her "could not safely count on our reciprocity, if she should solicit aid from us against Spain whose rights we have not yet solemnly disavowed. We ought to be independent," said Miranda, "we ought to run the risks and to enjoy the advantages of that status, in order that foreign nations may make firm compacts with Venezuela which will serve us by engaging directly the forces of the enemy against that nation which aids us. I believe that this reason ought to influence us strongly in favor of independence." [29] His clever suggestion that the Venezuelan nation might be able to negotiate a foreign alliance which would aid her against Spain must have made a strong appeal to his compatriots; for some of them felt that they could scarcely cope with Spanish power

---

[27] *El libro nacional,* pp. 50, 59-60.   [28] *Ibid.,* pp. 45, 49, 51.   [29] *Ibid.,* p. 49.

single-handed, while others thought that French soldiers would ultimately overrun Spain.

Francisco Javier Yanes, a delegate from Araure, declared that he could not add anything to what Miranda had said to demonstrate "the justice, necessity, utility, and convenience" of an immediate declaration of independence. He undertook to refute the arguments of its opponents. He maintained that Miranda had demonstrated that Venezuela had been for some time in a position to declare herself independent. He reasoned that a confederation could not properly be established before independence was proclaimed; for "a confederation was an association of free, sovereign, and independent states" united by a perpetual compact. He argued that a preliminary expression of the popular will concerning independence was not necessary: the people were represented in the Constituent Congress, and the decision of a majority of Congress was the national will. He asserted that, if the patriots had consulted the people about the measures of April 19, 1810, the Venezuelans would still be slaves. It would be more dangerous, he said, for Venezuela to postpone action in regard to independence than to make an immediate decision. He argued that independence of Spain would greatly benefit Venezuela, and asserted that the debate concerning independence had "perhaps been the most important discussion that had been witnessed by Spanish America since the melancholy epoch when it was enslaved." [30]

Just before this debate closed, Miranda rose to analyze the arguments that had been presented. In emphatic words he asserted that almost all the delegates agreed that certain advantages would accrue to Venezuela from an immediate declaration of absolute independence from Spain. He declared that Yanes had destroyed the argument that the formation of a confederation should precede a declaration. The plea that the delegates lacked authority to declare independence he stigmatized as sophistical.[31]

---

[30] *Ibid.*, pp. 50-55.   [31] *Ibid.*, p. 60.

The Patriotic Society had meantime undertaken to crystallize opinions about Venezuela's status. A member of Congress named Palacio Fajardo, who later wrote a sketch of the revolution in the Spanish Indies, recorded that on April 19 the members of that society "marched in procession through many of the principal streets, bearing ensigns appropriate to this festival." [32] It seems that on the evening of that joyous anniversary Miranda presided at the meeting of the club. Eloquent members argued in favor of the separation of Venezuela from Spain. Antonio Muñoz Tébar avowed that April 19 was "the natal day of the revolution" and that a year had been dissipated in dreams of love for the royal slave of Napoleon. "Let the first year of independence and liberty begin. Let us have a confederation of states or a centralized government, one legislature or many legislatures." A cyclopean patriot named Coto Paúl vehemently argued for immediate action. "We are here," he reasoned, "on the high mountain of holy demagogism, to reanimate the Dead Sea of Congress. When demagogism has destroyed the present régime, and when sanguinary spectres have come for us upon the field that has been torn by war, Liberty will arise." [33]

To counter the argument that the Patriotic Society was usurping the place of Congress Simón Bolívar pleaded as follows:

"There are not two Congresses. Will those who most fully realize the need of union foment discord? What we desire is that this union should become effective and should urge us on to the glorious enterprise of our liberty. To unite ourselves in order to repose, in order to sleep in the arms of apathy, was yesterday a disgrace,—today it is treason. The national Congress is debating what decision should be reached. And what do its members say? That we should commence by a confederation, as if we were all confederated against foreign tyranny. That we should await the results of the policy of Spain. What does

---

[32] *Outline of the Revolution in Spanish America,* p. 111.
[33] *El publicista de Venezuela,* no. 17, as quoted by González, *Biografía de José Félix Ribas,* pp. 33-35.

it matter to us whether Spain sells her slaves to Napoleon or keeps them, if we are resolved to become free? These doubts are the melancholy results of our former chains. What great projects should be prepared during the calm! Were not three hundred years of calm enough? The patriotic junta respects the national Congress, as it should, but Congress should listen to the patriotic junta, which is the center of all the revolutionary interests. Let us fearlessly lay the corner stone of South American liberty: to vacillate is to be lost. Let a committee representing this society convey these sentiments to the sovereign Congress." [34]

A committee of the Patriotic Society was accordingly chosen to make known to Congress its views concerning a declaration. On July 4 that committee expressed the sentiments of the society about this critical issue to a secret session of Congress. A member of the club named Miguel Peña presented a discourse which urged that an immediate declaration of independence should be made. Congress now suspended the debate upon independence until its President could confer with the Executive Power as to whether or not such a step would be compatible with public security.[35]

On the forenoon of the next day Cristóbal de Mendoza, who was now president of Congress, announced to it that the Executive Power had expressed the conviction that an immediate declaration of independence from Spain would not only put an end to the political ambiguity of Venezuela but would also spoil the schemes of her enemies. At once Miranda arose to reenforce this decision and to urge the need of immediate action because of conditions in Spain.[36] The delegate from La Grita again protested that his instructions would prevent him from agreeing to a declaration of independence. Two other delegates asserted that such a step was inconsistent with the oath of allegiance which had been taken to support Ferdinand VII. Among the speakers who tried to refute this argument was Roscio; he alleged that the Bourbon dynasty had virtually

---

[34] *Ibid.*, pp. 36-37. [35] *El libro nacional*, p. 62. [36] *Ibid.*, p. 63.

8—II

sold Spanish America to Napoleon. He further argued that
the justice and necessity of a declaration of independence had
been demonstrated. He frankly admitted, however, that publicists might well doubt whether Venezuela with only one million inhabitants was strong enough to take such a significant
step. Cabrera pointed out, however, that European nations
had recognized smaller states than Venezuela as having an
independent status.[37]

Miranda pleaded for definite action. Upon Roscio's half-
hearted argument about Venezuela's ability, he descanted in a
long, energetic speech that was fortified by concrete illustrations gathered during his travels. He asserted that when the
United States had "perfected her grand and immortal enterprise" she did not have three million white inhabitants. The
Republic of San Marino, he maintained, scarcely had a population of half a million. The City-Republic of Ragusa, which
he had admired while traveling in Europe, contained no more
than eighty thousand people. The Swiss Republic had only
two million inhabitants. The Republic of Genoa, which had
played a distinguished rôle in history, had about a million.
The Electorate of Hanover had fewer inhabitants than Venezuela. The United Provinces of Holland had struggled successfully against the tyrant Philip II. In fine, Miranda concluded that the Venezuelans, bordered as they were by New
Granada, should banish their fears and proceed immediately
to proclaim their independence.[38]

Cristóbal de Mendoza then spoke in favor of such a step.
He said that Venezuela would thus set an example which would
be immediately followed by the neighboring Viceroyalty, and
that a declaration of independence by the Venezuelans would
thwart their enemies. Juan José de Maya, the delegate from
San Felipe, stated, however, that although he favored independence, yet he was apprehensive that a declaration might
cause an exodus from Venezuela similar to that which once
took place in France.[39] To refute this objection Miranda

---

[37] *El libro nacional,* pp. 64, 65, 75-76.   [38] *Ibid.,* p. 78.   [39] *Ibid.,* pp. 78-79, 81.

sprang to his feet to declare that when the Republic was proclaimed, only the nobles had left French soil. In regard to Venezuela the orator argued that only a few undesirable Spaniards would emigrate if a republic should be proclaimed. He then asked a pertinent question:

"What evils will result if such men leave the country without agreeing to independence? Their departure would be the happy occasion of our perfect tranquillity. Let them embark in a happy hour! Let them go to Puerto Rico! Let them join Cortabarria, who is commissioned to represent the Spanish King! They will certainly do us less damage there than they could do amongst us." [40]

Thus Miranda became one of the foremost champions of an immediate declaration of independence. In the words of Roscio, who was not a kindly critic, Miranda "bore himself well and debated wisely." [41] After other congressmen had expressed themselves in favor of a declaration, with the exception of Maya of La Grita who still insisted that his instructions prevented him from supporting the measure, the delegates voted in favor of independence. The president promptly announced that "the absolute independence of Venezuela" had been declared. The official account of the congressional debates records that this "announcement was followed by the cheers and acclamations of the people who had been tranquil and respectful spectators of this august and memorable discussion." [42] A royalist contemporary was probably not exaggerating much when he declared that he then beheld dashing through the streets of the city of Caracas coatless, intoxicated, and jubilant young men who tore down the portraits of Ferdinand VII and trampled them under foot.[43] Patriots embraced one another.

On the afternoon of July 5, 1811, Congress appointed various committees. Francisco Isnardi, who had been acting as secretary, and Juan Roscio were chosen to draft an exposition

[40] *Ibid.*, p. 81.   [41] Amunátegui, p. 111.   [42] *El libro nacional,* p. 90.
[43] Díaz, *Recuerdos sobre la rebelión de Caracas*, p. 33.

stating the causes and motives that impelled the delegates to declare their independence of Spain. Felipe F. Paúl, a delegate from San Sebastián, was assigned the task of formulating an oath that would pledge officials and dignitaries to support the new régime.[44] Miranda and two other members were selected to choose the design for a cockade and a national flag. This committee evidently accepted Miranda's views: it soon decided that the standard of the new State should be red, blue, and yellow,—the very colors which in 1806 the arch-revolutionist had flown from the masthead of the *Leander*. The standard soon hoisted by Venezuelan vessels bore a unique design. In the upper inner corner was an Indian armed with a bow and arrow, who was seated upon a rock by the sea. Upon a staff he displayed a liberty cap. A crocodile's jaws protruded beyond his feet, while above the horizon a glorious sun was rising. Below the aboriginal figure was the legend "Colombia," and across the upper corner of the union were inscribed the words, "Venezuela Libre." [45]

On July 5 Juan Rodríguez Domínguez, who was serving as president of Congress, announced to the Executive Power that Congress had sanctioned a Declaration of Independence and was engaged in considering the formulation of an act that would elevate the Venezuelan provinces to the rank of free and sovereign states and would emancipate the people from the horrible slavery that they had suffered. The Executive Power promptly made the decision in favor of independence known to the officials of the province of Caracas, to the other provinces of Venezuela, to the archbishop, and to the army. In a proclamation addressed to the people of the province of Caracas the members of the Executive Power avowed that they now no longer recognized any superior authority upon earth, but that such a noble conception could only be executed by men

---

[44] *El libro nacional*, pp. 91, 92.
[45] Design inclosed in Hodgson to Liverpool, Aug. 11, 1811, W. O., 1/109. See further, Mendoza Solar, "Escudos de armas de Caracas, Miranda, Nueva Granada, la Gran Colombia y Venezuela, desde la conquista hasta el año 1911," in *El Cojo Ilustrado*, XXI, 327.

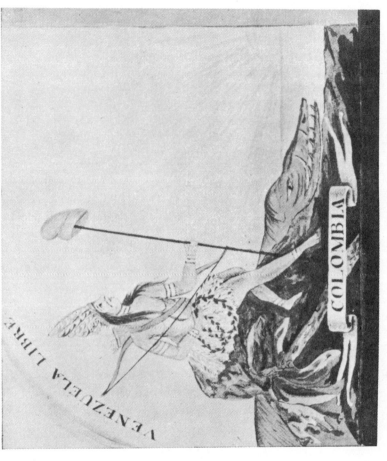

Design of the union on the flag hoisted by vessels of Venezuela soon after the Declaration of Independence was signed. From a colored sketch sent by Manuel Sanz to Governor Hodgson of Curaçao. In the Public Record Office, London.

animated by the spirit of liberty and disposed to make sacrifices for it.[46]

On July 7, 1811, the committee on the framing of a Declaration of Independence presented the "Solemn Act of Independence" to Congress. Although the congressional records for that day merely state that "the Act declaring independence framed by the secretary was read and approved," [47] yet it appears certain that Roscio rather than Isnardi was chiefly responsible for the vibrant phraseology of a document that became immortal in Venezuelan annals. Though acting as the secretary of Congress, Isnardi was not a member of that assembly. On the other hand, Roscio was a trusted, judicious, and patriotic congressman who was well versed in political theory. Further, when Congress appointed a committee composed of Roscio, Fernando del Toro, and the secretary to present the Declaration to the Executive Power, it was Roscio who acted as the spokesman for the deputation.[48] Still, to the writer it would seem strange if the Declaration of Independence of Venezuela were framed without the use of Miranda's knowledge of political thought and without the aid of his facile pen.

The "Solemn Act of Independence," began by invoking Almighty God. Its preamble continued thus: "The representatives of the United Provinces of Caracas, Cumaná, Barinas, Margarita, Barcelona, Mérida, and Trujillo, which form the American Confederation of Venezuela in the southern Continent, assembled in Congress, in view of full and absolute possession of our rights that we have recovered justly and legitimately since April 19, 1810, in consequence of the occurrences at Bayonne, the occupation of the Spanish throne by conquest, and the succession of a new dynasty instituted without

[46] Gil Fortoul, *Historia constitucional de Venezuela*, I, 535-36.

[47] *El libro nacional*, p. 94.

[48] Gil Fortoul *op. cit.*, pp. 536-37. The biographers of Roscio take the view that he took a large part or even an exclusive part in framing the Declaration, see Azpurúa, R., *Biografías de hombres notables de Hispano-América*, I, 159; Yanes, "Semblanzas de próceres civiles," in *El Cojo Ilustrado*, II, 16.

our consent, are desirous, before using the rights of which we have been forcibly deprived for more than three centuries but which are now restored to us by the political order of human events, to make known to the world the reasons arising from these events that authorize the free use which we are about to make of our sovereignty."

The Venezuelan Fathers politely drew a veil over the evils resulting from three hundred years of Spanish domination in America. The reasons for their Declaration of Independence were primarily based upon the distracted condition of Spain. The Solemn Act of Independence stated that by the abdication of the Spanish monarchs at Bayonne, they had failed in "the sacred duty which they had contracted with the Spaniards of both hemispheres," and had become incapable of ruling "a free people whom they transferred like a group of slaves." It argued that certain measures of the Spanish patriots had helped to conserve in America the illusion in favor of Ferdinand VII: they promised us liberty, equality, and fraternity in pompous discourses and studied phrases in order to conceal the snare of a cunning, useless, and degrading representation." It asserted that when the Venezuelans were compelled to take action to preserve the rights of the Spanish King, the Spaniards stigmatized as ungrateful, perfidious, and insurrectionary a measure identical with that which had been taken by the provisional governments of Spain, because that step put an end to the monopoly of administration which they had intended to perpetuate in Venezuela in "the name of an imaginary King."

The Act proceeded to say that the Venezuelans were then declared to be in a state of rebellion. They were blockaded, war was declared against them, and agents were dispatched from the Motherland to set them against each other. Their representation in the Cortes had been made a mockery. After spending three years in "a condition of indecision and political ambiguity," by the use of "the imprescriptible rights that people enjoy to destroy every pact, agreement, or association that does not answer the purpose for which governments were established, "they had reached the conclusion that they ought no longer to preserve the bonds which had united them to Spain, and that they were free to "take among the powers of the earth the place of equality assigned them by the Supreme Being and by nature." The climax of their intricate reasoning is presented in the following paragraph:

"We, the representatives of the United Provinces of Venezuela, beseeching the Supreme Being to witness the justice of our proceedings and the rectitude of our intentions, imploring His celestial aid, at the moment when we are born to the dignity that His Providence restores to us, express the desire to live and to die free and to believe and defend the Holy Catholic and Apostolic Religion of Jesus Christ, as the first of our duties. We, therefore, in the name and by the will and authority which we hold from the virtuous people of Venezuela, declare solemnly to the world that her United Provinces are and ought to be by fact and right, free, sovereign, and independent states, that they are absolved from any dependence on the Spanish crown or on those who call themselves its agents or representatives, that, as a free and independent State, Venezuela has full power to adopt that type of government which will conform to the general wish of the people, that she has power to declare war, to make peace, to form alliances, to negotiate treaties of commerce, limits, and navigation, and to make and execute all other acts performed by free and independent nations. To make this, our solemn Declaration, valid, firm, and durable, we hereby mutually bind each province to the other provinces and pledge our lives, our fortunes, and the sacred tie of our national honor." [49]

Though a few clauses of the Venezuelan Act of Independence vaguely re-echo immortal phrases of Thomas Jefferson, yet it can scarcely be said that this Act formulated a philosophy which justified the Spanish-American Revolution. Neither did the Venezuelan Declaration contain a terrible arraignment of the colonial policy of the Motherland. Stress was rather laid on those spectacular events that induced the

[49] *El libro nacional*, pp. 199-205.

wise political philosopher, James Bryce, to characterize Napoleon the Great as the "Liberator of Spanish America."

On July 8 Congress approved the oath of allegiance to the independent government. This oath contained an acknowledgment of the sovereignty and absolute independence of the "United Provinces of Venezuela" from the Spanish monarchy. It included a pledge of obedience to the magistrates and laws of Venezuela as well as a declaration that the Venezuelans would defend their Confederation and would preserve Roman Catholicism pure and undefiled as the exclusive religion of the country.[50] The Executive Power instructed the archbishop on July 8 that when the Declaration of Independence was formally made public the bells in all the churches of the capital city should ring.[51] In a number dated July 11 *El Publicista de Venezuela*, a periodical which served as the organ of Congress, printed the Declaration of Independence in the belief that it would thus fulfill the fervent wishes of a people who were "anxious to become acquainted with the most glorious act that had yet been performed in South America."[52]

The announcement of Venezuela's separation from Spain was published on July 14; at the same time the national flag was for the first time displayed. On the next day the oath of allegiance to the new system was taken on the gospels by such dignitaries as congressmen, judges of the supreme court, members of the Executive Power, and the archbishop of Caracas. Regulations were soon promulgated that relieved the press from many restrictions which had hampered it during the colonial régime. Other steps were taken that aimed at the regeneration of Venezuela. On July 30 Congress passed a bill which provided that treason was not to work corruption of blood or forfeiture except in the person of the traitor.[53] About a month later it sanctioned a law that absolutely prohibited

---

[50] *El libro nacional,* p. 210.
[51] Damiron, *Compendio de la historia de Venezuela,* p. 171.
[52] Sánchez, *El publicista de Venezuela,* p. 19.
[53] Blanco, III, 166-69, 188.

the use of torture in the United Provinces.[54]

The measures taken by the Venezuelans in the midsummer of 1811 constituted the most important step in their transition from the status of Spanish colonists to that of citizens of an independent republic. The Declaration of July 5, 1811, was indeed the complement of the measures of April 19, 1810. Leaders of Venezuela now boldly discarded the mask of their professed allegiance to Ferdinand VII and proclaimed their intention of establishing absolute independence of the Motherland.

As stated in their Declaration of Independence, the Venezuelans had been incited by provocative measures of the changing governments of Spain. There is reason to believe, however, that a number of determined radical leaders had for some time been directing their efforts toward a Declaration. On the other hand, as in the case of the United States, there is no certainty that a majority of the citizens of Venezuela would have favored such an extreme step at this juncture, if they had been asked to express their opinions in a referendum. In fact, it is doubtful whether the prospect of independence from Spain had even been considered in some of the elections for delegates to the Congress of 1811. Subsequent developments indeed raise the question as to whether the Venezuelan patriots who ardently desired absolute independence were not in a minority.

However that may be, Venezuela had now taken a decisive step. Henceforth her people had to range themselves either for the independent cause or against it. Though here and there in the Spanish Indies discontented individuals had indistinctly muttered the magic word *independencia*, though certain *cabildos* had dropped vague hints about separation, and though local juntas had made veiled statements about their secessionary designs, yet the clearest announcement with regard to the destiny of a Spanish-American people that had yet been made came from Caracas. Venezuela was the first of the

---

[54] *Ibid.*, p. 207.

Spanish colonies in America, through delegates assembled in a Congress, formally and absolutely to declare herself independent of the Motherland.

As an exposé of motives, the Declaration of Independence was supplemented by an exposition that had been framed by Roscio and Isnardi in accordance with the decision taken by Congress on July 5. On July 24 this justificatory address was approved by Congress, and six days later it decided that one thousand copies of the manifesto should be printed.[55] If we may judge by the emphasis and the reasoning employed in this document, it was, in the main, written by the same hand that framed the Act of Independence. Relatively slight attention was given to the despotic and monopolistic policy pursued by Spain toward her colonies. In reasoning that was occasionally inconsistent, attention was rather directed to the scandalous scenes that had taken place in distracted Spain, to the alleged declarations of Spanish patriots that upon the proclamation of a Napoleonic dynasty they had recovered their absolute liberty and independence, and to the thwarting of the project of Venezuelan leaders to institute a local junta in imitation of the juntas formed in the Motherland. The oppressive rule of Captain General Emparán was bitterly denounced. Resentment was displayed at reports that had been circulated in Venezuela of alleged victories of Spanish arms over the French intruders. The liberal promises held out to colonists by the Spanish Regency were ridiculed as illusory. April 19, 1810, was proudly mentioned as the day upon which the colossus of despotism in Venezuela had collapsed. The period intervening between that memorable day and July 5, 1811, was declared to have been marked by insults and hostilities on the part of Spain and by moderation and suffering on the part of Venezuela. The author announced that it was a principle of natural law that the Indies no longer belonged to the Spanish crown. He argued that emigrants who settled in a new country acquired a right to that territory. "It is well

---

[55] *El libro nacional,* pp. 128, 133.

known," he continued, "that in the natural order, it is the duty of the father to emancipate his son, when he ceases to be a minor and can make use of his powers and his reason to make a living; and that it is the right of the son to do this whenever the cruelty or dissipation of his father or his tutor compromises his fate or exposes his patrimony to be the prize of a covetous person or of a usurper." [56]

As in the case of the Thirteen Colonies, so also in Venezuela the Declaration of Independence was not signed on the day when it was adopted. Not until August 17, 1811, did those members who were then present in the halls of Congress solemnly affix their signatures and rubrics to the formal announcement that Venezuela had separated from Spain.[57] It was probably more than a tradition which impelled the talented Venezuelan artist, Martín Tovar y Tovar, in painting that memorable scene to portray Miranda standing in martial pose beside the desk at which the Venezuelan fathers were successively signing their Declaration of Independence.

Foreign opinion of this Declaration was various. A Spanish journalist in London stigmatized it as an imprudent and precipitate measure. "By this atrocious policy," said Blanco White, "our brothers have become insensible to our disgrace; they have armed themselves against us; they have blotted from their minds the sweet impressions of friendship and consanguinity, and have converted a part of our great family into enemies. * * * This imprudence has caused me as much dismay as the moderation of the first junta of Caracas caused me enthusiasm. I cannot apply any other name to a step that without producing any good effects may bring about many evils to the common cause of the Spanish Empire." [58] The editor of the *Correio Braziliense* took a different view: "When we turn our eyes to this new State," said he, "it appears to us that we behold there the elements of a powerful nation; for the provinces that enter into the Confederation include an ex-

---

[56] *Prólogo á los anales de Venezuela*, p. 117.
[57] *El libro nacional*, p. 173.   [58] *El Español*, IV, 42.

tensive territory with a fertile soil and healthful climate,—a domain endowed with many lakes, seaports, and navigable rivers." [59]

Newspapers in the United States made favorable comment. On September 3, 1811, in an article entitled "Independence of South America," the *Weekly Aurora* said: "We have this day the gratification of publishing the Declaration of Independence of the provinces formerly subjected to the Spanish yoke, in that part of South America called Venezuela, and the establishment of the only form of government, that of a *federal and representative republic,* founded on the equal rights of mankind, which is calculated to assure the liberty and happiness of the human species. The provinces consist of seven; but the spirit of liberty and independence is not confined to Venezuela; it extends to the whole of South America." In an editorial addressed to "the Friends of Good Government, Liberty, and Independence," after mentioning the revolutions that had taken place in France and North America, the *American Patriot* added: "South America now appears on the grand theatre, and has taken rank in the great scale of nations. Who amongst us does not exult at the intelligence received from that abused and long oppressed people?" [60] A sympathetic expression of sentiment came from the White House. President Madison declared, in his annual message to Congress on November 5, 1811, that it was impossible to overlook the scenes that were developing among "the great communities which occupy the southern portion of our own hemisphere and extend into our neighborhood. An enlarged philanthropy and an enlightened forecast concur in imposing on the national councils an obligation to take a deep interest in their destinies, to cherish reciprocal sentiments of good will, to regard the progress of events, and not to be unprepared for whatever order of things may be ultimately established." [61]

[59] *Correio Braziliense,* VII, 567.
[60] As quoted in the *National Intelligencer,* Sept. 26, 1811.
[61] Madison, *Writings,* VIII, 162-63.

The Signing of the Venezuelan Declaration of Independence. Painting by Martín Tovar y Tovar. In the Palacio de Justicia, Caracas. Engraving by George Profit in "El Cojo Ilustrado," July 1, 1911.

Chapter XX

PROBLEMS OF THE NEW NATION

THE NATION which thus sprang from the disintegrating Spanish Empire was confronted by delicate domestic and international problems. More than one of these problems were intimately related to the status of this new political entity. One problem was to determine the means to be adopted to promote the acknowledgment of Venezuela's independence. Another was concerned with the mode of establishing amicable relations with neighboring provinces that had not yet renounced their allegiance to Ferdinand VII. Again, the nascent commonwealth's fiscal system was crying aloud for proper organization. Further, an immediate decision was needed as to the policy that should be adopted toward those persons who still remained loyal to the Mother Country. Most important of all perhaps was the problem of national organization: it was imperatively necessary that the fledgling statesmen should frame a constitution for the provinces which had declared their independence of an Old-World monarchy. In a letter to James Monroe, secretary of state, Robert Lowry transmitted his diagnosis of the political condition in Venezuela. On June 9, 1811, he wrote "that from want of a proper application of the Public Money, through want of Talent; and Intrigue; the country is fast approaching to poverty, anarchy, and imbecility; which will most probably throw the Government into the hands of General Miranda. Some late occurrences have strengthened these suspicions, and the probability is that in less than a couple of months, there will be some further Revolution, perhaps more favorable to the real liberty of the Country." [1]

Prominent Venezuelans cherished sanguine hopes that they might, as Miranda had suggested, secure aid and recognition from foreign powers. In the flush of their revolutionary en-

---

[1] I. & A., Consular Letters, La Guayra, I.

thusiasm, the Venezuelans looked expectantly to their grand exemplar in the North. Early in 1811 José R. Revenga had been sent as an agent to Washington in place of Juan V. Bolívar who took ship for La Guaira. Juan de Escalona, the provisional president of Venezuela, informed the American Secretary of State that Orea and Revenga were to promote intimate relations between North and South America. Escalona even expressed the hope that Venezuela and the United States might form an alliance based on free principles and mutual interest.

After learning of the decisive step taken by Venezuela, Telésforo de Orea sent an announcement of this event to Secretary of State James Monroe. Orea inclosed a copy of Venezuela's Declaration of Independence as well as the design of her national flag. In this letter of November 6, 1811, Orea expressed the hope that the United States would recognize the Venezuelan Confederation as an independent nation which would prepare the way for a commercial treaty.[2] In accordance with a suggestion in President Madison's message to Congress, a committee of the House of Representatives framed a resolution which declared that when the Spanish-American provinces had attained "the condition of nations," Congress and the President would establish with them friendly relations and commercial intercourse. Monroe made Orea acquainted with this resolution and informed him that the ministers of the United States in Europe had been instructed concerning the sentiments entertained by their government.[3]

With respect to the court of London, however, Luis López Méndez could hold out no prospect of the acknowledgment of independence in the face of England's policy to maintain the integrity of the Spanish dominions in both hemispheres. Nor did Miranda's intimate correspondence with Vansittart hold out any promise of recognition. The new-born statesmen were

[2] Manning, *Diplomatic Correspondence of the United States,* II, 1148-49, 1154.
[3] Robertson, "Beginnings of Spanish-American Diplomacy," *loc. cit.,* pp. 252-55.

indeed fortunate that Cortabarria failed in his attempt to induce the English governor of Curaçao to adopt hostile measures against Venezuela.[4] On the other side, upon returning from a trip to New Granada, on May 11, 1811, in words that often rang false, Pavia warned the English Government that Miranda was "incessantly employed in framing a code of laws taken from those that were in force in the worst period of the French Revolution." In conclusion he avowed that the heart of Miranda was "entirely French, his disposition tyrannical; and he will never conform himself to the ruler England may think proper to dictate unless it pleases his fancy or favours his ambition! For my part I have always considered him a madman, for I have frequently heard him say . . . that he was born to be Emperor of Peru." [5] As though further to poison the minds of English statesmen, on August 1, 1811, an enthusiast named William Jacob presented a memoir concerning the Spanish colonies. Jacob asserted that Miranda was "enraged against the government of England, which nourished him too cordially and too long, his whole scheme is to encourage the wildest flights of democracy, till if he cannot rule himself, make his peace with Buonaparte by delivering the province to the power of France." [6]

After England became the ally of the Spanish patriots, the French Emperor developed a keen interest in the Spanish Indies. Soon after Venezuela declared her independence, the French Minister of Foreign Affairs, the Duke of Bassano, informed the American Minister at Paris that Napoleon had decided "to acknowledge and support" the independence of "the Spanish continental possessions in America so far as they have the spirit and strength to assert it with a reasonable probability of success." [7] In a dispatch to Serurier, the French minister at Washington, Bassano declared that it was the Em-

---

[4] Hodgson to Liverpool, Oct. 12, 1811, W. O., 1/108.
[5] Memoir addressed to Peel, W. O., I, misc. series 3, vol. 1125.
[6] Jacob to Perceval, inclosing a "Memorial respecting the American Colonies of Spain," F. O., 72/122.
[7] Russell to Bassano, Sept. 4, 1811, A. A. E., États-Unis, vol. 66.

peror's intention to favor the independence of Spanish America, and that Napoleon would aid this movement not only by
the dispatch of arms but also in every other way, provided
that Spanish-American patriots did not form any special
relations with the English. Serurier was to suggest to the
United States that she should join with France and furnish
aid publicly or secretly to the Spanish-American revolutionists. Bassano then added a passage that was pregnant with
meaning; for he declared that just as at an earlier epoch
France had promoted the independence of the United States,
so now she would "carry on this glorious work in favor of all the
Americas. This policy is worthy of the power of France and
of the soul of her Emperor. France keenly desires a success
that should promote anew the civilization, the commerce, and
the prosperity of peoples." [8]

On January 8, 1812, Joel Barlow, who had become American minister at Paris, wrote a letter to Bassano which contained a significant statement that the President of the United
States was happy to find by diplomatic correspondence that
the Emperor was animated by "good will towards the Spanish colonies in America, and that he harmonizes with the President in the desire to see them independent." [9] Yet, although
Orea entered into relations with Serurier, and received assurances that a Venezuelan minister would be well received by
France, these negotiations proved fruitless because of calamitous events in South America.

The new government of Venezuela also took measures to
improve relations with revolutionists in New Granada. The
Executive Power appointed Madariaga as agent to the junta
of Bogotá. In addition to his credentials he was intrusted with
a letter from Miranda that suggested the necessity of a political union between New Granada and Venezuela. "Canon Dr.
José Cortés Madariaga," wrote Miranda, "is charged with a
most important commission, and will tell you all that I could

[8] Sept. 16, 1811, A. A. E., États-Unis., vol. 66.
[9] Manning, op. cit., II, 1373.

suggest in regard to a political reunion between the kingdom of Santa Fé de Bogotá and the province of Venezuela in order that coalesced into a single social body, we may presently enjoy the greatest security and respect and that in the future we may enjoy glory and permanent happiness." [10] In accordance with his cherished plan of government, Miranda was thus attempting to confederate two sister states.

As a result of Madariaga's mission, in May, 1811, a convention of alliance and confederation was signed between Venezuela and the State of Cundinamarca, a political entity that had been formed from an important province of the Viceroyalty of New Granada. This convention contained provisions for the admission of other states into the proposed Spanish-American federation. It stipulated that in a separate treaty the boundary between Cundinamarca and Venezuela should be delimited. The capital of the projected federal republic was to be located in the center of her territory.[11] When this treaty was submitted to the Venezuelan Congress objections were made to certain clauses; but on October 22, 1811, it was ratified with some modifications. In regard to a federal union between the two states, this Congress deferred action, however, until the people of Cundinamarca through their representatives might have an opportunity to consider the plan.[12] Though no immediate step was taken to establish a common government and Miranda's dream of a South American confederation thus failed of realization, yet he had promoted a measure that dimly foreshadowed the formation of "Great Colombia."

The Venezuelans were forced to consider the readjustment of their finances. Their currency soon became demoralized for specie disappeared from the marts of trade. Still a bill providing for the coinage of copper money was not enacted by Congress.[13] Here, again, the Venezuelan Fathers were forced

---

[10] Rojas, *El general Miranda*, p. 615.
[11] Austria, *Bosquejo de la historia militar de Venezuela*, pp. 95-96.
[12] *El libro nacional de los Venezolanos*, pp. 172, 253, 270, 285-86.
[13] *Ibid.*, p. 171.

to call upon their long-exiled compatriot. On July 14, in response to a message from the Executive Power advocating the establishment of a national currency, Congress appointed Miranda and Ustáriz members of a commission that was to formulate a plan for the issue of both metallic and paper money.[14] About two weeks later, General Miranda having marched against Valencia, Congress authorized Ustáriz to ask for certain documents relating to monetary problems from the secretary of that general.[15] Accordingly it seems not unlikely that, as a Venezuelan writer has declared, the project for the issue of paper money was favored, if not indeed partly formulated, by the general who had witnessed the use of assignats during the French Revolution.[16]

On August 17, 1811, Congress enacted a law stipulating that 1,000,000 pesos of paper money should be issued in denominations of 1, 2, 4, 8, and 16 pesos for the "United States of Venezuela." The national revenues, and in particular the import duties and the money accruing from the tobacco monopoly, were to guarantee the redemption of this currency. The paper was to be equal in value to the gold money in circulation and should be legal tender for all debts. Penalties were provided for the punishment of such persons as might refuse to accept the notes. Counterfeiters were to be put to death. The amount of paper money in circulation was subsequently increased by the printing of notes of 2 reals amounting to 20,000 pesos.[17] As funds for redemption were lacking, the paper currency steadily depreciated in value. A well informed citizen of Caracas said of the fundamental act that aimed to reform the currency: "It was an unfortunate law * * * calculated to disaffect the public mind towards the revolution, and to exercise a malignant influence in unhinging the State." [18]

As already suggested, the debates in Congress had made evident the existence of different shades of political opinion

---

[14] *El libro nacional*, p. 103.   [15] *Ibid.*, p. 133.   [16] Soto Hall, *Venezuela*, p. 5.
[17] *Ibid.*, pp. 5-9.   [18] Robertson, *Miranda*, p. 454.

among patriot leaders. The attitude of Miranda towards politico-religious reforms also encouraged the crystallization of
parties. The intriguing attitude that he had assumed in a
violent controversy which was provoked by the publication of
Burke's articles advocating religious toleration did not diminish the resentment with which some of his compatriots viewed
him. Jealousy of the general's talent was not decreased in
view of his obvious yearning for political power and prestige.

By one means or another Miranda was striving to make
himself the central figure of a clique that evidently included
Madariaga and members of the influential Bolívar family.[19]
In opposition to Miranda's increasing influence, scions of the
aristocracy were ranging themselves in the so-called *Man-
tuano* party. The *Mantuanos* expressed much displeasure
when he attempted to win support from the colored people
who had been set free. In June, 1811, Roscio wrote to Bello
and declared that the returned exile was aiming to form a
party among the negroes and mulattoes by "flattering them
excessively with his views, conversations, and words expres-
sive of the most liberal ideas." [20]

Signs of dissension in Venezuela had long been apparent.
In certain sections, as Coro and Guiana, a faction that may
be termed the loyalist party reared its head in opposition
to the Declaration of Independence. The cities of Caracas and
Valencia became hotbeds of royalist plots. At Caracas on July
11, 1811, discontented natives of the Canary Islands rose in
revolt. There is a tradition that their rallying cry was "Death
to the traitors! Long live the King and the Inquisition!" [21]
They were soon overpowered, however, and thrust into prison.
About a dozen of the ringleaders were executed. Certain contemporaries declared that at the instigation of Miranda the
heads of these unfortunate conspirators were severed from
their bodies and stuck on poles in the avenues of the capital.[22]

---

[19] Amunátegui, *Vida de Don Andrés Bello,* pp. 99-102, 109-10.
[20] *Ibid.,* p. 102.
[21] Larrazábal, *Vida y correspondencia general del libertador,* I, 99.
[22] Poudenx and Mayer, *Mémoire pour servir à l'histoire de la révolution de
la capitainerie générale de Caracas,* pp. 47-48.

The royalist uprising in the city of Valencia was more difficult to suppress. As it found that the local government was unable to check the counter-revolution, on July 13 Congress issued a decree declaring that the Executive Power was authorized to take any measures necessary for the public welfare.[23] The Executive Power accordingly summoned Miranda from his seat in Congress and placed him at the head of the army. On July 19 General Miranda accordingly marched out of the capital city with an army of some four thousand men.[24] He soon established his headquarters at Maracay. When the besieged royalists sent Pedro de Peñalver with proposals for an armistice the patriot commander expressed his willingness to agree to their terms with certain modifications. Miranda stipulated that the insurgents should give up their arms and that the *cabildo* should be reëstablished. In regard to the proposal of the Valencians that they should be allowed to treat with Congress during the truce with respect to the acceptance of independence, he rejected this and responded that he was fully authorized by the Government to decide that matter.

According to Miranda's official report dated July 24, the insurgents now invited him to draw near the city. Hence he marched to the Morro, where the Valencians treacherously opened fire on his soldiers. Then the besiegers captured that fort and drove the garrison into the city. An incautious attack on the quarter occupied by the colored people and on the Franciscan convent whence the enemy had retired, however, was repulsed and several patriot officers were wounded. Among those officers who had distinguished themselves in action, Miranda mentioned Colonel Simón Bolívar, which would seem to discredit a tradition that the jealous generalissimo had tried to relieve that ardent patriot of his command.[25]

---

[23] Blanco, *Documentos para la historia de la vida pública del libertador,* III, 161.   [24] Poudenx and Mayer, p. 49.

[25] "Extract from a Spanish Gazette dated Caracas the 30th of July 1811, Translation," W. O., 1/109.

The besiegers now withdrew beyond the city walls. The surrounding region was subjugated, cannon were brought from the capital, and some Valencians deserted to the enemy. It seems that insurgent leaders now proposed that, as the revolt had been fomented by priests, a capitulation should be arranged with the archbishop. Miranda retorted, however, that "if they did not surrender unconditionally, he would see that the arrival of the archbishop was hastened by cannon and bullets." [26] On August 12 a general assault was made and the besieged were driven to their inmost intrenchments. At dawn of the following day the attack was resumed, and at ten o'clock the insurgents, whose supply of water had been cut off, proposed a capitulation. However, warned by his previous experience, the patriot general refused to consider their proposals unless they first relinquished their arms. Thus, said Miranda, they were obliged "to surrender at discretion, and to trust entirely to our humanity and generosity." At noon the Venezuelan tricolor was hoisted over the city. The rest of the story shall be taken from a French version of Miranda's dispatch of August 13 to the Secretary of War:

"After brief negotiations, the flotilla of four to six small armed vessels that had plagued the lagoon of Valencia and its environs also surrendered. Thus all the people who were in arms against Caracas on July 21 are either subjugated or pacified. In later dispatches I will send a list of the small number of killed and wounded that we suffered in this action, an encounter which has covered our troops with glory. Colonel Don Simón Bolívar, who with his companions in arms has distinguished himself on this patriotic occasion, and my aide-de-camp, Captain Francisco Salias, who emerged from a prison to serve his country, will inform your highness of other details which time does not permit me to state in this dispatch." [27]

The next measure of the government was to provide for the punishment of the reactionary Valencians. Priests as well as

---

[26] Poudenx and Mayer, pp. 50-51.   [27] *Journal de l'Empire,* Nov. 20, 1811.

laymen who had fomented the loyalist uprising were thrust
into prison. On August 10 the Executive Power had issued a
proclamation establishing a special court for the trial of the
royalists. Of this tribunal Miranda was made the presiding
judge.[28] Eight days later Congress issued a decree praising
"the excellent conduct" of the national commander at the siege
of Valencia. "The humanity shown by the commander in chief
toward the inhabitants of the city," ran the decree, "deserves
the highest praise, while the firmness that he displayed toward
those Valencians who persisted in their opposition to the cause
of justice, and the skill with which he reduced them to submission prove that he unites to high military talents those
benevolent sentiments which may happily promote the designs
of the independent provinces." [29]

Yet the commander's conduct during the Valencian campaign was bitterly criticized. He was accused of having caused
unnecessary bloodshed. Assertions were made that his discipline had been extremely harsh and that he had levied forced
contributions without authority.[30] For the second time in his
career Miranda was summoned from the head of an army to
present himself before the bar of a nation. The accused general successfully defended himself against his critics. His rôle
was graphically described by a citizen of the United States in
these words: "Miranda was forced to vindicate himself before
the congress, when he ought to have been employed in the
field. His friends delight in descanting upon his accomplish-
ments * * * and ascribe to him a promptness in argument, ingenuity in debate, and an eloquence not inferior to that of the
great Pericles, when he harangued the citizens of Athens, and
moved the multitude by his irresistible force of persuasion, as
a tempest heaves the billows of the main." [31]

In a dispatch dated August 21, 1811, Lowry declared that
the success of the revolution depended "in a great measure on
succor from abroad." He predicted that Miranda would "e'er

[28] Austria, pp. 83-84.   [29] *Correio Braziliense,* VII, 653.
[30] Amunátegui, p. 111; *El libro nacional,* pp. 303, 305, 307.
[31] Robertson, *Miranda,* p. 452.

long be at the head of this Government which will most probably be a benefit to the Country, as he may be safely pro-
nounced the fittest person in it for the station." [32] "General
Miranda, whose conduct at first caused suspicions," said another observer, "enjoys at present the greatest popularity.
The people know that he is ambitious and enterprising; but he
has given such unequivocal proofs of his attachment to the
cause of the revolution that they have complete confidence in
him." [33]

Even before Miranda landed on Venezuelan soil some of
his fellow countrymen had dreamed of forming a constitution.
Before the Declaration of Independence was adopted Congress had intrusted to a committee headed by Francisco Javier
Ustáriz of San Sebastián the task of preparing for its consideration a "plan of a constitution on the bases of a confederation." Besides Ustáriz, this committee included Paúl, Ponte,
Roscio, Sanz, and Miranda.[34] Evidently it was deliberating
about a democratic project of government while Congress was
discussing the policy that should be adopted in respect to independence.[35]

To this committee the returned exile submitted that scheme
of government for liberated Spanish America which he had
formulated in 1801. In that connection Roscio wrote to Bello
that Miranda wished that "a project should be adopted which
he had brought with him in which the executive authority was
to be vested in two Incas whose term of office should be ten
years." Roscio declared that it was neither possible to agree
to such a pretension nor to bring Miranda's scheme into harmony with the plan formed by the committee on a constitution.
Hence the resentful constitution-maker conceived the idea of
ridiculing the committee's plan and "formed a club of seven
persons, who, without being censors, undertook as their task
the criticism of our plan. Compared with the project of the
two Incas, it merited approval. Miranda neither showed his

---

[32] Manning, *op. cit.*, II, 1151-52.
[34] Amunátegui, p. 98.
[33] *Journal de l' Empire*, Nov. 20, 1811.
[35] *El libro nacional*, pp. 26, 44, 45.

scheme to the government nor to other persons who might at least have praised his arduous labor." [36]

Unfortunately for Miranda's plans a propaganda had been launched in favor of a federal scheme of government. In December, 1810, at Philadelphia, García de Sena, a native of Venezuela, had dedicated to his fellow countrymen a volume which contained not only translations from Paine's *Common Sense* but also translations of the Articles of Confederation and the United States Constitution. In his dedication, addressed to the Spanish Americans, García de Sena declared that in dedicating to them his first attempt to translate the works of Thomas Paine, he wished to justify their conduct and to promote their liberty and prosperity. The very title of this treatise, *The Independence of Terra Firma Justified by Thomas Paine Thirty Years Ago*, doubtless inspired and flattered the sentiments of Venezuelan leaders. [37]

In his articles in the *Gaceta de Caracas* Burke pleaded for the establishment of a federal government in Venezuela, and for the formation in Spanish America of a United States of Mexico and a United States of South America. The following passage will suggest the way in which he used the Republic of the North as an exemplar: "This nation, which is as great as all Europe, demonstrates by experience, which is the best proof, that extent of territory is not an obstacle to union if a free and representative plan is adopted, and that this system is, on the contrary, susceptible of including a much greater territory without the least inconvenience or danger to the liberty of any citizen. In the North American Confederation, as we have already indicated, each State retains its independence and individual sovereignty, and having the constitution, government, and laws that are suitable is only subject to the general government in what concerns the union, defence, and prosperity of the confederation." [38] Such leaders as Ustáriz

---

[36] Amunátegui, pp. 98-99.
[37] García de Sena, *La independencia de Costa Firme justificado por Thomas Paine treinta años ha,* pp. 67-154, 176-97, 200-40; Austria, p. 119.
[38] *Derechos de la América del Sur y México,* p. 44.

and Roscio corresponded with other patriots concerning the type of government to be established, which became the great theme of the hour.[39] In a copy of *El Publicista de Venezuela*, the rare periodical which printed congressional debates, Roscio is quoted as having said that there could be "little doubt of the advantages of the federal system, for these advantages had been so well proved by the experience of the United States." [40]

On September 2, 1811, Francisco Javier Ustáriz laid the committee's plan of a constitution before Congress.[41] Although this project was more than once designated the plan of Ustáriz, yet presumably other members of the committee had taken part in framing it.[42] Interrupted at various times by other pressing business, discussions about this plan took place in Congress from September 2 to December 21. Such fragmentary records of the debates as have come down to us indicate that some Venezuelan leaders did not feel that the federal republican plan, which they considered the most perfect type of political organization, was adapted to the needs of a people who were just liberating themselves from the shackles of Spanish rule. This was the opinion of both Bolívar and Miranda.[43] As already suggested, Miranda still clung tenaciously to his project that placed supreme executive authority in the hands of two "Incas" and provided for a dictator in case of extreme necessity. In all likelihood Bolívar already entertained the view that the federal Constitution of the United States was not suited to Venezuela. Several years later he declared that it was a marvel that the United States Constitution had endured and that the idea had never entered his head "to consider as identical the characteristics of two peoples so different as the Anglo-American and the Spanish-American." [44]

Hints of the debates in Congress about the plan of a consti-

---

[39] Palacio Fajardo, *Outline of the Revolution in Spanish America*, p. 119.
[40] Aug. 1, 1811.   [41] *El libro nacional*, p. 214.   [42] *Ibid.*, pp. 250, 251.
[43] Larrazábal, I, 99; Austria, p. 119.
[44] Robertson, *Rise of the Spanish-American Republics*, p. 236.

tution indicate that some members objected to a proposal to establish a council of the ancients and expressed a preference for a tribunal of censors. The adoption of a fundamental law was for a time entangled with a project for the division of the province of Caracas. A bone of contention was the relation that should exist between Church and State under the new régime. This issue involved the problem of the patronage, that is to say, the right to make those ecclesiastical appointments which in colonial days had been controlled by the Spanish crown,—a problem that often occasioned difficulties in Spanish-American states when they set out on their independent careers. Most serious perhaps of the politico-religious problems was the question as to the extent to which a priest should be allowed to enjoy his peculiar privileges or exemptions by an immunity styled the *fuero*. On December 16, despite the insistent opposition of certain priests, Congress voted that the *fueros* of ecclesiastics should be completely abolished.[45]

"The Constitution as drawn up by the Congress," said Gregor McGregor, "was signed by all the members on Saturday the 21st. December and immediately signified to the people by the discharge of cannon and an illumination at the house of Congress, in other respects there was little appearance of rejoicing. General Miranda protested against it generally, and the priests (who are members) against the abolition of their privileges named *fueros*." [46] In fact certain priests accompanied their signatures with protests against the abolition of their ancient privileges. A few lay members of Congress also objected to the article abolishing the *fueros*.[47] Miranda, who was now vice president of Congress, entered a protest against the general character of the fundamental law in this cryptic passage: "As I believe that in the present Constitution the powers of government are not properly bal-

---

[45] *El libro nacional*, pp. 349-50.
[46] McGregor to Perceval, Jan. 18, 1812, F. O., 72/171.
[47] *El libro nacional*, pp. 359-70.

anced, that its structure and general organization are not sufficiently clear and sensible to remain permanent, and further that it is not adapted to the population, habits, and customs of this country,—from which the result may flow that instead of uniting us in a general mass or social body it will divide and separate us to the prejudice of our common security and independence,—I inscribe these reservations in the fulfillment of my duty." [48]

A letter by the chairman of the committee on a constitution furnishes an illuminating commentary on the old man's protest. Ustáriz interpreted the allegation that the powers of government were not properly balanced to mean that Miranda wished the Executive Power to be sacred and inviolable with a term lasting ten years. The allegation that the structure and organization of government were not clear and sensible, Ustáriz interpreted to mean that Miranda either did not understand them or did not wish to understand them. The allegation that the Constitution was not adapted to the country, Ustáriz interpreted to mean that Miranda wished the Venezuelans to continue to live under a monarchical régime, and perhaps even that they should seek a substitute for Ferdinand VII. "It should also be noticed." proceeded Ustáriz, "that Miranda emitted neither protest nor objection, which I know of while listening to the reading, discussion, and debate of the Constitution, except in one particular. This repugnance was shown toward a clause that prohibited him from becoming an official of the government, as indeed it prohibited all persons who had not resided here, which is a common practice everywhere. Afterwards he suddenly emphasized his protest at the time of signing the Constitution as if to embarrass us and to keep us constantly in a state of uncertainty, while he might utilize a good transaction or a fortunate event." [49]

The Constitution of 1811 provided that the seven provinces which had formed the Captaincy General of Venezuela should compose a federal republic. Evidently the Venezuelan Fathers

---

[48] *Ibid.*, p. 359.   [49] Rojas, *El general Miranda* p. 617.

favored a régime that would permit the provinces to choose their own executive authorities. The Constitution declared that the provinces,—which were virtually recognized as states, —preserved their sovereignty, liberty, and independence except when these were expressly delegated to the Confederation by the Constitution. Under no circumstances was the seat of the national government to be located at the capital of a province. Under certain conditions any other section of Spanish America might be admitted to the Confederation.

The Constitution vested executive authority in three persons chosen by indirect election who were to be styled the Supreme Executive Power. Among the functions of the chief executive magistrates were specified the command of the land and naval forces, the appointment of ambassadors, consuls, and supreme judges, and, subject to the consent of the Senate, the negotiation of treaties with foreign nations.

Legislative power was vested in a Senate and a House of Representatives. The Senate was to be composed of members elected by the provincial legislatures. The House of Representatives was to be made up of members chosen by electors in the provinces. All bills concerning revenue should originate in the lower house but the Senate might sanction, modify, or reject such measures. A bill might become a law, in spite of the vote of the executive, if it passed both houses by a two-thirds majority. Among the powers granted to Congress was the right to declare war or to make peace, the right to call the militia of the provinces into the service of the nation, and the right to establish inferior judicial tribunals throughout the Confederation. The highest judicial power was vested in a supreme court which was to be located in the capital city. The jurisdiction of this court was to extend to differences arising between two or more provinces, to differences between one province and the citizens of another, and to differences between a province and a foreign state or citizen. In some of its clauses this Constitution showed the pervasive influence of the United States Constitution.

In matters concerning religion, however, the Venezuelan Constitution reflected the colonial régime. Chapter I provided that Roman Catholicism was not only to be the religion of State but also the sole religion of the people. One of the first duties of Congress should be to protect that faith and to maintain its purity and inviolability. Though Congress had apparently decided to extinguish the right of patronage as hitherto exercised, yet no solution of this problem was formulated in the Constitution. Neither did the Venezuelan Fathers provide for the negotiation of a concordat, although they recognized the need of readjusting their relations with the Papacy.

Chapter VIII of the Venezuelan Constitution, which was devoted to a formulation of the rights of man in the new State, was obviously inspired by the example of France. It seems possible that Miranda had proposed some of its doctrines. Philosophy of the French Revolution was discernible in introductory phrases declaring that after "men were organized in society they renounced the unlimited and licentious liberty induced by passions which were only proper in a condition of savagery. The establishment of society presupposes the renunciation of these fatal rights and the acquisition of other rights that are more sweet and pacific. It also presupposes subjection to certain mutual duties." [50] Besides an enumeration of the rights of citizens to liberty, equality, property, and security, this chapter guaranteed liberty of thought and freedom of the press so long as public tranquillity, private honor, or Christian morality were not attacked. Aliens were to enjoy the same protection in person and property as natives of Venezuela, provided that they respected the religion, independence, and government of the country. With regard to Indians and mestizos, caste distinctions were swept away. The slave trade was prohibited. An Hispanic-American ideal embodied in this Constitution was a desire to unite with the people of other portions of Spanish America in defense

---

[50] *El libro nacional*, p. 402.

of their religion, sovereignty, and independence.

In a proclamation dated December 23, 1811, the President of Congress declared that "the project of a social contract" which was presented to the people for approval had been formed to promote their felicity.[51] The signing of the Constitution was made known to the citizens of Caracas by the ringing of bells and by a salute of twenty-one guns.[52] With the exception of the province of Cundinamarca, which had just adopted a fundamental law that contemplated the erection of a constitutional monarchy professing fidelity to Ferdinand VII, Venezuela was the first State of Spanish America to frame a Constitution. Influenced by the example of France and the United States, the Venezuelan Fathers rejected monarchical forms.

As Miranda had suggested, the first Constitution adopted by a Spanish-American state that claimed to be independent was, in certain particulars, unsuited to the stage of political development which the people had attained. In Anglo-Saxon eyes perhaps its most glaring defect was the fact that it attempted artificially to construct states that were to function in a federal scheme of government from provinces which during the Spanish régime had been little more than administrative divisions of a Captaincy General. The first Constituent Congress of Venezuela has not inappropriately been compared to an architect who wished "to construct a sumptuous palace without having the necessary materials at his disposal." [53]

About the time that the national Congress adopted a Constitution other important changes took place. Certain provinces of the former Captaincy General proceeded to frame their fundamental laws. In the autumn of 1811 the provinces of Mérida and Trujillo adopted constitutions. By a peculiar procedure the constitution of the province of Caracas was

---

[51] *Prólogo á los anales de Venezuela*, p. 201.
[52] *Boletín de la academia nacional de la historia*, VI, 985.
[53] Poudenx and Mayer, p. 46.

formed by its delegates in the national Congress. This frame of government was patterned after the federal scheme. The province was divided into departments which were subdivided into cantons and districts. A large measure of autonomy was granted to the cities.[54]

Early in January, 1812, news reached Caracas that the province of Cartagena in New Granada had declared its independence. To manifest their joy the patriots illuminated their houses. Gregor McGregor delighted the populace by directing a piper to play in the patio of his house where his servants danced Highland reels.[55] A letter from Caracas, probably by a Frenchman, stated that the patriot leader Miranda was now dedicated to "the great and glorious task of establishing the independence of all Spanish America." [56]

In the beautiful valley of Caracas, at least, signs of prosperity and progress were manifest. Emigrants were arriving, especially from the Antilles. Arts and sciences were stimulated. Agriculture and industry revived; factories of various sorts were established. In the capital city promenades were laid out, roads repaired, and bridges constructed. Partly because of the encouragement accorded to foreigners by new legislation, commerce developed rapidly. Religious toleration had been "tacitly conceded." Under the fostering care of the new government, public instruction made notable progress. Academies of anatomy and mathematics were opened. Freed from the trammels of the colonial régime, the press had a surprising activity: gazettes were founded; satirical poems were published; pamphlets appeared which "were written with elegance and purity but which contained words rather than solid thoughts." [57] The bright side of the shield was vividly depicted by an inhabitant of the capital city who declared that the revolution "had now assumed a grand, brilliant, and imposing aspect. People everywhere discoursed about their rights with the same familiarity that they used to converse

---

[54] Blanco, III, 491-526.
[55] McGregor to Perceval, Jan. 18, 1812, F. O., 72/171.
[56] *Journal de l'Empire,* May 8, 1812.   [57] Poudenx and Mayer, p. 58.

about God and the King. * * * A numerous and sprightly youth, assiduously imbibing knowledge by education, gave hopeful promise of furnishing future pillars to the State." [58]

This description of developments in the first republic founded in Spanish or Portuguese America is obviously flattering. It suggests that, besides convoking the earliest Congress held in Spanish America, signing a Declaration of Independence, framing a federal Constitution, and initiating social reforms, the patriots of Venezuela were contemplating other steps in national progress. Their sanguine hopes were suddenly dashed to earth, however, by a strange concatenation of circumstances which brought Miranda to the center of the stage as the man of destiny.

---

[58] Robertson, *Miranda,* p. 458.

Chapter XXI

THE FIRST DICTATOR OF VENEZUELA

EVEN BEFORE the Constitution of Venezuela had been framed, signs of dissatisfaction with the patriots had been displayed in regions outside the province of Caracas. The emergence of a dissident party corresponding to the Tories of the Thirteen Colonies became a dangerous factor in the situation. In the provinces of Coro, Guiana, and Maracaibo the loyalists composed a large element of the population. To lead the royalist reaction there appeared Domingo de Monteverde, an aspiring naval captain who in February, 1812, was intrusted by Fernando Miyares, the titular captain general of Venezuela, with the command of a small expedition. Early in the following month Monteverde marched from Coro. On March 23 he captured Carora. Influenced by his success, some of the inhabitants of the invaded region soon enrolled under the Spanish flag.

The Congress of Venezuela had been transferred to Valencia which had been made the seat of the Confederate Government. In accordance with the Constitution, Fernando del Toro, Francisco Espejo, and Francisco Javier Ustáriz were now installed as the Executive Power. The new statesmen began to occupy themselves with the legislation and administration of the Republic.

A tendency to desert the patriot cause was much stimulated by an unfortunate, unforeseen event. On the afternoon of Thursday, March 26, 1812, when devout Catholics were preparing for the solemnities of Good Friday, an ominous rumbling was heard in the distant Andes. Terrible quivers of the earth took place. In the province of Caracas the first quake occurred a few minutes after four o'clock in the afternoon. This shock was followed by repeated upheavals which were felt in most of the important towns and cities. At La Guaira the forts were either seriously damaged or completely destroyed and some two thousand people perished. An English captain named Forrest who visited this port shortly after the earthquake said that only three houses were left standing. He found the terror-stricken survivors preparing to dig the dead bodies of their friends and relatives out of the awful ruins so that they might burn them on funeral pyres.[1]

There is no better way to describe the effects of the earthquake than to adapt a vivid account by an inhabitant of the city of Caracas. He declared that a "multitude perished in the churches, whither they had gone on this festival to adore the Supreme Being." He avowed that no pen could depict "the dreaded disaster in half its multiformity of shapes. Men were maimed and bruised; our finest youth crushed to death; streets, temples, houses, bridges, public edifices, all destroyed. Every form of wretchedness passed in tragic review." The "doleful groans and lamentations of the dying" were heard, as well as the moans of "persons imploring succor from beneath the ruins"; horror was depicted upon every countenance; people abandoned "their homes, their interests and dearest objects of their care" and fled "in crowds to the neighboring mountains. All these scenes of affliction and sorrow formed an assemblage so lamentable, as has no parallel in the annals of Venezuela. In twenty seconds all was overturned." [2]

Among other cities or towns that were partly or entirely destroyed by the earthquake were Puerto Cabello, Maracaibo, Mérida, Trujillo, Barquisimeto, Tocuyo, Carora, San Carlos, and San Felipe. As this calamity occurred on the ecclesiastical anniversary of the very feast day upon which the Captain General had been deposed by the patriots of Caracas, many devout Catholics felt that it was a punishment from Heaven. "In short this [is] a death blow to Miranda, and his followers," said Captain Forrest, "if the adherents of Ferdinand the Seventh do not lose time in taking advantage of the effect which this calamitous visitation has had on the minds of the populace, it having happened upon Holy Thursday, a solemn

[1] Forrest to Stirling, March 30, 1812, F. O., 72/139.
[2] Robertson, *Miranda*, pp. 460-61.

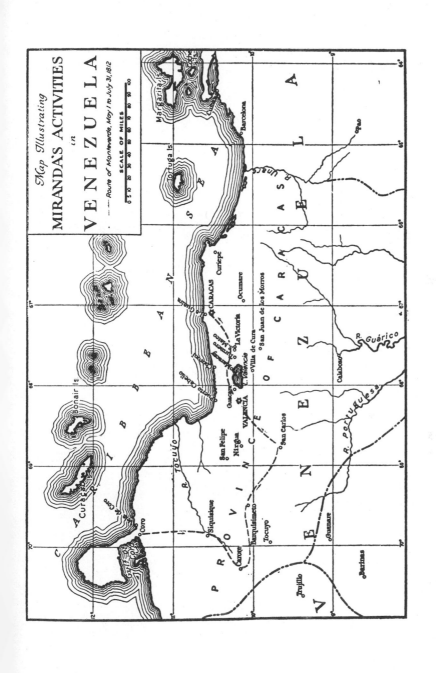

Map Illustrating
MIRANDA'S ACTIVITIES
in
VENEZUELA

----- Route of Monteverde, May 1 to July 31, 1812

SCALE OF MILES
0 5 10 20 30 40 50 60 70 80 90 100

Festival, and while they were all in Church, gave a degree of solemnity to the calamity which was truly awful, and inspired very generally an Idea that it was a Judgment of the Almighty upon them, manifesting his displeasure at their defection from Loyalty to their Sovereign." [3]

The earthquake had a very depressing effect upon the partisans of independence because certain towns that were most damaged were among those in which they had held the mastery. Again, in some cases those parts of cities in which patriot soldiers were quartered were ruined, while other portions were miraculously spared. Further, the loyalist stronghold at Coro escaped the calamity as if by a miracle. In his account of this disaster a royalist contemporary named José Díaz stated that upon the most elevated part of the ruins of the capital city, he beheld Simón Bolívar whose countenance depicted the utmost terror but who notwithstanding dauntlessly ejaculated: "If nature opposes herself to us, we will wrestle with her, and force her to obey!" [4]

A conservative estimate would have placed the number of fatalities in the capital city at ten thousand. A large number of patriot soldiers lost their lives by the destruction of barracks or fortifications. Certain churches were reduced to heaps of ruins. Terror-stricken people cast themselves upon their knees in the Great Square and implored the divine mercy. The priests who were mostly devoted royalists, took advantage of the fact that the calamity had occurred on a feast day; they tried to convince the people that the earthquake was a sign of God's displeasure at the secession of Venezuela from Spain. Narciso Coll y Prat, archbishop of Caracas, issued a pastoral letter in which he avowed that the earthquake was a divine retribution for the vices of the Venezuelans.[5] A revolutionary memoir illustrates the spirit of fanaticism:

"We should notice here a singular event that took place

---

[3] Forrest to Stirling, March 30, 1812, F. O., 72/139.
[4] Díaz, *Recuerdos sobre la rebelión de Caracas,* p. 39.
[5] Urquinaona, *Memorias,* p. 91.

after the earthquake; it will serve to show the influence of the clergy upon the spirit of the people of these countries. After several priests had exhorted the people to public repentance, persons who had lived in concubinage hastened to get married. It is claimed that during the two months that followed the earthquake as many as five hundred marriages were solemnized. Adroit priests used the calamity to lead people to support their political system. They pointed out that the catastrophe had taken place on the anniversary of the day on which the Captain General was deposed. Nothing more was necessary to make the credulous inhabitants hate the new government." [6]

Many people now forsook the patriot cause and joined the royalists. This reactionary tendency became so manifest that the legislature of the province of Caracas published a proclamation which aimed to counteract the fanatical exhortations of priests and to strengthen the spirit of allegiance to the new government.[7] Congress enacted a Draconian law that was designed to punish soldiers who deserted the army. As desertions from the patriot ranks did not decrease, the Executive Power issued a decree which proclaimed martial law in the province of Caracas and provided that all deserters should be punished with death.[8]

Yet manifestations of terror or piety did not cease. "The sacred cause of freedom was neglected," said a Venezuelan, "for a blind, puerile, fearful, and extravagant devotion. Multitudes thronged the churches day and night: public prayer and penitences were the occupation of the people; agriculture, commerce, and the arts stood still; he who did not surrender himself to the ridiculous mania of living in penance was regarded as a dissolute libertine who provoked the anger of heaven. This dismal contagion extended to the people of the interior; so that Venezuela was suddenly converted into a vast

---

[6] Poudenx and Mayer, *Mémoire pour servir à la histoire de la révolution de la capitainerie générale de Caracas*, p. 65.
[7] Rojas, *El general Miranda*, pp. 619-23. [8] *Ibid.*, pp. 623-26.

camp, presenting to the eyes of the philosopher, nothing but caravans of pilgrims trooping to Mecca, or hordes of inhabitants in religious frenzy." In describing the activities of the priests this contemporary avowed that "they exhibited in their hands a Jesus on the cross, but in their hearts were chains of slavery." [9] When news of the calamity reached Telésforo de Orea, he sent to Secretary Monroe a plea that began with this passage:

"It is in the name of humanity that I desire your attention on this occasion. I ask it with confidence, for just and sensible persons cannot be indifferent to the calamities suffered by human beings. The unfortunate fate of the cities of Caracas, La Guaira, Puerto Cabello, and the adjacent towns has become well known; and I regret that its effects should be so far-reaching. Those persons who have survived the catastrophe not only have to regret the loss of their parents, children, friends, and thousands of their fellow citizens but they behold their very existence threatened in a thousand ways. Without protection against storms, deprived of the products of their land which have been buried beneath the ruins, and deprived of all immediate succor,—hunger, helplessness, and the rigors of the season will end their misery and desolation, if some providential hand does not save them from so great a calamity!" [10]

Upon becoming aware of the calamitous effects of the earthquake, the Congress of the United States passed an act appropriating money for the purchase of provisions for the relief of the unfortunate sufferers. Orea was informed that steps had been taken for carrying this law into force immediately, and that Alexander Scott, "a very respectable citizen of the United States," would soon sail for South America to execute the commission. [11]

The earthquake gave fresh *élan* to the troops of Monte-

[9] Irvine's Notes, I. & A., Consular Letters, La Guayra, I.

[10] Urrutia, *Páginas de historia diplomática*, p. 22. Other impressions of the effects of the earthquake may be found in Key-Ayala, "Apuntes sobre el terremoto de 1812," in *El Cojo Ilustrado*, XXI, 158.

[11] Robertson, "Beginnings of Spanish-American Diplomacy," *loc. cit.*, p. 258.

verde. His forces were increased not only by deserters but also by fresh recruits. When news reached Venezuela that the Cortes at Cadiz had promulgated a liberal Constitution which provided that delegates representing the Indies should sit in the national legislature, the disaffection did not decrease. Congress took steps to check the royalist advance. It placed the Marquis of Toro in charge of the military forces. As events soon showed, however, that this commander was not able to cope with the emergency, the leaders of the independent movement in Venezuela were compelled again to place Miranda in command of their army.[12] On April 23, 1812, the Secretary of War addressed a significant letter to the veteran general to announce that the Executive Power of the Union had just appointed him "general in chief of the soldiers of the Venezuelan Confederation with absolute power to take any steps" that he might judge necessary to preserve the national territory which was invaded "by the enemies of Colombian liberty. In so doing it does not make you subject to any laws or regulations previously in force in the Republic. On the contrary, you are to consult only the supreme law of the salvation of the Fatherland; and for this purpose the Executive Power of the Union delegates to you, under your responsibility, its ordinary authority as well as the extraordinary functions which on the fourth of this month were conferred upon it by the national representatives." [13]

The appointment of Miranda as generalissimo was soon approved by the government of the province of Caracas. The *Gaceta de Caracas* explained that this step had been taken because of Miranda's "well-known military knowledge, his valor, and decided patriotism." [14] By a secret order dated May 4 the Executive Power placed the national funds at the disposal of the commander in chief for the purpose of this campaign.[15]

---

[12] Austria, *Bosquejo de la historia militar de Venezuela,* p. 127.
[13] Rojas, *El general Miranda,* p. 628.
[14] Extracts from the *Gaceta de Caracas,* April 28, 1812, in W. O., 1/111.
[15] Rojas, *op. cit.,* pp. 628-29.

Meantime Miranda had taken measures to reorganize the army. Some adventurous Englishmen joined the patriot forces. A legion of Frenchmen was formed under Colonel du Cayla. To command the fort at Puerto Cabello the general-issimo selected the dashing colonel, Simón Bolívar. José de Austria, the author of a military history of Venezuela, who stated that he was present at the meeting between General Miranda and the members of the Executive Power, asserted that the general asked that this selection should be made because Bolívar was a dangerous youth.[16] Whether or not Miranda thus wished to deprive that colonel of an opportunity to distinguish himself on the battle line, there is no doubt that he gave the ambitious leader a prominent post. Puerto Cabello was perhaps the most important fortified city in Venezuela: its magazines held large stores of munitions; and in its fortress were incarcerated some unflinching royalists. Yet, as a confidant of the Liberator later suggested, this command was not suited to the bold genius of Bolívar who perhaps felt that the appointment was a reflection on his dignity and valor.[17]

Although the eastern provinces of Venezuela did not rally to the defense of the national government, and although disaffection had spread among the patriots, yet it seems likely that the most daring soldiers in the Republic proceeded to range themselves under the veteran general, "anxious to distinguish themselves in the defense of the Fatherland." [18] From Caracas on April 30 Miranda issued an allocution to his soldiers which has come to hand in a poor English translation. He declared that Venezuela, "threatened by some malevolent individuals," invited them to the field of battle and expected salvation from their bravery and patriotism. He exhorted them to march "to Triumph under the Banners of Liberty and to conquer that which some of your fellow Countrymen (who were sold in a cruel manner by individuals unworthy of the name of Venezuelans) lost." He told them that they might

---

[16] Austria, p. 128.   [17] O'Leary, *Memorias,* XXVII, 55.   [18] *Ibid.*

"be sure of the Victory," for the "God of Hosts ever protects
the cause of Justice." He asked them to commend their wives
and children to "a Paternal Government which will take immediate care for their preservation and provide the neces-
saries for their subsistence while you are covering yourselves
with immortal Glory. Trust in your General who shall always
lead you thro' the Path of Virtue and Honor to the enjoyment
of your Liberty." [19]

At daybreak on May 1, 1812, General Miranda led the van-
guard of his army out of the capital city. From La Laja he
sent a detachment on a reconnaissance to Valencia. Meantime
that important city had been evacuated by its patriot garrison, and attempts to recover it were altogether vain. For on
May 3, after capturing San Carlos, Monteverde had entered
Valencia in the midst of popular acclamations.[20] Yet, despite
his elation at this triumph, the royalist commander was apprehensive of an attack by the patriots. He sent letters to
the governor of Coro describing his position as very critical;
he asked for munitions and reënforcements. "I have reliable
information that Miranda expects artillery of large calibre
in order to undertake a formal siege of this city," said Monteverde, "and that his army is composed of more than 3,000
men determined to conquer it. You can imagine what my situation will be: my army is excessively fatigued with extraordinary exertions; for more than eight days it has not rested
a moment; it has become so debilitated by great fatigue and
lack of clothing that I am moved to compassion. But all this
vigilance is necessary; for the astute Miranda only awaits a
chance to attack me on all sides." [21]

For the time being, however, the patriot commander was
not inclined to take aggressive measures. From Guacara on
May 8 he issued a proclamation asking the Valencians to expel

---

[19] "Copy Translation," inclosure in Hodgson to Liverpool, June 18, 1812,
W. O., 1/111.
[20] Urquinaona, *Resumen de las causas principales que preparon y dieron
impulso á la emancipación de la América Española*, p. 25.
[21] Blanco, *Documentos para la historia de la vida pública del libertador*,
IV, 21.

the royalists and to reunite themselves with the people of Caracas. "Choose Valencians between the two extremes: either to be free or to die; this is the vow that the Republicans whom I have the honor to command have made; and the same which you must adopt for yourselves either by force or good will." Yet he declared that, as in his previous campaign against them, he loved humanity. Bulletins of the independent army that were published in the *Gaceta de Caracas* reported minor engagements between the patriots and the royalists. A bulletin dated May 14 indicated that Miranda had decided to form a camp at Maracay "where he established his headquarters in order to organize, discipline, and complete a necessary number of Troops to render them calculated to re-establish our affairs, and to destroy at once (and if possible forever) the Enemies of the Liberty and independence of the Province of Venezuela." [22] On May 15 he promulgated a series of army regulations that were almost Draconian in their severity. Theft was to be punished by death. An officer caught playing cards was to be demoted. A soldier who became drunk was for the first offence to be imprisoned for eight days on bread and water.[23] The generalissimo also directed that steps should be taken to fortify the outposts which protected his position. At Maracay men, provisions, and munitions were gathered for the projected movement.[24]

An officer named José de Austria, who wrote an instructive history of those trying times, skilfully diagnosed the situation. He declared that the "defenders of the Fatherland" had demonstrated their valor "in various encounters with the enemy." He explained that "the rapid and progressive occupation of the country was made possible for the enemy not by triumphs on the field of battle but by repeated and inexplicable retreats." He presented the view that either "the generalissimo believed that the authority which had been transferred to him needed greater force and latitude or else he

[22] Translation, W. O., 1/111.
[23] Rojas, *El general Miranda,* pp. 629-30.   [24] Austria, pp. 133-34.

wished to reinvest it with new forms." Hence Miranda requested a conference with the chief officials of the Republic through selected commissioners. " 'It is necessary,' he said, 'to have conferences about impending events and about the perils that threaten the country, while it is neither possible nor prudent for me to leave the headquarters at Maracay from which I can survey the theatre of operations.' Under these circumstances nothing could be denied to the leader to whom had been confided the most important mission of saving Venezuela's liberty." [25]

The Executive Power now decided to take radical steps to save the Republic. On May 17 President Francisco Espejo asked Roscio, who was now a member of the Executive Power, to go to Maracay in order to confer with Miranda and not only to decide upon a military and political program which would promote the success of the patriot arms but also upon the measures that should be taken to reëstablish public confidence which had been destroyed in certain quarters by fanaticism and persecution.[26] In addition, the executive and the legislative authorities of the province of Caracas selected José V. Mercader and Francisco Talavera to proceed to Maracay on a similar mission.[27]

Those commissioners met in solemn conclave with the commander in chief in a house at La Trinidad that belonged to the Marquis of Casa León. In a précis signed on May 18 they expressed the view that the military and political administration of the province of Caracas and of the Venezuelan Confederation should be remodeled. They resolved that martial law should be proclaimed and that Miranda should have the sole power to appoint both military and political officials throughout Venezuela. They determined that her financial system should be reorganized, and selected the Marquis of Casa León to direct that task. In addition, they decided that "besides the powers intrusted to the generalissimo by the Executive Power of the Union, which are the same as those conferred

[25] Austria, p. 134.   [26] Rojas, *El general Miranda,* p. 502.   [27] *Ibid.,* p. 631.

upon him by the honorable Congress, there is expressly conceded to him the authority to treat directly with European powers and with those American nations that are free from Spanish domination, in order to obtain the means that he may judge appropriate for the defense of these states. He is to give to the government of the Union an account of those negotiations and of the appointment of the persons to whom they are intrusted." [28] In the words of José de Austria, "the result was to enlarge the powers that without authority had been conferred upon the general in chief and to constitute him in reality a Dictator,—in fact the other constitutional authorities of the Republic were swept away, as was even the Constitution itself." [29]

There is no reason to suppose that this large and significant increase of authority was contrary to the wishes of the generalissimo. Miranda had attained the climax of his career. The agitator and idealist, who had planned and dreamed for many years of directing a revolution in South America, was now virtually made the chief civil and military executive of Venezuela. It was not simply the hand of fate that had invested him with the dictatorial authority ascribed in an emergency to the chief executive in his own governmental scheme. Such a dénouement had been anticipated by divers contemporaries who had avowed that Miranda was insistently striving to attain supreme power.

On May 21 the Dictator issued a trenchant manifesto to his compatriots. After mentioning the circumstances that had caused the government by a series of measures to confer upon him unlimited powers, he said:

"These measures have vested in my person a great and extraordinary authority; but my responsibility increases in the same proportion, and I can only endure this authority and responsibility because the liberty and independence of my native land is their sole object. Therefore, fellow citizens, I shall labor for the reëstablishment of liberty and independence. In

[28] *Ibid.*, p. 632.   [29] *Bosquejo*, p. 135.

this task I count upon the uniform and simultaneous coöperation of the governments and the people of Venezuela. The energy and prudence of those governments in the execution of orders, and the ardor and patriotic enthusiasm of the people for the preservation of their properties, persons, and lives,— these constitute the indispensable conduct that I expect and which I shall venture to exact. The result will be the organization and equipment of a republican army, the destruction of our enemies, the reunion of the insurrectionary provinces under the standard of liberty, and ultimately peace and amity among the people of Venezuela who ought to form one family.

"In order to secure these advantages it has become necessary to correct some great evils that militate against them. Among the chief defects from which the Republic has suffered and which most prevented her perfection have been the complete disorder of our fiscal department and the depreciation of our paper money. Both of these defects will be remedied at once; at the head of the department of finance will be placed wise and intelligent men who will reform it by establishing banks that will promote the circulation of national money and thus stimulate the sources of general prosperity. The scarcity of certain supplies that are needed to carry on the war with activity and success makes it necessary to devise a proper mode of acquiring them. In consequence I find myself vested with the express power to treat directly with European states and with the independent nations of America in order that through contracts or other arrangements the Republic may be provided with the arms, soldiers, and munitions which will insure her liberty and independence.

"Chief magistrates of the provinces and all their inhabitants! I pledge my solemn word not to lay down the sword that you have confided to me until I have avenged the injuries of our enemies and have reëstablished a rational liberty throughout the territory of Venezuela. I will never abandon the important position in which you have placed me without satisfying your confidence and your desires. Then I shall again become a simple citizen. With pleasure I shall behold you enjoying the felicity that I so much desire,—a felicity which I shall have aided to establish. The Venezuelan Republic will then be governed tranquilly by her own constitutions, which were only momentarily altered by circumstances and imminent perils, and I shall always be ready to relinquish my life and my repose to conserve and defend them." [30]

This manifesto outlined Miranda's policy. He had decided to reorganize and reënforce his army before taking offensive measures. On May 29 he supplemented this pronunciamiento by an address to the people of the province of Caracas in which he declared that the enemy had invaded the very heart of the province, and that it had pillaged towns, devasted the country, and committed terrible excesses. He said that through seduction and fanaticism Monteverde had gained possession of advantageous positions. Then he made this impassioned appeal:

"Citizens:—with anxiety we await you in order that you may share the laurels with us or that we may live in the memory of men as having exhaled the last breath together. It is not to be concealed that the Fatherland is in danger and that the peril will increase every day, if we do not combine our forces. Martial law, which was imperiously demanded by circumstances, has been proclaimed. Let there not be an able-bodied man who does not march to the field of glory with those arms which he is able to procure. Let him carry at least a sword or a lance or a dagger; or let him come armed only with anger! With anger the hearts of good republicans is illumined, and the fire of offended honor penetrates and inflames them. Citizens: what injuries you have to avenge, what assassins to destroy, what beloved objects to defend, what triumphs to obtain! The time for vengeance has arrived; let the slaves tremble who came to attack free men! * * * Citizens! from their tombs the dead ask you to avenge their blood, while the sick call upon you to display the wounds inflicted in glorious actions! Women, children, and old men summon you in order that they may escape the assassin's dagger; and we invite you to take up arms in order that the flag of Venezuela may wave over Valencia, Coro, and Maracaibo!" [31]

---

[30] Austria, pp. 135-36.
[31] Rojas, *El general Miranda,* pp. 634-35.

Dictator Miranda soon decided to use the diplomatic powers that had been conferred upon him. On May 20 he wrote a letter to Madariaga indicating his intention to dispatch an agent to Bogotá.[32] Some days later he instructed Delpech to proceed to the English Antilles on a mission to his old friend Admiral Cochrane. In a letter to the admiral Miranda reminded him of the relations of friendship and harmony that had existed between Venezuela and England. He asked Cochrane to permit any person who might so desire to proceed from the West Indies to Venezuela.[33] Early in June the Dictator determined to send agents to Cundinamarca, Cartagena, England, and the United States.[34]

On June 2 Miranda sent a letter to Governor Hodgson of Curaçao that ran as follows: "I have the honor to inform your Excellency of my appointment as Generalissimo of Venezuela, with full powers to treat with Foreign States, and to take such other measures as I may deem necessary, for the interest and security of these Provinces. Being animated with the desire of promoting by all means in my power, the friendly dispositions existing between the two Governments, which I conceive for the mutual interest and advantage of both,—I shall most willingly contribute to cement the present union, and to form if possible a more intimate connexion; and have no doubt I shall meet with a similar disposition on your part." However, Governor Hodgson, who had been instructed by Lord Liverpool not to enter into any intercourse with Miranda made this non-committal reply: "I had the honor of receiving your Letter of the 2nd. instant yesterday, a copy of which I shall take the earliest opportunity of transmitting to His Majesty's Government." [35] Because of the alliance existing between England and Spain, English officials in the West Indies were loath to take steps to aid the South American revolutionists.

It was perhaps only natural that, as in former years, Mi-

---

[32] Rojas, *El general Miranda,* pp. 664-65.   [33] Austria, pp. 137-38.
[34] Rojas, *op. cit.* p. 267.
[35] By a mistake the copies of both letters bear the date of June 2, 1812, W. O., 1/111.

randa should have fixed his highest hopes of succor upon England. In a confidential letter to Blanco White on May 29 the Dictator expressed the hope that he would aid the Venezuelans. This note was intrusted to Delpech who was instructed to proceed to England where he was to have a secret interview with that journalist about the mode of raising volunteers in England for the Venezuelan army. Such recruits, said Miranda, would become citizens of Venezuela; according to their services, they would be recompensed by grants of land and by other rewards. Delpech was authorized to purchase arms which the Dictator agreed to pay for upon their delivery in South America.[36]

As agent to the English ministry Miranda selected Molini, who had been serving as his confidential secretary. The Dictator's intention in dispatching his secretary to London was indicated in epistles of June 2 to Spencer Perceval and Lord Castlereagh. As the letter to Castlereagh was almost identical with the letter to Governor Hodgson, we shall quote the letter addressed to Perceval:

"My correspondence with H. M. Ministers has been for some time suspended, owing to my not having a direct influence in the Government—I have within these few days been appointed Generalissimo of Venezuela, with full Powers to treat with Foreign States, and take such measures as I may judge necessary for the interest and security of these Provinces. Being always animated with the same views toward Great Britain, whose interests I conceive are intimately connected with the safety and prosperity of this Country, I am very desirous of cimenting by all means in my power the existing friendship and forming if possible a closer union between both Countries. The Bearer of this Letter is my Secretary, Mr. Thomas Molini, who will be able to give H. M. Ministers every information they may desire, relative to the actual state of these Provinces." [37]

---

[36] O'Leary, XIII, 43-44.
[37] Add. MSS., 38, 249, f. 72; the letter to Castlereagh is quoted in Robertson, *Miranda*, pp. 466-67.

On June 2 the Venezuelan commander sent a missive of similar tenor to Richard Wellesley. The latter was informed that Miranda had written to English ministers about the improvement of relations between England and Venezuela; and he was solicited to use his influence "to obtain so desirable an end." [38] On the same day the Dictator wrote to Jeremy Bentham expressing the hope that the day was not far distant, when he would see "the liberty and happiness" of Venezuela established "upon a solid and permanent footing." [39]

These letters indicate that in June, 1812, Miranda still cherished the hope of winning the independence of his native land. Apparently he thought that an influential factor in the accomplishment of this end would be the aid secured from foreign nations. It was evidently with the intention of stimulating the attempt to secure munitions from the United States that early in July the Dictator expressed his intention of sending Pedro Gual to replace Orea at Washington. Possibly Miranda may also have had in mind thus to promote the pending negotiations with Serurier. Colonel du Cayla and a patriot named Martín Tovar were sent to the West Indies to get recruits and munitions. [40] As an inducement Tovar was instructed to offer to volunteers the rights of Venezuelan citizenship after three campaigns and a grant of land when the revolutionary war had terminated. [41]

Meanwhile through correspondence with his officers the Dictator attempted to obtain information about the movements of the enemy. It is evident that he was forming a plan of campaign which he intended to follow in case the royalists were expelled from Valencia. On May 21 Miranda wrote to Bolívar to instruct him that he should not relinquish certain advance posts near Nirgua; for when the Spaniards evacuated Valencia they would presumably try to withdraw in that direction. Under such circumstances Bolívar was to form a

---

[38] Copy, F. O., 72/157.   [39] Bentham, *Works*, X, 468.
[40] Rojas, *El general Miranda*, pp. 586-89, 687.
[41] Miranda to Tovar, July 2, 1812 (copy), W. O., 1/112.

flying squadron with which to pursue the retreating royalists.[42]

The impressions which the condition of the new nation made upon an unprejudiced foreigner are reflected in a letter of June 5, 1812, to Secretary Monroe from Robert K. Lowry, who had been sent to La Guaira as consul of the United States:

"Since the communication I had the honor of making on the 2d. Feby. the Commission of Consul in due form which it has pleased the President of the United States to forward to me, has been received.

"On the 23 of March, I forwarded the patent to Caracas to the Executive Power, being prevented from personally presenting myself by indisposition. It was gladly received, and the usual forms of recognition nearly gone through when the dreadful convulsion of Nature of the 26 March threw everything into confusion and dismay. The Earthquake has been followed by the invasion of the Province from the side of Coro. The Enemy has penetrated as far as Valencia, and has been joined by a considerable portion of the Inhabitants of the Interior, among whom the superstitious idea, principally excited by the Priesthood, that the Earthquake is a chastisement of Heaven for abandoning the Cause of Ferdinand the Seventh, has pretty generally spread itself—General Miranda has succeeded in stopping the progress of the enemy and there is now reasonable hope that they will be defeated.

"In the meantime the General has been invested with the powers of a Dictator, and I believe an organization of this government distinct from that which has been given to the world in the shape of a Constitution, will shortly take place.

"Circumstanced as the authorities of the Country are, I have deferred making any further application for the present relative to the recognition of my powers but purpose doing so ere long and with this view have written to Genl. Miranda." [43]

Drastic measures that the Dictator deemed necessary to take at this time, however, did not increase his prestige. Cer-

---

[42] Rojas, *op. cit.*, p. 669.   [43] I. & A., Consular Letters, La Guayra, I.

11—II

tain military officers of Spanish descent were deprived of their commands and confined at La Victoria. In consequence of such measures some republican leaders, like the Toro brothers, even declined to serve in Miranda's army. Madariaga and two military officers were instructed to seize the royalist archbishop Narciso Coll y Prat and to confine him in a castle at La Guaira. At the instance of Miranda steps were taken to incarcerate all Spaniards and natives of the Canary Islands in that port. Two dictatorial decrees added to the growing discontent. One decree proclaimed that martial law existed throughout the Republic, while the other offered freedom to those slaves who would enlist in the patriot army for ten years.

In an account of the Dictator's proceedings a fellow countryman made a commentary that suggests the spirit of mistrust that was now growing in the independent ranks. Austria avowed that all "the acts and arrangements of the generalissimo produced fear and a lack of confidence in many patriots. What contributed to excite hatred and to make him even more unpopular was his secrecy in regard to certain measures,—a secrecy strange among republicans who were pursuing the same end in the midst of perils. In view of the dispiriting inertia of the republican arms that was apparently the result of unknown plans, his intimate relations with the governor of Curaçao and with other important foreigners produced a species of jealousy and increased the lack of confidence that would probably have completely disappeared if the conference at La Trinidad had resulted otherwise." [44]

At this critical juncture Miranda was apparently in a dubious or vacillating frame of mind. Although some of his compatriots undoubtedly disapproved of his Fabian policy, yet there were others who felt that Venezuela could not successfully terminate the struggle for independence without foreign aid. Perhaps the best analysis of the situation is that afforded by a friendly letter that a patriot official named Miguel J. Sanz sent to the Dictator on June 14:

---

[44] *Op. cit.*, p. 140.

"After I became acquainted in the department of state with the political condition of Venezuela, I formed the idea that her liberty and independence could not be achieved without effective aid from European powers. The situation in which our soldiers, our agriculture, our commerce, and our revenues are placed, the partisan spirit that animates our compatriots, and the scarcity of men to carry out the enterprise have practically convinced me of that truth. In such conditions it is impossible to furnish and equip the necessary military forces with so small a population and with only the revenues that the province of Caracas actually affords. * * * Should we not prefer to negotiate with the Grand Turk rather than to be again enchained? The situation is clear: we cannot sustain ourselves without agriculture, commerce, arms, and money. The greater part of our territory is occupied by our royalist enemies, while our internal enemies make cruel and perilous war upon us. These internal enemies are ignorance, envy, and pride. Such evils not only render your measures inefficacious but disturb and confound everything. If you wish to have the glory of making your native land independent and of securing to her the enjoyment of liberty, do not depend upon the means available here,—seek means abroad." [45]

Threatening advances of the royalists soon caused Miranda to remove his military headquarters from Maracay to La Victoria, which because of its strategic position was the key to the capital city. Further, the Dictator learned that the slaves and the colored inhabitants of Curiepe and other towns on the coast had risen tumultuously and were committing divers excesses against both patriots and royalists. Shortly afterwards Miranda received news of an untoward event that had happened in Puerto Cabello, a post which his "confidential aide-de-camp" described as "the bulwark of liberty in which the Patriots might defy all the power of Spain." [46]

On the forenoon of June 30, during the absence of the commander of the castle of San Felipe that dominated Puerto

[45] Rojas, *El general Miranda,* pp. 275-77.
[46] Leleux to Vansittart, Aug. 26, 1812, F. O., 72/140.

Cabello, the ranking patriot officer, Lieutenant Francisco
Fernández Vinoni, joined forces with the royalist prisoners
who were incarcerated there, and hoisted the Spanish flag.
Commanders of other forts soon followed Vinoni's example.
Many soldiers in the patriot garrison, some inhabitants of the
city, and the crews of certain Venezuelan vessels in the harbor
joined this uprising. Puerto Cabello refused to surrender. The
royalists then opened fire on the city, while Colonel Simón
Bolívar tried to defend it with a small contingent. In course
of the ensuing struggle that force was diminished through
desertion, capture, and death. On July 4 soldiers arrived from
Coro to reënforce the royalists, while no help came to succor
the beleaguered patriots.[47] Bolívar had sent a courier to the
generalissimo on July 1 and declared that if he did not "immediately attack the enemy" Puerto Cabello would be lost.
The Dictator received this disastrous news on July 5.[48] On the
next day, in despair of receiving timely succor from Miranda,
his force having been reduced to some forty men, the patriot
colonel reluctantly decided to give up the struggle.

In deep dejection Colonel Bolívar notified Miranda of the
fall of Puerto Cabello. He avowed that he had performed his
duty and alleged that if one soldier had remained with him
he would have continued to combat the enemy. "If the soldiers
deserted," added Bolívar, "that was not my fault. There was
nothing which I could do to prevent this desertion and to com-
pel them to save the country; but, alas! the post has been lost
in my hands!"[49] In an incoherent letter transmitting his account of the struggle for Puerto Cabello, the defeated commander avowed that he was filled "with a species of shame,"
and that he desired a respite of a few days to see if his spirit
might not regain possession of "its ordinary temper. After
having lost the best position in the country, how can I help
being demented, my general?"[50] The last passage of this lament ran in these words: "With respect to myself, I have ful-

---

[47] Istueta's deposition, July 5, 1812, W. O., 1/111.
[48] Rojas, op. cit., pp. 647, 687.   [49] Ibid., p. 648.   [50] Ibid., pp. 648-49.

filled my duty, and, although I have lost Puerto Cabello, I am blameless; and I have saved my honor. I regret that I have saved my life and that I was not left dead under the ruins of a city which should have been the last asylum of the liberty and the glory of Venezuela!" [51]

The loss of Puerto Cabello broke Miranda's spirit. In reminiscences written many years later Pedro Gual stated that the commander in chief had just been discussing the new mission to the United States and had promised him letters of introduction to John Adams and Thomas Jefferson when Bolívar's first portentous letter came to hand. Upon entering the military headquarters to which the Dictator had retired, said Gual, he was startled to see members of Miranda's staff in odd poses. Roscio was striking one hand against the other, Espejo was sunk in profound meditation, while Sata y Bussy was frozen like a statue:

"Filled with the presentiment of an unexpected calamity, I approached the generalissimo. 'Well,' I said to him, 'what news is there?' Even to a second inquiry, he made no response but to a third inquiry, made after an instant had elapsed, drawing a letter from his vest pocket, he said to me in French: *'Tenez: Venezuela est blessée au coeur!'* Never shall I forget the pathetic picture presented at that critical moment by those venerable patriarchs of American emancipation who were profoundly depressed by the intensity of actual misfortune and by a foreboding of other calamities that were about to afflict unfortunate Venezuela! * * * After the first surprise was over, General Miranda broke silence to say: 'You see gentlemen, how things happen in this world. A short time ago all was safe:—now all is uncertain and ominous. Yesterday Monteverde had neither powder nor lead nor muskets; today he can count on forty thousand pounds of powder, lead in abundance, and three thousand muskets! Bolívar told me that the royalists were making an attack but by this time they should be in the possession of everything!' " [52]

The effects of the royalist coup were thus described to Mo-

---

[51] *Ibid.*, pp. 660-61.   [52] Blanco, III, 759.

lini by Delpech: "It was the surrender of Puerto Cabello that caused all the evils, put the climax to the discouragement, the disorder, and the confusion, at the same time that it increased almost ten-fold the audacity and the resources of the enemy, who at that moment were actually without any kind of munitions and had determined to make their retreat within two days; but scarcely had this important place been delivered to them with the immense magazines and munitions of war which it contained, when a swarm of hostile vessels arrived there carrying troops, émigrés, and opponents to the system of Venezuela." [53] In his classic account of the revolution the Colombian historian José M. Restrepo reënforced the views of Delpech with this judicious summary: "Colonel Bolívar had to endure the mortification of returning to Caracas to give his commander such ominous news after having done all that he could on his part to hold Puerto Cabello, which was impossible. This fatal blow delivered by the enemies of the Venezuelan Confederation put them in possession of a strong point of support, of munitions, and of all that was necessary to continue the war with advantage." [54]

---

[53] "Relation succincte des évènements dernièrement survenus à Caracas par L. Delpech de Caracas," Feb. 27, 1813, F. O., 72/151.

[54] Restrepo, *Historia de la revolución de la república de Colombia,* III, 129-30.

Chapter XXII

THE FATEFUL CAPITULATION OF SAN MATEO

IN VIEW of the fratricidal conflict that was being waged in Spanish America, the English Government had early suggested to Spain that its good offices might be employed between her and the revolutionists. This offer was partly due to a keen desire by England to conserve the trade that had been developing between her merchants and the Spanish colonists. In June, 1811, the Spanish Cortes agreed to allow England to act as a mediator on certain conditions. So far did these negotiations progress that a few months later the English Government appointed Sir Charles Stuart, John P. Morier, and Admiral George Cochrane to serve as commissioners for the mediation between the revolted colonists and Spain. To aid him in the execution of his mission Nicholas Vansittart forwarded to Stuart a letter of introduction to General Miranda. In addition Vansittart sent that commissioner "such particulars respecting the character and views of that officer" as he thought might be of service in the proposed negotiations.[1] A copy of an unofficial memorandum concerning the South American Revolution that was prepared for the commissioners depicted the Dictator of Venezuela in colors which were not attractive. Miranda was denounced as the leader of a radical faction from which "no sort of conciliation" was to be expected. "The terror upon which they ground their power will not avail them for a long time, but the state to which they will have rendered the Country, is truly dreadful. * * * As terror has been their instrument of Power, Anarchy and Destruction will be their last resource when they find themselves in distress to preserve it."[2]

Commissioner Morier proceeded to Jamaica which he reached in March, 1812.[3] Instructions prepared for the Eng-

---

[1] Stuart to Vansittart, May 8, 1812, Add. MSS., 31, 230, f. 236.
[2] "Memorandum of the Revolutions of Caracas and Buenos Ayres," endorsed "Mr. Blanco," F. O., 72/124.
[3] Morier to Wellesley, March 14, 1812, *ibid.*, 72/156.

lish commissioners by Lord Castlereagh on April 2 declared that England's desire in the proposed negotiations was "to see the whole of the Spanish Monarchy united in common obedience to their lawful Sovereign Ferdinand the Seventh, and the entire power and resources of the Monarchy in all parts of the world concentrated under a common Government and directed with unanimity and effect against the common Enemy." [4] Meantime, however, a Cortes at Cadiz had promulgated a liberal Constitution which not only declared that the Spanish nation included all Spaniards in both hemispheres but also that the legislature was to include deputies from the Indies. However this Cortes did not wish to see Mexico included in the projected mediation on the ground that this Viceroyalty was not in rebellion when England proferred her good offices. Hence it declined to sanction the mediatory policy. Nevertheless rumors of this project for a reconciliation between Spain and her revolted colonies reached Miranda and influenced his policy during the fateful days that came upon Venezuela.

The crucial condition of affairs that resulted from the slave uprising, the surrender of Puerto Cabello, and the advance of Monteverde, dispirited the patriots. Nevertheless, as contemporaries suggested, the horizon became clear, and the conduct of General Miranda became less enigmatic.[5] He decided to hold a conference with Venezuelan leaders.

On July 12 at Miranda's headquarters at La Victoria, there assembled two members of the National Executive Power, Francisco Espejo and Juan G. Roscio; the Secretary of War, José Sata y Bussy; the Director of the Finances, the Marquis of Casa León; and the Minister of Justice of the province of Caracas, Francisco Antonio Paúl. To them the generalissimo described the disastrous situation produced by the fall of Puerto Cabello and the occupation of the coasts of

[4] F. O., 72/124.
[5] Poudenx and Mayer, *Mémoire pour servir à l'histoire de la révolution de la capitainerie générale de Caracas*, p. 81.

Choroní and Ocumare by the royalists, "less by force of arms than by the influence of perfidy, fanaticism, and fraud which instead of diminishing were increasing and offering new advantages to the enemy." He made clear that the patriots had neither received aid from other nations nor was there any prospect that they would receive such assistance. Further, some Venezuelan provinces were in the hands of the enemy, while others were not aware of their duties under the Constitution or were without arms with which to aid the confederate soldiers. He pointed out that in reality there were then free from occupation by royalist soldiers little more than those regions adjacent to the cities of Caracas and La Guaira. Let us read an extract from the document that embodied his decision as accepted by other leaders:

"Because of these reasons, because of the poverty of our armament, and the absence of any hope of foreign aid, I have decided to initiate negotiations with the commander of the enemies' forces. In the perilous circumstances in which Venezuelan liberty is placed this policy is imperative in order to secure the lives and properties of those persons who have not yet fallen into the hands of the enemy. We must propose an armistice and negotiate an agreement with the enemy that will stop bloodshed and assure peace according to the mediation offered by the generous English Government. They all agreed to the proposition of the generalissimo; and its execution was left to his prudence and to his military and political genius." [6]

Accordingly on the same day Miranda, declaring that he wished to avoid the bloodshed which would accompany an obstinate struggle, proposed an armistice to Monteverde.[7] In response the royalist commander stated that, in accordance with the desire of the Spanish Cortes, he also wished to avoid a bloody war. He declared that he was willing to engage in negotiations for an armistice but maintained that a cessation of hostilities ought not to hinder the advance of his soldiers

[6] Rojas, *El general Miranda*, pp. 738-39.   [7] *Ibid.*, pp. 739-40.

who were moving by land and sea to occupy positions near
the capital city. Further, Monteverde stipulated that a conference on this subject should take place at his convenience.
To these conditions Miranda could not agree, but he commissioned Lieutenant Manuel Aldao to confer with the Spanish commander. As Monteverde expressed his desire to follow
the humane policy recommended by the Cortes, on July 17
the Dictator authorized Aldao and Sata y Bussy to treat
with him.

Their instructions provided that, an armistice being agreed
upon, "the decision of the conflict should be left to those mediators selected by the court of England who were momentarily expected." The Dictator held that if this procedure was
not followed, a treaty of peace might not conform to the instructions of the English mediators. Miranda proposed that
if mediation was acceptable, then the patriot army should be
allowed to re-occupy the posts it had held when stationed at
Maracay. "If this cannot be obtained," said he, "you will proceed to a decorous capitulation that will conserve the lives
and properties of all persons who have promoted or followed
the just cause of Caracas in these provinces and that will leave
them in liberty to remain here or to depart and to dispose of
their property within three months." The patriot commander
also proposed that all prisoners of war should be set free and
that the partisans of independence should not be molested because of their conduct or political opinions. To insure the security of those persons who contemplated leaving Venezuela,
Miranda proposed that the opposing armies should remain in
their present lines for thirty days. In the meantime the money
of the Confederation should continue to circulate. The island
of Margarita ought to be excluded from the capitulation in
order that partisans of Venezuelan independence might there
seek an asylum.[8]

Though the proposal for English mediation was not acceptable to the Spanish commander, yet at Valencia on July

---

[8] Rojas, *El general Miranda,* pp. 740-45.

20 the patriot commissioners reached a partial and tentative understanding with him. All prisoners of war held by either party were to be declared free at once. In the territory that had not been reconquered persons and property should be protected. No one should be imprisoned or deprived of his property because of his political conduct. All persons who desired to leave Venezuela should be furnished with passports. Among the propositions of Monteverde which were not accepted by the patriots were demands that the former Captaincy General should be governed by the laws and regulations of Spain, that all the unconquered territory should be placed at his disposal, and that his proposals should be accepted within two days. To Miranda these seemed like hard terms from an unforgiving enemy.

In the belief that the acceptance of these terms would cause many evils, in the fear that the unfortunate inhabitants of the unconquered portions of Venezuela might justly have occasion to complain that he had made their torments heavier, and in the hope that the Spaniard might modify his demands, on July 22 Miranda appointed the Marquis of Casa León to continue the negotiations.[9] Two days later the Marquis agreed to an adjustment of the disputed points with Monteverde: soon afterwards he passed over to the royalist camp. On July 25, 1812, having consulted the National Executive Power, Miranda accepted Monteverde's terms; he appointed Colonel Sata y Bussy as agent to complete the arrangements.

According to the protocol which marked the climax of the negotiations, the agreement was reached that nothing in the treaty was to exclude Venezuelans from enjoying the provisions of the Constitution of Cadiz in regard to Spanish America. All inhabitants of territory that was unconquered by the Spaniards were to be considered as sacred in their persons and properties. A final and definitive act of capitulation was to be signed by Miranda and Monteverde in Caracas or wherever they might judge convenient.[10] Shortly afterwards the Span-

---

[9] *Ibid.*, pp. 745-48.   [10] *Ibid.*, pp. 750-53.

ish commander transmitted to his government the protocol of the Capitulation of San Mateo. Careful scrutiny of its articles reveals the surprising fact that, although they were signed by a Spanish naval officer, yet they did not mention certain small vessels belonging to the patriots. Later explanations by Miranda show that by virtue of this omission from the capitulatory articles it was his intention to make possible the withdrawal from Venezuela of his unfortunate followers.[11]

By these articles the generalissimo of a revolutionary army of some four thousand five hundred men capitulated to an upstart loyalist who commanded forces that were evidently inferior in numbers. But the royalists were rapidly increasing in strength, while, largely because of desertions, the patriots were steadily dwindling away. Miranda's prestige had been injured by his dilatory policy; and his fondness for foreign military officers had increased the jealousy with which he was viewed by some of his comrades. Certain Venezuelan leaders were evidently convinced that their cause was lost. Yet others indulged in the hope that by a vigorous stroke they might still emerge victorious.

Among Miranda's associates and contemporaries grave differences of opinion prevailed about the wisdom of the Capitulation of San Mateo. Some Venezuelans naturally questioned the authority of the Dictator to determine the fate of the new nation. The capitulation was thus interpreted by Austria:

"The spirit of the generalissimo was fatigued. Ever since the commencement of the campaign he had been censured because of plans that were more or less mysterious. He lacked support in public opinion for the exercise of his unlimited authority. He was keenly and justly irritated at the defection from the patriot cause of persons with fame and reputation, a defection that had been going on ever since the first uprising. He was oppressed by years. In fine, his fame and his person were threatened. Hence he conceived the project to lay down his arms and to restore a shameful peace to Venezuela through

---

[11] Statement of G. Robertson, July 31, 1812, F. O., 73/153.

a negotiation with the Spanish commander that would subject her anew to the Peninsular Government. A terrible idea! A pusillanimous thought,—insufficient to save the dignity of the Republic and to extinguish the fire of liberty which patriotism had lit in one glorious day!" [12]

Alexander Scott, who had been intrusted by the United States with the shipment of provisions for persons who had suffered by the earthquake, was also unfavorably impressed by Miranda's conduct. On November 16, 1812, he wrote to Secretary Monroe as follows:

"Miranda by a shameful and treacherous capitulation surrendered the liberties of his country—Whether he was an agent of the British Government as he now states, or whether this conduct resulted from a base and cowardly heart, I cannot decide. As to myself, a short acquaintance with him convinced me that he was not only a brutal and capricious tyrant but destitute of courage, honor, and abilities. Thus has terminated this unfortunate revolution, nor has the evil ended here—" [13]

One of the most illuminating commentaries is that of Dr. Felipe Fermín Paúl, who witnessed the capitulation:

"The surrender of General Miranda was a mystery to all. It was said that he would sign the articles on shipboard. None of the officials in Caracas or La Guaira heard of the capitulation until after Spanish troops had occupied the territory. The anxiety and suspense in which everybody was placed inevitably provoked reactionary projects that were mainly directed against this chief because he had not lived up to the confidence that had been reposed in him, because he had acted against the general opinion of the people, and because he had compromised a multitude of citizens who were exposed to sufferings and outrages. Certain proceedings against Miranda in which there were involved some of the most illustrious supporters of independence cannot properly be attributed to their lack of patriotism but rather to an irresistible impulse

---

[12] *Bosquejo de la historia militar de Venezuela*, pp. 148-49.
[13] Manning, *Diplomatic Correspondence of the United States*, II, 1160.

for their own preservation; they evidently calculated that, if their chieftain could save himself, they might command the same fortune." [14]

Comments on the Dictator's conduct were often colored because of events that occurred after the Capitulation of San Mateo was signed. Miranda was bitterly criticized because he had selected the Marquis of Casa León as his agent in the negotiations. Delpech stigmatized Casa León as a "traitor,"—[15] a judgment which is supported by the fact that the Marquis was rewarded for his conduct by the Spanish commander.[16] The charge brought against Miranda that he betrayed his native land indeed hinges on his relations with that nobleman. Seventeen years after the Capitulation of San Mateo was signed, a striking formulation of this accusation was made by the royalist writer Díaz in his recollections of the Venezuelan rebellion. He presented the view that Miranda "meditated concerning the plight of Venezuela and agreed with the Marquis of Casa León about the necessity for a capitulation." However, the rebel chieftain represented to the Marquis that as he was "without means to return to England, he could not undertake what he wished." Casa León seized this opportunity: "he proposed to furnish Miranda with a thousand ounces of gold, and, when the latter accepted the offer, he at once informed me in order that I might remit a part of the gold to La Victoria, while the remainder was soon to follow to Caracas and La Guaira. In consequence negotiations for a capitulation were begun. * * * I sent two hundred and fifty ounces of gold to La Victoria." [17]

The view that the patriot leader was thus induced to betray his native land for selfish gain was elaborated by the Spanish historian Torrente. He alleged that "at the very

---

[14] Casas, *Defensa documentada de la conducta del comandante de La Guaira*, p. 35, note.
[15] "Relation succincte des évènements dernièrement survenus à Caracas par L. Delpech de Caracas," Feb. 27, 1813, F. O., 72/151.
[16] Robertson, *Miranda*, p. 472, note a.
[17] Díaz, *Recuerdos sobre la rebelión de Caracas*, p. 47.

juncture when the royalist commander took possession of the capital city Miranda went to La Guaira in order to embark, with the expectation of receiving seven hundred and fifty of the thousand ounces of gold which had been offered him to lay down his arms, and of which only two hundred and fifty had been sent to La Victoria by Don José Domingo Díaz." [18] After Díaz had published his recollections, Felipe F. Paúl stated that León gave orders for money to the generalissimo which the latter never cashed.[19] With the exception of this allegation which was repeated by Austria, there has not been found in the writings of contemporaries any support for the accusation that the Dictator surrendered because he was promised financial aid, unless indeed the fact,—which may have been attributable to other causes,—that in Miranda's property which was carried off from Venezuela there should have been, according to his own later statement, a thousand ounces of gold.[20]

While his agents were negotiating about a capitulation, the Dictator had arranged for the removal of his books, papers, and other property from Caracas to La Guaira. On July 15 Casa León informed Miranda that his trusted aide-de-camp, Antonio Leleux, had cautiously conveyed most of his papers to that port; and on the following day the Marquis reported that other belongings of the Dictator had been likewise transferred. Apparently Leleux obtained assurances from Manuel María de las Casas, the military commander of La Guaira, that the Dictator's wishes concerning the disposal of his property would be obeyed. At the instance of Miranda, steps were also taken to secure for the use of Venezuelan patriots the *Zeloso* and other small vessels that might constitute a naval force.[21] It was evidently in conformity with Miranda's wishes that on July 18 by order of Casa León ten thousand pesos in specie from funds belonging to the tottering Republic were

[18] *Historia de la revolución hispano-americana*, I, 308.
[19] Casas, p. 35, note.
[20] Miranda to Vansittart, May 21, 1814, Add. MSS., 31, 231, f. 74.
[21] Rojas, *El general Miranda*, pp. 392-94.

delivered by Casas to an English merchant named George Robertson who planned to leave Venezuela.[22] After the tentative Capitulation of San Mateo had been signed, twelve thousand pesos in specie were likewise delivered by Casas to the same merchant.[23]

Possibly the general may have intended for his own use the specie which was thus transferred to the English merchant. Yet it seems more likely that Miranda considered that he was consigning this treasure in virtue of the agreement by which he had been made Dictator of Venezuela. Evidently he had scrupulously refrained from any discussion with Monteverde about certain property of the Venezuelan Republic. George Robertson, who overheard a conversation between Captain Haynes and the Dictator, declared that "Gen'l. Miranda stated that the floating property of the State of Venezuela was not at all stipulated to be given up (he having carefully kept free of all discussions on that head) but that he intended it should afford a conveyance for the unfortunate Inhabitants to some friendly or allied Port." [24] This statement harmonizes with an interpretation of Miranda's actions that was later made by Pedro Gual. He declared that in the course of his decision with the Dictator about a capitulation, Miranda thus forecast his future steps:

"Let us direct our views toward New Granada where I count upon Nariño who is my friend. With the resources that we can probably obtain in that Viceroyalty, and with the officers and munitions that we can take from Venezuela, we shall again regain Caracas without risking the dangers by which we are menaced at the present moment. It is necessary to allow Venezuela to recover from the effect of the earthquake and the depredations of the royalists." [25]

To the writer this interpretation seems quite credible. The

---

[22] Casas, pp. 32-33 and note.
[23] Receipt, July 30, 1812 (copy), F. O., 72/153.
[24] Statement of G. Robertson, July 31, 1812, copy, *ibid*.
[25] Blanco, *Documentos para la historia de la vida pública del libertador*, III, 761.

idea of renewing the attack on the royalists from New Granada as a base was in accordance with the life-purpose of Miranda. Yet, as the Dictator did not make known his intention to all of his colleagues, when those patriots who were not aware of the real character of his negotiations learned that they were pledged to lay down their arms and to relinquish the unconquered portion of Venezuela to an inferior force of royalists, they naturally became disgusted.

Few of the distracted Venezuelans realized that their generalissimo was confronted by a dilemma: either to surrender to the royalists, or to resort to a desultory warfare by independent bands. The idea of becoming an irregular fighter, however, was presumably no less distasteful to Miranda than to Napoleon. The Venezuelan who had been trained as a professional soldier in European wars was not attracted by the alternative of guerilla warfare. In this respect he furnished a singular contrast with Bolívar.

On July 26, having intrusted the final arrangements of the capitulation to Sata y Bussy, General Miranda quietly withdrew from the headquarters of the Venezuelan army at La Victoria and proceeded to the capital city. He later declared that he duly informed the municipal authorities of Caracas of the terms of the surrender and that they gave that agreement their sanction.[26] If this were true, it was extremely unfortunate for the general that, apparently awaiting a notice of the final adjustment of the terms of the capitulation by Monteverde and Sata y Bussy, he did not make it public. On July 28 Carlos Soublette, who was now acting as Miranda's aide-de-camp, published an order of the day that provided for the disbandment of the patriot soldiers who were encamped near the capital city.[27] The anxiety of the Dictator concerning his precious papers at this juncture is shown by the fact that on the same day Soublette sent a letter to Leleux that ran as follows:

---

[26] Rojas, *El general Miranda*, pp. 754-56.   [27] *Ibid.*, p. 699.

12—II

"The general orders me to write to urge you again to pack properly his papers and maps that are in trunks. You are to have these trunks transported immediately to La Guaira and embarked upon the brig *Watson* which is soon to set sail for Curaçao. You are to address the trunks to the firm of Robertson and Belt who are to be directed to keep them in their possession. It will be necessary that you should yourself go to La Guaira in order that all this should be done with the greatest order and safety as a matter of much concern to the general. You shall likewise proceed to pack the books that are left in Caracas in order that they may be forwarded upon another occasion, if this should prove necessary." [28]

When the surrender was made known to the Venezuelans they scattered or destroyed their military stores and dispersed wildly over the country.[29] The resulting disturbances did not facilitate negotiations with the Spanish commander about the remaining articles of the capitulation that were concerned with the surrender of military supplies and the relinquishment of territory unconquered by the royalists. It appears that those articles were never sanctioned by the fallen Dictator.[30] In the end of July, 1812, Monteverde entered the distracted city of Caracas.

The air of mystery enveloping Miranda's departure from La Victoria as well as his failure to publish the terms of the surrender combined to provoke intense dissatisfaction among patriot leaders. Even before the jubilant royalists had entered the capital city, Miranda, who despite the express terms of the capitulation seemed unwilling to trust his own person to the mercy of his enemies, had departed from Caracas for La Guaira. The goal of disheartened patriots fleeing from the menace of Spanish conquerors, that port has not inaptly been compared to the Tower of Babel.

---

[28] Rojas, *op. cit.*, pp. 699-700. Recently the inference has been made that Leleux was a son of Miranda, see Gonzáles, "Tras la pista de Leleux," in *Boletín de la academia nacional de la historia*, X, 196-98. Leleux dropped no hint of such relationship when in 1815 he conversed with Lord Glenbervie about his former commander, see Glenbervie, *The Diaries of Sylvester Douglas*, II, 194-95. Neither has any evidence to support this absurd view been found in the Mir. MSS. [29] Rojas, *op. cit.*, p. 756. [30] *Ibid.*, pp. 756-59.

On July 29 there had opportunely arrived at that port His Majesty's brig *Sapphire* commanded by Captain Haynes. At the request of the *Zeloso's* captain, Haynes sent an officer and men on board that brig to maintain order until the capitulation became known. The English captain also found much consternation among English merchants at La Guaira because of an embargo that the patriots had laid upon commerce and a fear that Spanish troops might enter the city before the prohibition was lifted. Haynes accordingly wrote to Miranda to ask what steps he intended to take about English property that was afloat in the harbor. To this letter the Dictator replied from Caracas on July 30 to state that such property was not in the least danger as it was not only protected by the independent batteries of La Guaira but also by a solemn capitulation which had thus far been respected by the enemy. In conclusion Miranda expressed hope that Haynes would protect the patriots instead of augmenting their afflictions.[31] On the same day Leleux embarked his master's books and papers on board the *Sapphire*. For greater protection this luggage was addressed to George Robertson of the English firm of Robertson and Belt of Curaçao with which Miranda had had business transactions.[32] George Robertson on the same day embarked on the *Sapphire* twenty-two thousand pesos that he had received from Miranda.[33] Meantime there arrived at La Guaira other revolutionists, including José Antepara, Gregor McGregor, and Simón Bolívar, who planned to emigrate from Venezuela. It seems that the military commander of La Guaira originally intended to take refuge on the *Sapphire* under the protection of the British flag.

At eight o'clock on July 30 General Miranda reached La Guaira. Captain Haynes recorded that the general immediately declared the embargo at an end. "As soon as I could

---

[31] Haynes to Stirling, Aug. 4, 1812, with inclosures nos. 2 and 3, Ad. R., 1/263. [32] Captain Haynes's Log, July 30, 1812, S. L., 1245. [33] Robertson's receipts, July 26 and 30, 1812, translations, W. O., 1/112.

disengage him from the Crowd, who encircled him," continued
Haynes, "I informed him of my Officer and Crew being on
board the *Zeloso*, and that as matters were so well arranged I
should withdraw them. He entreated me not to do so and informed me that he had every reason to fear that I should have
full exercise for my Humanity; that he did not expect the inci-
dental arrival of a British Ship of War, and had consequently
kept that Brig as the mainstay of the unfortunate adventurers who had embarked in the cause of Independence under
him." [34] The English captain urged the ex-Dictator to embark on the *Sapphire* at once, but unfortunately he decided
to pass the night on Venezuelan soil.

The momentous decision to remain on shore furnished the
disgruntled compatriots of Miranda with the desired opportunity. Even before he reached La Guaira the military
commander of that port had been in secret communication
with Monteverde. On the other hand it seems that, after General Miranda reached the coast, Casas had solicited from him
four thousand pesos of the specie which had been quietly embarked upon the *Sapphire*.[35] After Miranda had unsuspect-
ingly retired, Casas intrigued against him with certain patriots who had fled from the wrath of the Spaniards. Prominent among them was the former commander of Puerto
Cabello, Simón Bolívar. These refugees felt that they were
being betrayed, for their homeland was being given up to
the royalists although the capitulation had not been ratified.
It seems that certain patriots were further incensed because
of Miranda's heated replies to their inquiries about the surrender. Insane with fury, they denounced their commander
and vehemently demanded that he should be detained. They
decided to seize him before dawn on the morning of July 31.[36]

We continue the sombre story by the aid of fairly well authenticated tradition. It appears that after placing pickets

[34] Haynes to Stirling, July 31, 1812, Ad. R., 1/263.
[35] See *infra,* p. 182.
[36] Austria, pp. 159-60, 163-64.

in the street and in Casas' house, conspirators led by Bolívar stealthily proceeded to the chamber in this house where Miranda was asleep in bed. The fatigued general seems at first to have expostulated to his new secretary, Carlos Soublette, at being awakened at so early an hour, but recognizing the voices of former comrades, he arose and soon appeared before the intruders in a challenging attitude. Bolívar then stepped forth and in a loud voice told the fallen chieftain of their decision that he was to be made a prisoner. By the light of a lantern held by Soublette, Miranda thereupon haughtily surveyed one after another of the conspirators who encircled him, and passionately ejaculated: "A tumult! A tumult! These people are only capable of stirring up tumults!" [37] He relinquished his sword. Then the conspirators insolently escorted him to the castle of San Carlos.

A letter from Antonio Leleux, the officer to whom the Dictator had entrusted his treasured memorabilia, thus rehearsed the dramatic circumstances that happened after the capitulation:

"The Soldiers for the greatest part deposited their arms with the greatest reluctance; and the General came to La Guayra, to embark himself and go to Curaçao, having previously sent me with his books and papers, etc., to have them put on board an English vessel, and direct or accompany them if I found an opportunity before he came to Messrs. Robertson and Belt of Curaçao. According they were put on board H. M. S. *Sapphire* Capt. Haynes, and to secure the effects I thought prudent to make them out to Mr. Robertson, who was at that time at La Guayra, sure they would be respected as being British effects and the General arriving on the 30 in the evening spoke to Cap[n] Haynes, telling him in presence of the Governor of Guayra that the embargo which had been laid for some time on the merchant vessels, was raised; and that they might all go, the next day intending himself to take his

---

[37] Becerra, *Ensayo histórico documentado de la vida de Don Francisco de Miranda*, II, 263; *Documentos históricos sobres la vida del generalísimo Miranda*, pp. 97-98.

passage on board the *Sapphire*.

"The Governor of Guayra whose name is Casas, a mean man whom the Gl. had raised from the dust and loaded with favors, had with that indifferent coolness considered for a few days past, what line of conduct would be most advantageous to him. He nevertheless appear'd determined to follow the Gl. if he should order four thousand dollars in specie to be given him, out of twenty-two thousand the Gl. had embarked as his private property. This was declined and he was only offered $800. on the ground that the Gl. having to provide for a great number, he could give but little to every one. Casas made no answer; but from this very moment determined to stay and make his peace with Monteverde. He caballed, intrigued, the very moment the Gl. went to bed, with some other malcontents and at three o'clock in the next morning he arrested the unsuspecting gl. who was quietly sleeping in bed, put [him] in a Castle, gave immediately advice of what he had done to Monteverde; ordered by his own authority those Vessels that had permission from Miranda, not to go out the harbor, sunk an English one that attempted it; detained every stranger and natives on Shore till the enemies entered the town." [38]

On the same morning a courier seems to have reached Casas with a peremptory message from Monteverde commanding him to prevent the patriots from sailing from the port.[39] On July 31 the independent colors that had been flying over the forts at La Guaira were replaced by the Spanish flag.[40] The military commander of that port had now definitely decided to cast in his lot with the royalists. Casas promptly laid an embargo on all vessels in the harbor and sent word of his proceedings to the Spanish commander. Further, he kept the patriot refugees inside the walls of the city until the advancing royalists had entered its gates. In a dispatch to his government Monteverde thus described the capture of Dictator Miranda:

---

[38] Leleux to Vansittart, Aug. 26, 1812, F. O., 72/140; in part in Robertson, *Miranda,* p. 475. Leleux's later account of the commission with which Miranda intrusted him is found in Glenbervie, II, 194-95.   [39] Austria, pp. 160-61.
[40] Captain Haynes's Log, July 30, 1812, S. L., 1245.

"As soon as I reached Caracas I gave the most peremptory orders for the detention of the rebel leaders who were at La Guaira, but fortunately by the time that I reached that port, although I had marched with the greatest rapidity, Casas had with the advice of Peña and by the aid of Bolívar thrust Miranda into a prison and also detained all of his companions who were in that port. In this transaction Casas risked his life, which he would have lost if his orders had not been carried out. Peña and Bolívar ran a similar risk. Casas finished his task in a most satisfactory manner. He had previously disobeyed the orders of the Despot that he should place the Europeans and Canary Islanders of that vicinity on a pontoon that should be scuttled upon the slightest occasion. * * * I cannot forget the interesting services of Casas, nor those of Bolívar and Peña; because of these services I have not touched their persons, simply conceding to Bolívar passports for foreign countries; for his influence and connections here might be dangerous in the present circumstances." [41]

In this manner the future Liberator was able to escape to the West Indies. The betrayal of Miranda to his implacable enemies was a tragic incident which has besmirched the fame of certain Venezuelans. On their behalf it should be said that they could scarcely have been aware of Miranda's hidden motives. Of the three men who were primarily responsible for this foul deed, Peña, Bolívar, and Casas, only the civil commander of La Guaira died without making an attempt to explain his motives or to justify his conduct. However, it seems that Peña was disaffected to the patriot cause; for in ominous words he had recently asked the Dictator to be relieved of his post. It appears that when Simón Bolívar was complimented by Monteverde about his conduct at La Guaira, he responded that he had "seized Miranda in order to punish a traitor to his country, not to serve the King!" [42] Many years later Colonel Wilson, the Liberator's aide-de-camp, thus elucidated Bolívar's motives: "To the last hour of his life he rejoiced of that event,

[41] Robertson, *Miranda*, p. 528.
[42] Larrazábal, *Vida y correspondencia general del libertador*, I, 138.

which, he always asserted, was solely his own act, to punish the *treachery* and *treason* of Miranda in capitulating to an inferior force, and then intending to embark, himself knowing the capitulation would not be observed." Wilson even asserted that Bolívar always gloried in the fact that he had "risked his own safety which he might have secured, by embarking on board a vessel, in order to secure the punishment of Miranda for his alleged treason. His plea was not altogether ill founded; for he argued that if Miranda believed the Spaniards would observe the treaty he should have remained to keep them to their word; if he did not, he was a traitor to have sacrificed his army to it. General Bolívar invariably added, that he wished to shoot Miranda as a traitor but was withheld by others." [43]

Because of reflections by Bolívar, who stigmatized his conduct in preventing the departure of the patriots from La Guaira as traitorous, at one time Manuel María de las Casas contemplated the publication of an exposition that would justify his conduct. As he was hospitably treated by the Liberator in 1827, however, Casas discarded this idea. Still, after Restrepo had characterized that commander as a most ungrateful and perfidious wretch, his relatives undertook to vindicate him.[44] They composed a careful, documented defense of his conduct which at certain points was supported by letters embodying the recollections of Venezuelan patriots who had actually been at La Guaira on the fateful days following the Capitulation of San Mateo.

One of the most judicial of these letters was that of Juan P. Ayala who interpreted the action of the patriots as an attempt to detain the Dictator because of their "just suspicions" that he would not sign the capitulation "until after he had embarked, thus leaving all the patriots unprotected and compromised." Ayala made some wise observations that are worthy of notice. He declared that "almost all revolutions

---

[43] O'Leary, *Memorias*, XXVII, 75-76, note.
[44] *Historia de la revolución de la república de Colombia*, III, 141.

terminated in attempts of the participants to calumniate each other in order to justify and save themselves; that they were wont to cast in each others' faces in a vile manner the faults and political errors committed because of the factions formed among them to profit by revolutionary purposes and results. From these dissensions originated the calumnious accusation of treason to their country against Señor Casas and General Miranda. This ignominious idea had never occurred to them, especially to Miranda, except in so far as, being a man of strong character, he thought of carrying out plans of government that he cherished,—plans that were not suited to his compatriots." [45] In our own times, however, a great-granddaughter of Casas spoke the truth when she said that his conduct was due to the fact that he was a royalist.[46]

In fine, the evidence indicates that at this crisis Casas was a traitor to Venezuelan independence. Peña had become a recreant to that cause even before Miranda reached La Guaira. As regards the ardent revolutionist Bolívar,—who in his afterthoughts seems to have utterly forgotten the disastrous effects of the loss of Puerto Cabello,—it is likely that he was animated by bitter resentment toward the fallen leader. "There are not lacking persons," said General Briceño Méndez, "who accuse Bolívar, because of the imprisonment of Miranda, of having wished to ingratiate himself with the Spaniards and obtain his own pardon at the cost of the life of his general; but the truth is that Bolívar had no other object than to avenge his country, and to avenge himself for the evil of having been detained in Venezuela so that he should fall a victim to the enemy." [47] Because of his incarceration the ex-Dictator was evidently not allowed a chance either to reject or to sanction the final articles of the fateful Capitulation of San Mateo. While meditating about the strange turn which the wheel of fortune had suddenly taken General Miranda must have felt that his long and arduous labors as apostle and

---

[45] Casas, p. 64, note.
[46] Rivas Vicuña, *Las guerras de Bolívar*, p. 86.   [47] Austria, p. 164.

promoter of Spanish-American independence had been rewarded by base ingratitude.

Meantime what had become of the *Sapphire?* Soon after Miranda had been betrayed, that brig escaped from La Guaira. A number of patriots who had prudently embarked on that vessel, including Antepara and McGregor, were accordingly transported to Curaçao.[48] The actions of Captain Haynes, who claimed to have left that port while the Venezuelan flag was still flying over the castle, greatly provoked the Spanish commander who complained to the English admiral at Barbadoes.[49] On August 9 in a letter to Pedro Labrador, the Spanish secretary of state, General Monteverde made the following accusation: "The chief of the rebels, the cursed Francisco Miranda, in his premeditated flight in conjunction with his companions has carried off the money that was left in an exhausted treasury and also a small amount of silver plate and jewels belonging to the churches which he could lay his hands upon as they had been collected because of the earthquake." [50]

Ten days later Monteverde addressed a protest to Governor Hodgson of Curaçao. Emphatically he demanded the property that Casas had transferred to George Robertson before Miranda's betrayal. Monteverde argued that the twenty-two thousand dollars which had been carried off on the *Sapphire* was the property of the Spanish crown, and formed a "part of the Funds taken off by the Traitor Miranda, from La Guayra, after this Province was restored to the Dominion of my Sovereign." After asserting that Miranda and Robertson had combined to export these funds in a fraudulent manner, the Spanish commander added: "Very happily the Military Commander Don Manuel Mᵃ. de las Casas who was appointed by Miranda to the Command of La Guayra (but already corresponded with me knowing that I was coming to take pos-

---

[48] Haynes's "List of Passengers," Aug. 3, 1812, W. O., 1/112.
[49] Monteverde to the secretary of state, Aug. 7, 1812, A. G. S., estado, 8174.   [50] Robertson, *Miranda,* p. 477, note b.

session of said City from the Town of Victoria) had the very
wise and prudent precaution to demand two obligations from
Mr. Robertson for the said amount of Twenty-Two Thousand
Dollars which said Robertson obliged himself to pay to the
order of said Casas on presenting said Documents." After in-
forming Hodgson that he had sent an agent to Curaçao to
receive these funds, Monteverde added: "He is likewise intrusted by me to take charge of the Boxes with Plate, Trunks,
Packages, etc., containing the Interests of His Catholic Majesty carried by the said Ship *Sapphire* to your Island." [51] In
a letter to Lord Bathurst, who became secretary of state for
war and the colonies in the Liverpool ministry that was formed
in June, 1812, Governor Hodgson transmitted the correspondence which he had had with Monteverde about the boxes
and trunks that had been transported by the *Sapphire* from
La Guaira to Curaçao. The governor's explanation ran as
follows:

"The Plate is claimed by a Don. S. Bolívar, but having been
landed in a clandestine manner, it has been seized by the Col-
lector of His Majesty's Customs, and is now under prosecution; several of the Trunks found empty at the seizure, report
says, contained Church Plate when they were first landed;
however no satisfactory proof on this point can be adduced.

"Miranda's correspondence with many distinguished Characters in Europe is inclosed in one of them, it is carefully preserved, and I beg to be honored with your Lordship's orders
respecting it, as well as the other subjects of this Letter.

"I am sorry to say that several Letters from very high
Characters in England to Miranda, have been made public in
this Island, with a view, no doubt, of disseminating the opinion
that Great Britain is friendly to a Revolution in South
America." [52]

Fortunately for Miranda's fame, there reposes in the English archives an explanatory list, which was prepared by customs officers at Curaçao in September, 1812, of the trunks and

---

[51] "Copy of a Translation," W. O., 1/112.   [52] Sept. 27, 1812, *ibid.*

packages carried from Venezuela to that island which were "clandestinely landed from His Majesty's Sloop *Sapphire* and were not declared at His Majesty's Customs, first claimed as the private Luggage of George Robertson, Esquire, and now claimed by Foreigners." [53] This list clearly shows that two trunks bearing the name of Simón Bolívar contained some silver plate, that a portmanteau, a box, and a trunk bearing Miranda's initials contained atlases, books, and wearing apparel, while three other trunks bearing the initials "F. M." on a brass plate contained the bound volumes of Miranda's manuscripts.[54] Some of the silver plate that was taken from Venezuela therefore seems to have been Bolívar's instead of Miranda's. The specie that was transported from La Guaira to Curaçao was, for the time being, retained by Robertson and Belt who maintained that the major portion of it rightly belonged to them because of debts incurred by the first Dictator of Venezuela. By direction of the Secretary of State for War and the Colonies the fallen leader's papers were soon carefully transported to England. A century later the author, to whom the present Lord Bathurst generously gave access to the papers of his famous ancestor, identified the sixty-three tomes as the lost manuscripts of Miranda.[55]

The English Government obviously realized the need of guarding the papers of the revolutioner who had so long lived on its bounty. On November 2, 1812, William Prince, the postmaster of Curaçao, informed the general postoffice at London that after Miranda had been betrayed he had "received a Letter and Some Packages of Newspapers" addressed to that general but that as it was not "deemed advisable to forward them as they would certainly come into the hands of the Spanish Government of Caracas, and perhaps be prejudicial to him," and as he had been instructed not to recognize "any Agents of the late Independent Government of Venezuela,"

---

[53] Lloyd and De Larrey, "List of Trunks, Packages, etc.," undated, inclosure in Hodgson's letter to Lord Bathurst, Sept. 27, 1812. W. O., 1/112.
[54] *Ibid.*, Miranda, *Diary,* p. xxii.   [55] Miranda, *Diary,* p. xxvi.

he desired to know what action he should take.[56] On January 11, 1813, the secretary of the London postoffice transmitted "the Packet from London addressed to Gen'l. Miranda" to the Foreign Office.[57] An indorsement on Prince's letter signed with the initials of Henry Goulburn, under secretary for war and the colonies, reads thus: "When you get it let me see it." [58] Unfortunately this mysterious packet, which was perhaps sent from 27 Grafton Street, has not come into our hands.

By virtue of a clause of the Treaty of San Mateo which provided that he should retain command in Venezuela until the treaty was carried into effect, Monteverde succeeded in maintaining control of the subjugated region, despite the arrival of Fernando Miyares, the captain general of Venezuela. On August 3 Monteverde issued a proclamation to the people of Caracas in which he declared that one of the proofs of the justice and the legitimacy of governments was good faith and exactness in the fulfillment of their agreements. He proclaimed that his promises were "sacred" and his word "inviolable." Yet he announced that his pledges did not extend to all epochs of Venezuela's unfortunate history; for they terminated at the moment when the capitulation was signed and sanctioned. "Subsequent occurrences," he maintained, "are included in another circle in which there should operate the absolute authority of the law and of your security." [59] In spite of these assurances, however, eight prominent patriots, including Isnardi, Madariaga, and Roscio, were seized by order of the conqueror, cast into prison, and transported to Spain. To justify this proceeding Monteverde maintained, without presenting proof of his allegation, that these "eight monsters" had conspired to violate the Treaty of San Mateo.[60] As a contemporary said, the shouts of liberty were thus replaced by the groans of slavery.

In a dispatch to the Secretary of State on October 1, 1812,

---

[56] F. O., 72/150.   [57] *Ibid.*
[58] *Ibid.* In regard to the return to Vansittart of certain letters that he had written to Miranda, see Miranda, *Diary,* p. 144.
[59] Blanco, III, 708.   [60] *Ibid.,* pp. 710-12.

Monteverde justified his proceedings. He took the view that, as a result of his measures, conditions in Venezuela had much improved. He maintained that he had not forgotten the promises made in the Capitulation of San Mateo, as he had set free some of the least blameworthy of the imprisoned Venezuelans under pledges for good conduct. "Nevertheless," he went on to say, "as there are a certain number of these prisoners whose opinions are well known, whose activities have been exceedingly notorious, and whose conduct even after the capitulation did not leave any doubt in the minds of faithful servants of the King respecting their conduct, I have arranged that they shall be kept safely until His Majesty deigns to make known his sovereign wish in regard to them."[61] In a letter to Secretary Monroe dated November 16, 1812, Alexander Scott described the policy that Monteverde had adopted toward the unfortunate Venezuelans. "A system of proscription, sequestration, imprisonment, and cruelty almost unexampled, has been adopted and practiced toward the unhappy republicans—Loaded with irons, and deprived of the necessities of life, many have fallen victims to the contaminated air of crowded dungeons, noxious in all countries, but doubly fatal in a climate like this—" [62]

On October 21, 1812, a communication was read to the Spanish Cortes from the Secretary of the Navy that announced "the submission and pacification" of Venezuela and the imprisonment of "the rebel Miranda" and some of his partisans. At the motion of José M. Calatrava, the Regency was instructed to inform Monteverde of the great satisfaction with which the legislators had learned "the happy result" of his measures for the pacification of Venezuela.[63] The Spanish Government thus gave the Treaty of San Mateo its tacit approval.

In December, 1812, after publishing the liberal Constitution that had been formed for Spain by the Cortes of Cadiz,

---

[61] A. G. I., audiencia de Caracas, 133-3-12.   [62] Manning, *op. cit.*, II, 1160.
[63] *Diario de las discusiones y actas de las cortes*, XV, 472.

General Monteverde directed a junta to prepare a list of Venezuelans who were dangerous to public security or who were suspected of disloyalty and to include those who had participated in "the criminal act of April 19, 1810." A royalist writer estimated that as a result some fifteen hundred persons were incarcerated.[64] Certain patriots likened Monteverde to a ravening wolf. In consequence of the violation of his public pledges by the Spanish commander many maledictions fell upon the head of the captive Venezuelan leader. On April 8, 1814, Simón Bolívar, who had been proclaimed the Liberator of Venezuela, declared that the shameful Capitulation of San Mateo was not the work of Monteverde but the result of circumstances and of the cowardice of the commander of the Venezuelan army.[65] In his manifesto addressed to the nations of the world, the Liberator denounced his former comrade by declaring that in 1812 the "only force which restrained Monteverde was unfortunately commanded by a chief, who, obsessed by ambition and violent passions, either did not recognize the risk or else wished to sacrifice to his own feelings the liberty of his country. Despotic and arbitrary to excess, not only did Miranda make the soldiers discontented but he disorganized all the branches of public administration." [66] Yet, on the other hand, when Madariaga was summoned from a Spanish prison cell to answer certain questions he declared that the Treaty of San Mateo was negotiated by the Dictator of Venezuela with the consent of the magistrates of that country and the universal approval of the inhabitants.[67] The truth evidently lies between these two extreme views.

Divers opinions have been expressed about Miranda's conduct by Spanish-American writers. These verdicts have varied according to their notions of the imminence of the peril which in July, 1812, confronted the Republic of Venezuela, and according to the conceptions that their authors entertained of

[64] Blanco, IV, 117.   [65] O'Leary, XIII, 178-79.   [66] Blanco, IV, 11.
[67] Robertson, *Miranda*, p. 478, note c.

Miranda's character. A Venezuelan patriot who linked the Capitulation of San Mateo to earlier chapters of the revolutionist's life later maintained that Miranda was more disposed to be a faithful interpreter of the policy of the English cabinet than to consecrate himself to the cause of Venezuelan liberty.[68] Contemporaneously, however, J. P. Morier, who had returned to England from the West Indies whither he had gone on a fruitless mission as a commissioner of the projected mediation between Spain and her colonies, thus expressed his views: "The progress of the revolution in the Caracas has for the moment been arrested by the Successes of General Monteverde. But the little good faith, observed by him in the Treaty of Capitulation with Miranda, has tended as little to reëstablish the Credit of the Royal Party, as it has that of Miranda individually, who is now universally abhorred as having by that Treaty, surrendered the Cause he had pledged himself to support." [69] Certain Spanish historians have not been able to refrain from denunciations of the rôle played by Bolívar: they have characterized him as a false friend, and have intimated that he desired to ingratiate himself with Monteverde.

It is worth while to quote the verdict of certain foreigners who were serving under the patriot banner, for their judgments are less apt to be biased by prejudice than those of either Spaniards or Venezuelans. In a memoir by two Frenchmen concerning the Venezuelan revolution they stigmatized the generalissimo as a traitor both to Venezuela and to Spain. "In an instant," they wrote, "Miranda lost the fruit of thirty years of intrigues, his honor, and his liberty. Such is the deplorable fate of political adventurers." [70] Delpech thus vented his spleen in a précis addressed to Molini: "Finally, my friend, everything became ignominy, confusion, and vileness; this immoral and despicable people richly deserve chains and humiliation. So much shame could only be covered by an earthquake

---

[68] Austria, p. 162.   [69] Feb. 13, 1813, to Castlereagh, F. O., 72/156.
[70] Poudenx and Mayer, *Mémoire pour servir à l'histoire de la révolution de la capitainerie générale de Caracas*, pp. 83-84.

that would swallow them up in its abyss." In justificatory words Delpech declared that much "time would be needed to respond to the calumnies, the sophistries, and the outrages" with which people had overwhelmed Miranda, and to struggle with "the multiform hydra of imposture, fanaticism, and ig-norance." In an interpretative spirit he added that the public generally judged events by their results: "they have said that Miranda was a traitor because the villain Monteverde in-fringed the capitulation, and all the people of property have been delivered up to the assassinous dagger of the infamous Spaniards. But without discussing these unfounded asser-tions, I venture to believe that, if Miranda had been a traitor, he would certainly not have deceived himself by partaking of the fate of those whom they said he sold to Monteverde. If I did not have the conviction that he was incapable of such a base action, I would say that it is impossible, that a man who laboured all his life for the independence of America was able at the end of his career to forget this glorious enterprise, to stain his white hair, and to dishonor forever his memory in de-scending to the tomb, and in return for so much ignominy and crime to receive no other recompense than chains and death."[71]

The policy of Monteverde was not altogether negative. He speedily selected the Marquis of Casa León to take charge of the fiscal administration of the colony as intendant. He soon reëstablished the *audiencia* of Caracas. In accordance with Spanish law and custom he ordered all foreigners to depart from Venezuelan soil. So arbitrary were certain measures of Monteverde that occasionally even the Spanish Government could not refrain from censuring his conduct; for he assumed that the former Captaincy General should be treated like a conquered province. In particular, Monteverde's disregard of the Treaty of San Mateo aroused a vengeful spirit among South Americans. Its wanton violation was sometimes cited by Venezuelan leaders as a justification for the war to the

[71] "Relation succincte des évènements dernièrement survenus à Caracas par L. Delpech de Caracas," Feb. 27, 1813, F. O., 72/151.

death which subsequently raged in their country between patriots and royalists. Even the unfortunate, unforeseen results of Miranda's greatest failure thus stimulated among the people of northern South America that love of liberty which had been the obsession of his mature life.

To the writer it seems that in agreeing to the Capitulation of San Mateo, the first Dictator of Venezuela was influenced by the idea that such a course was the best policy which he could adopt for the welfare of his native land. In the succession of calamities that had befallen the new State he found ample justification for the negotiation of a treaty so generous to the vanquished. After the fall of Puerto Cabello, in view of the desertions from the patriot army and the increase of Monteverde's forces, the prospect of victory for the Venezuelans steadily declined. Miranda's judgment may be questioned but not his patriotism.

Available sources for the study of this period indicate that some Venezuelans were not truly converted to the cause of independence while many others were anxious to be enrolled on the winning side rather than on the side that was fighting for liberty. In view of the circumstances Miranda could scarcely be blamed if he had lost confidence in the military efficiency of his raw recruits.

Then, too, in justice to the Venezulean patriots, it should be stated that they did not all cheerfully submit themselves to the domineering leadership of a son of Caracas who had long lived on foreign gold. Not the least of Miranda's mistakes,— at least in the eyes of his countrymen who knew little or nothing of his long duel with the ubiquitous agents of Spain,— was his inexplicable decision to await neither at his military headquarters nor in the capital city the termination of the definitive negotiations for peace. The epic of his life supports the interpretation that, animated by a keen desire to avoid falling into the merciless clutches of those inveterate foes who had persecuted and hunted him since 1783, he had resolved to leave his post. It was an ironic fate that consigned the apostle and promoter of Spanish-American independence to a Spanish dungeon as a result of the unworthy measures of his own compatriots. This débâcle presents some resemblance to the downfall of José Artigas, the enigmatical hero of the revolution in Uruguay, who, after being routed by the traitor Francisco Ramírez, relinquished the struggle for independence and passed his last years as an exile in Paraguay.

The repeated attempts of Francisco de Miranda to establish the liberty of his native land terminated in a tragedy. Nevertheless the last effort of the revolutionary promoter to establish a free state in Spanish America had not been altogether in vain. Venezuelans like Bolívar and Sucre, who under his leadership had received training in warfare against the royalists, became the champions of a new struggle for independence. That war was waged while Francisco de Miranda was fretting his life away in lonely prison cells.

Chapter XXIII

CAPTIVITY IN SPANISH DUNGEONS

ON JULY 31, 1812, an accusation had been framed against General Miranda by Casas charging that he had conspired to leave Venezuela without having completed and published the Capitulation of San Mateo. After Monteverde took possession of La Guaira the captive was taken from the castle of San Carlos and thrust into a dungeon. Rumors were soon circulated in the West Indies that he was being examined by a commission of Spanish officers.[1] In a vile prison, loaded with chains, "up to his ankles in water,"[2] deprived of all communication, and in fear of being poisoned, Miranda was for a time reduced to subsistence on bread and water. It was presumably his son Leander who described the conduct of the Spaniards in these words: "Deaf to the common dictates of humanity, they chained this martyr to the cause of liberty to the floor of the prison in which he was confined." [3]

The other side of the shield is presented in the correspondence of the royalist commander. In December, 1812, Monteverde wrote to the Spanish Secretary of War and stated that to keep Miranda a prisoner in Venezuela was very dangerous to public tranquillity. The commander urged that the prisoner of state should be transported to Spain at once.[4] On January 20, 1813, in another letter to the same Minister the conqueror gave the fullest interpretation of his conduct after the Capitulation of San Mateo which has come into our hands. Monteverde declared that he had thrust the insurgent leaders into dungeons in order to free Venezuela of "these dangerous men," revolutionists by habit and ambition, who had brought many misfortunes upon their country. In regard to the conquered people, he wrote that each day he was more and more unde-

---

[1] Hodgson to Bathurst, Sept. 15, 1812, W. O., 1/112.
[2] Leleux to Vansittart, Aug. 26, 1812, F. O., 72/140; Rojas, *El general Miranda*, p. 774.   [3] Walker and Miranda, *Colombia*, p. 335.
[4] *Boletín de la academia nacional de la historia*, IV, 471; Figueredo, "Para pagar la cabeza del 'Traidor Miranda'," in *El Cojo Ilustrado*, XX, 656.

ceived in regard to their disposition. "They will do nothing for
mild and gentle treatment," he said, "and any punishment
administered to them ought to be accompanied by a certain
amount of force which will make the Government respected
and which will prevent vengeance from those who are punished. This condition explains why, on entering this city, not
finding myself with sufficient troops, and dreading to undertake their subjugation with my soldiers, who were engaged at
that juncture against the uprising of the negroes of Curiepe
since happily subdued, I did not have Miranda and other revolutionists who were imprisoned on their departure from La
Guaira—revolutionists who had planned to flee with him and
to abscond with property of the State—judged by a military
tribunal and shot. This condition explains why I had to dissimulate and regretfully to give passports to three or four
Venezuelans in spite of all my fears." [5]

Early in 1813 the ex-Dictator was transported from La
Guaira to Puerto Cabello where he was cast into another dungeon. He was confined in a cell of the fortress of San Felipe,
the very castle that had witnessed Vinoni's betrayal of the patriot cause. On March 8, when a commissioner of the *audiencia*
of Caracas was inspecting the prisoners who were rigorously
confined at Puerto Cabello, he visited that castle. In his official report there appears the following entry: "Another
vault: Don Francisco de Miranda, who has been a prisoner
for the space of eight months or thereabouts, in chains; his
case pending in the *audiencia*." [6]

Soon afterwards a report reached Curaçao that Miranda's
condition had been somewhat improved, as his friends had been
allowed to furnish him with provisions. A rumor was also circulated in this isle that during an examination the prisoner
of state had declared that he was "a General in the British
Service, and that he had acted under the orders of that Government." [7] Although presumably ignorant of the strange

---

[5] *Boletín de la academia nacional de la historia*, IV, 464.
[6] *Causas de infidencia*, p. 5.
[7] Hodgson to Bathurst, March 16, 1813, W. O., 1/113.

stories in circulation about him, yet Miranda deemed it wise
to address a petition to the colonial authorities. On May 19,
when the governor of Puerto Cabello was making a visit to
the dungeons of San Felipe, this prisoner who was confined in
one of its upper cells implored him for permission to have authentic copies made of two memorials that he had prepared
for the *audiencia* of Caracas. After describing the events that
preceded the Capitulation of San Mateo, in a memorial dated
March 8, 1813, Miranda explained his conduct in the campaign of 1812.

"The events of this campaign are so notorious that I shall
not analyze them. I shall only say that Venezuela, recognizing the imminent peril to her security, by a general and spon-
taneous act of all her authorities, appointed me generalissimo
of her soldiers and invested me with all the supreme authority
that she possessed. I used this authority, it appears to me, with
all the honor and zeal in my power, and exercised all my resources to procure a happy outcome. Yet, in spite of the repeated successes that our arms obtained at the port of Guay-
aca and the town of La Victoria, on the other side I was convinced of the calamitous condition to which the capital city and
the port of La Guaira had been reduced because of the lack of
provisions, and because of the sudden invasion which was
made at that time by slaves from the valleys and coasts of the
northern region. Stimulated by offers of liberty made by our
enemies, they had begun to perpetrate at Guatire and at other
places the most horrid assassinations. These events made me
realize that it was absolutely necessary to adopt a policy dependent upon my honor and responsibility which would avert
those awful evils, which would restore peace and tranquillity
to the people, which would in some manner repair the disasters
caused by the earthquake, and which, in fine, would reconcile
Americans and Europeans so that in the future they might
form one society, one family, and one interest. Thus Venezuela
would furnish to the rest of the Continent an example of her
political views; she would show that she preferred an honorable reconciliation to the calamities of a desolating civil war." [8]

[8] O'Leary, *Memorias*, XIII, 61-62.

The petitioner asserted that this idea had been approved by the chief citizens of Caracas, and that, after a short armistice, a Treaty of Capitulation was negotiated, printed, and distributed in the province of Caracas. In consequence the patriot soldiers laid down their arms and the Venezuelans submitted to a new order. "With what pleasure," proceeded Miranda, "did I flatter myself that I had fulfilled my duties with the greatest satisfaction, when in the midst of disastrous circumstances I ratified with my signature a treaty which was so beneficent and advantageous to the public good, a treaty which was sanctioned with all the formalities known to the law of nations, a treaty which Great Britain would also view with pleasure because of the conveniences that her ally gained, a treaty which, in fine, would open to peninsular Spaniards a secure and permanent asylum, no matter in what mode the struggle that they were waging with France might terminate. Such were my ideas, such my sentiments, and such the firm bases of this pacification that I proposed, negotiated, and brought to a proper end." [9]

Miranda then expressed surprise that at the very juncture when Spain announced that the Treaty of San Mateo was inviolable, he beheld her government infringing that capitulation, and "conducting various persons to prison who had been arrested arbitrarily or by sinister and tortuous means." He declared that these excesses stimulated the passions of certain persons who merely sought an excuse to unbridle them. "Denunciations multiplied," he continued, "political opinions which had been entertained before the signing of the armistice and which had been consigned by that contract to oblivion were now described as crimes against the State, and finally by inter-relating certain crimes the Spaniards prepared the lists of an almost general proscription." The ex-Dictator alleged that to justify those crimes various pretexts were maliciously trumped up. He thus described the treatment of the hapless victims:

---

[9] *Ibid.*, p. 63.

"All these prisoners were conducted to the port of La Guaira. Some victims mounted on beasts of burden were tied hand and foot on pack saddles. Others were driven on foot. All were threatened, outraged, and exposed to the indignities of the persons who escorted them; while in transit they were even prevented from responding to the demands of nature. They presented to spectators objects most worthy of interest and compassion.

"Then with horror I beheld scenes repeated in Venezuela which my eyes had witnessed in France. I saw arrive at La Guaira droves of men belonging to the most illustrious classes, who were treated like bandits. I saw them buried near me in those terrible prisons. I saw both rich and poor, venerable old men, tender maidens, artisans, and even priests bound with chains and condemned to breathe the mephitic air that extinguished artificial light, contaminated the blood, and inevitably prepared the way for death. Lastly, I saw sacrificed to this cruelty citizens distinguished for probity and talent who perished almost immediately in those dungeons, not only deprived of the aid that humanity dictates for the alleviation of physical suffering, but also deprived of the spiritual succor prescribed by our holy religion, and dying in the arms of their comrades,—citizens who would a thousand times rather have died with arms in their hands when they generously capitulated than have submitted to such outrages!" [10]

In the midst of such occurrences, added Miranda, there was promulgated in Venezuela "the wise and liberal Constitution" which had been sanctioned by the Cortes. Yet instead of dungeons being opened and tranquillity being restored, other unfortunate persons of all classes and ages were cast into prison. The ex-Dictator then asked whether this policy of prescription could be in conformity with the intentions of Spain. He stated that the Spanish Government had avowed principles that were diametrically opposed to those which were now being followed in Venezuela. "In such critical circumstances," he urged, "I claim the empire of the law, I invoke the judg-

---

[10] O'Leary, *Memorias*, XIII, pp. 63-64.

ment of the entire world, and, above all, I appeal respectfully to the authority of Your Highness in whose hands there resides exclusively and constitutionally the supreme judicial power of this district, who are the organ of the laws and the instrument for their application: to Your Highness, I repeat, I address my pleas for the first time in defense of the people of Venezuela who have not done anything since the capitulation to justify the Spaniards in treating them as criminals. My own honor, highly compromised in favor of their security and liberty, demands rigorous justice; a wise policy inculcates this, sane morality prescribes it, and reason dictates it! Otherwise I shall appear to be the most despicable being in the sight of the entire universe!" [11]

This appeal was duly presented to the *audiencia* of Caracas. "From Puerto Cabello," said José F. Hereida, regent of that tribunal, "I sent vigorous representations to the *audiencia* that it should take cognizance of Miranda's case in order that Spanish honor might not be stigmatized as Punic faith." [12] But these efforts were in vain. Still it appears that in May, 1813, the prisoner's condition was somewhat improved. A report was circulated in Curaçao that his fetters had been removed.

Early in the following month victories won by Simón Bolívar, who had led patriots into Venezuela from New Granada, gradually forced the royalist soldiers to retreat toward the city of Caracas. A prospect that the inveterate revolutionist might be liberated by his own compatriots evidently frightened Monteverde; for he suddenly decided to transport Miranda to the West Indies. "With another officer who at that time was imprisoned in the castle of Puerto Cabello, I was seized," said Miranda, "on June 4 in the dead of night, without our friends or agents being given any notice, hurried on board a small vessel, and conveyed precipitately to Puerto Rico. When we inquired of the governor of that island, who received us with proper humanity, the reason for our deporta-

[11] *Ibid.*, pp. 64-66. [12] Hereida, *Memorias,* p. 55.

tion, he informed us, without mentioning any specific cause, that we had been transferred by direction of the Captain General of Venezuela, and that we were to remain there until the receipt of new orders." [13]

On the following day a Spanish colonial official sent a note to the Secretary of War that explained the slow procedure of the *audiencia* of Caracas in respect to Miranda. He reported that this case had been opened on November 3, 1812, by a judge of that tribunal, as a result of an order from the Captain General. A demand was made for additional documents, especially those dealing with the sentence passed upon the filibuster in 1806. Meantime a charge had been framed by the faithless Casas to justify the seizure and incarceration of the fallen Dictator at La Guaira on the suspicion that he was about to flee from Venezuela without concluding and publishing the Capitulation of San Mateo. Delay in the prosecution of Miranda was inevitable, it was declared, because of the multitude of criminal cases pending before the *audiencia*. Further, the conclusion of this case was not deemed urgent because from its very inception Monteverde had shown that he wished to have the chief conspirators transported from the country.[14]

At Puerto Rico the prisoner of state was confined in Morro Castle. There he framed a memorial to the Spanish Cortes. In that document, which was dated June 30, 1813, he declared that two events had incited him to protest: first, the infringement of the Treaty of San Mateo by Monteverde; and second, the scandalous violations of the Spanish Constitution in Venezuela. As an illustration of these violations he mentioned his deportation from Puerto Cabello to Puerto Rico. He maintained that, if there were any charges against him he should be tried by the *audiencia* of Caracas, as provided by the Constitution, and that, if there were no accusations against him, he should be set free. He argued that the Capitulation of San

---

[13] Becerra, *Ensayo histórico documentado de la vida de Don Francisco de Miranda*, II, 303.

[14] Fiscar to the secretary of war, June 5, 1813, A. G. I., audiencia de Caracas, 133-3-12; Becerra, II, 293-94.

Mateo should be fulfilled, that the Spanish Government should appoint impartial officials who would observe it, and that the Constitution should be enforced throughout Venezuela. With indignation he declared that the policy which the Spaniards had followed in regard to his native land was more in conformity with the rules of the Inquisition than with the clauses of the Constitution. He asserted that Monteverde had persisted in violating the terms of the solemn Treaty of San Mateo with the exception of a single clause which he as patriot commander had never ratified. The adaptable mood of the fallen Dictator is shown by the fact that while declaring that, although his devotion to the cause of human liberty was notorious, yet he congratulated Spain upon the Constitution that had been drawn up at Cadiz. He avowed that he now considered himself "as one of those liberal Spaniards who sincerely desire the triumph and prosperity of true liberty in both hemispheres." He maintained that all Liberals, "whether Americans or Europeans, wish to be free and equal in rights." The responsibility for the failure to bring about a reconciliation between Spain and the Indies he laid at the door of those Spanish officials who oppressed the colonists.[15]

This appeal for justice and reconciliation from Miranda undoubtedly reached the Spanish Cortes. Comments written in Spanish fashion on the margins of the petition indicate that in September and October, 1813, it was successively referred to three committees of the Cortes which was in session at Cadiz: the committee on memorials, the judicial committee, and the committee on legislation. The last endorsement by a Spanish official on this memorial dated at Madrid, March 19, 1814, reads, "the Rebel," and, after giving a summary of his plea, the statement is made that the matter was then pending before the legislative committee.[16] On that very day the "ex-generalissimo of Venezuela," as he subscribed himself, again petitioned that the capitulation which he had made with Monteverde should be fulfilled. He also asked that impartial

---

[15] Becerra, II, 305-6.   [16] A. G. I., audiencia de Caracas, 133-3-12.

judges should be appointed to see that the Constitution of 1812 was observed in Venezuela.[17] Any action on these petitions was effectively prevented, however, by the policy of Ferdinand VII who, upon being restored to the Spanish throne on the downfall of Napoleon, promptly incarcerated the leaders of the Cortes, and discarded the liberal Constitution. Fairly to present the case of Spain, we should notice that during the following year Pedro Cevallos, the Spanish secretary of state, extenuated his Government's policy toward the Venezuelans by the technical plea that as the Capitulation of San Mateo had never been sanctioned by the insurgents it had no binding force.[18]

In the meantime Miranda's friends and acquaintances in England had become aware of the tragic results of his revolutionary activity. On October 5, 1812, the English Government published a notice of the surrender of the Venezuelan patriots and of Miranda's imprisonment. This news was translated into Portuguese and printed in the *Correio Braziliense*.[19] On October 12 Luis López Méndez appealed to Lord Castlereagh on behalf of the unfortunate inhabitants of Caracas.[20] Two days later he sent a memorial to Castlereagh to reënforce his previous arguments and to ask that the English Government should interpose to protect the conquered Venezuelans from Spanish vengeance!

"Your Excellency can easily imagine to what point the desolation and misery of Venezuela have increased by the possession of the capital city and all its resources by the hostile faction. Only England, by interposing in favor of the vanquished in order that at least Spain should fulfill scrupulously the capitulation that has been agreed to, can put a stop to the rage of the Spanish faction that is thirsting for vengeance. This is the favor which the memorialist beseeches of the English Government, convinced that if at an earlier period it raised its voice in favor of the Spanish Americans with the

---

[17] "Lista de los expedientes y papeles que tratan de la Revolución de Caracas," A. G. I., audiencia de Caracas, 133-3-12.
[18] Cevallos to Vaughn, Sept. 10, 1815, F. O., 72/176.
[19] IX, 671.   [20] F. O., 72/157.

sole purpose of ending the civil war, that now when to this fatal scourge there have been added in Caracas the effects of an even more horrible calamity, Great Britain cannot refrain from alleviating them by the easy and secure means that are at hand by virtue of her powerful influence in Europe and America. The interposition which Don Luis López Méndez respectfully asks on behalf of General Miranda and his other compatriots would beyond doubt be of great utility in the reëstablishment of order, peace, and confidence in Venezuela; it would at least avoid the continuation of those horrors which will soon complete the destruction of her people, and it would necessarily augment the popularity of England in the New World."

An official of the Foreign Office endorsed this communication as follows: "D. L. López Méndez * * * requests the countenance of England to the cause of Venezuela and Miranda's Person." [21] On November 28 of the same year Méndez sent another appeal to Castlereagh in which he besought the English government to mediate with Spain in order that the Capitulation of San Mateo might be faithfully carried out: "The petitioner does not conceive it necessary to recall to Your Excellency the motives that commend the people of Caracas to the generous compassion and friendly offices of Great Britain, but persuaded that only England can alleviate the burden of the calamities beneath which his compatriots are groaning, and convinced that her interposition with the Spanish Government would at least preserve the existence of a large number of victims, whom national honor, public faith, and all that is sacred among men cannot protect, he again appeals to Your Excellency beseeching him to submit this petition to the Prince Regent in order that His Royal Highness may judge it feasible, as the undersigned respectfully hopes from the frank and noble sentiments of His Royal Highness, to interpose his august mediation with the Spanish Government in order that by carrying out the capitulation which

---

[21] *Ibid.*

evidently preceded the entry of the royalist soldiers into Caracas some relief can be furnished to the unfortunate inhabitants
of that province, and a check can be given to the consummation of acts of perfidy and cruelty that have no precedent in
the history of civilized nations." In Downing Street this plea
was indorsed "further application in favor of Miranda, & c." [22]

Though no formal response was made by English publicists
to these appeals, yet they were not indifferent to Miranda's
fate. When in January, 1813, he sent to Lord Bathurst a
letter which made a plea on behalf of Miranda, Lord Grenville expressed the view that some consideration should be
paid to the fact that the prisoner had at one time been coun-
tenanced by Pitt. Besides he declared that he did not feel himself "at liberty in a case where a man's life is at stake to omit
any step that can on my part be useful to him, nor will you,
I am very certain, ever neglect an act of humanity if the case
be one in which you can with propriety interfere." [23] Another
clue to the attitude of English ministers toward Miranda is
afforded by a letter from Nicholas Vansittart to Lord Castlereagh that inclosed an appeal of Méndez for financial aid.
Vansittart stated that he wished that something could be done
for the unfortunate Venezuelans but that he realized how
difficult it would be to aid them.[24]

After Miranda's faithful secretary reached London, he undertook to champion the Venezuelan cause. On March 11,
1813, Thomas Molini transmitted to Richard Wellesley an
account by Delpech of the events in Venezuela that led to the
Capitulation of San Mateo. "Mr. M. has long been desirous,"
said Molini, "to submit to General Miranda's friends, some
account of those transactions, and particularly so, from having seen various statements in which the General's character
has been most grossly calumniated." [25] Delpech's sympathetic
and justificatory explanation of Miranda's conduct promptly
found its way into the files of the Foreign Office. There it lay

---

[22] F. O., 72/157.   [23] *Report on the Manuscripts of Earl Bathurst,* p. 226.
[24] Jan. 12, 1813, F. O., 72/150.   [25] *Ibid.,* 72/151.

almost unheeded; for the alliance between England and Spain compelled English statesmen to turn a deaf ear to appeals in favor of their former protégé.

Perhaps it was Delpech, who was now seeking to interest France in the fortunes of Spanish America, that transmitted a strange rumor to Paris about his master. This tale was that when Miranda was presented to a Spanish-American court for trial he had presented in his defense a commission from the English Government empowering him to act as a pacificator in the internecine struggle, and that, in consequence, the Spaniards had set him at liberty. It was even rumored that the ex-Dictator had departed from Venezuela for Puerto Rico with the avowed intention of presenting himself before the Spanish Regency and Lord Wellington.[26]

As the months passed, both López and Molini must have realized that England, the faithful ally of Spain, was not in a position to intercede in behalf of the promoter whom she had sheltered for so many years. Ambassador Wellesley, who seems to have been informed of Miranda's sad plight, later declared to Secretary Cevallos, that England had decided not to interfere between Spain and her revolted colonies "in any other manner than with a view to reconcile the differences between the two Parties by amicable Negotiation." [27]

Meantime the ex-generalissimo had traveled the last stage in his *via dolorosa*. In the latter part of 1813 Miranda was transported from Puerto Rico to Cadiz. There he was conducted to the castle of La Carraca which was located on an island in the harbor. On January 8, 1814, *El Redactor General* of Cadiz mentioned that the famous conspirator was incarcerated in La Carraca. As a prisoner who was deemed dangerous to the security of the State, Miranda was cast into a dungeon of the fort of the Four Towers, a two-storied structure that was surmounted by a tower on each corner. Shackles were again fastened to his ankles. Tradition records that, in

---

[26] "Nouvelles reçus des Indies Occidentales par lettres de Caracas, en date du 19 Janvier, 1813," A. A. E., Colombie, 1.   [27] Feb. 14, 1815, F. O., 72/173.

response to an inquiry by a Peruvian named Sauri who was a fellow prisoner, Miranda exclaimed that his Spanish chains burdened him less than the shackles with which he had been bound by his own comrades at La Guaira! Likewise there has been preserved a story to the effect that on a certain occasion while taking exercise in the narrow patio of his prison, Miranda lifted his fetters in his hand and mournfully lamented that the first link in his chain had been forged by his own compatriots. An official of the English navy who visited La Caracca even avowed that he had beheld "the venerable and distinguished prisoner" fettered to the wall by a chain that was fastened around his neck.[28]

Under the close surveillance of Spanish gaolers, the state prisoner did not find it easy to inform English friends of his whereabouts. However, before many months had elapsed, Miranda succeeded in smuggling out of his prison a letter in French addressed to his "dear and worthy friend," Nicholas Vansittart, who was now chancellor of the exchequer in the Liverpool ministry. In this letter from La Carraca, on May 21, 1814, the astute prisoner said that, as he was writing "unrobed and clandestinely," it would be necessary for Vansittart to divine his meaning. The ex-Dictator mentioned the stipulation of the Treaty of San Mateo providing that no person should be persecuted because of his previous political opinions. He alleged that this capitulation had been approved by the Spanish Government, put into force "very religiously" in Venezuela, and "with all the world, except with me, who was, however, the chief author of the scene. The Spaniards evaded this difficulty by sending me to Puerto Rico, and by transporting me from that port to Cadiz where the Spanish Government was then located. Upon our arrival its officials had left Cadiz for Madrid, and the evilly-disposed governor confined me in this arsenal from which I can have no communication with the English who are my friends.

---

[28] Becerra, II, 513; Larrazábal, *Vida y correspondencia general del libertador*, I, 140.

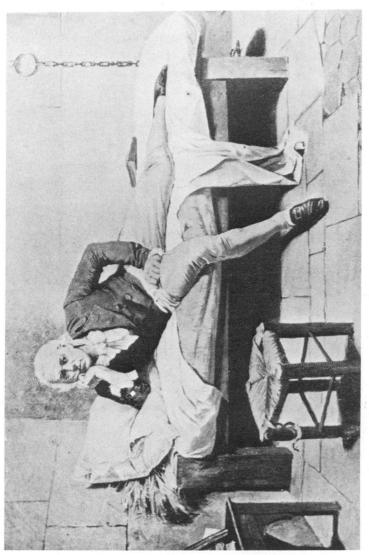

Miranda in the prison of La Caracca. Painting by Arturo Michelena. In the Museo Indígena, Caracas. From O'Kelly de Galway, "Francisco de Miranda." Reproduced by courtesy of Honoré Champion, Paris.

"If the Spanish King has approved the Constitution, I should be considered free because of its guarantee of personal liberty and by virtue of my right; but as all this is falling to the ground, and as the old government has regained its terrible place, a very powerful friend is needed to rescue me from the clutches of despotism. I can find nothing else that will explain why I suffer this persecution and hatred. England, all powerful today in Spain, can easily render me that service by demanding through Lord Wellington or through her Ambassador at Madrid that Spain should carry out the Capitulation with respect to me as she has fulfilled it with the others.

"Be so good as to talk with your friends and with my friends, His Royal Highness the Duke of Gloucester, Mr. Wilberforce, &c.,—in order to obtain a prompt and efficacious recommendation. * * * By the annexed proclamation you will see with what emphasis the Spaniards ratified the Capitulation and promised not to persecute anyone for what had transpired in the epoch previous to that contract. * * * All my papers, which in large part are also those of the English Government on account of my correspondence, are safe at Curaçao with the English firm of Robertson, Belt, and Company, as well as my books and baggage, with 22,000 pesos in silver and 1,200 ounces in gold. I beg you to secure this as well as you can. Molini knows all about it and will indicate the best action to take. I believe that these merchants are known to the firm of Murton in London; and I think that they will act honorably. I ask you to see that Mr. Tayler send me credit to the house of Duff at Cadiz, for he is the only person that knows how to communicate with me. Do not allow any of the Spaniards to learn anything about this affair; for they are abominable people, whom I have come to understand thoroughly and to my cost. Let your reply come in an envelope of Mr. Duff, and always with reserve." [29]

Months seems to have elapsed before the ex-Dictator's friends could aid him. In September, 1814, Peter Turnbull,

---

[29] Add. MSS., 31, 231, ff. 73-74.

14—II

the son of Miranda's old friend, the retired London merchant, secretly made arrangements that the prisoner should be furnished with sums of money. On December 8, 1814, John Turnbull wrote to Vansittart to inform him that he had received news of their "old and unfortunate friend" from his oldest son at Algeciras. Peter Turnbull had reported that he had found General Miranda "in prison at Cadiz, where he will probably remain all his life, unless means can be found to effect his Escape—I wrote him some days since a letter, merely giving him accounts of the health of his friends in London; which I sent open thro' the governor of this place.—and it has been communicated to me, thro' an authentic Channel, which I can mention when I get home, that for £1,000 Sterling his liberty could be effected." [30]

On April 13, 1815, Miranda addressed another letter to Vansittart which reached its destination.

"This is the third letter that I have been able to write you since being confined here; but unfortunately I have addressed my letters through Sir J. Duff whom I have discovered to be a strange and detestable personage with respect to myself. Finally he insultingly refused to let me have five pounds sterling. * * * The letter or order that I last sent him, made out to you for one hundred pounds sterling, he retained, as well as a receipt for one hundred and fifty pesos, without sending me a sou. If he had done what I wished, I would now actually be free from all embarrassments, and very probably reposing in Grafton Street. Some days ago I wrote to Rutherfurd at Gibraltar to ask credit for two hundred pounds sterling on some commercial house at Cadiz, excluding that of Duff, but, as yet, I have received no response. It seems that adversity pursues me everywhere and in every possible manner. * * * Finally, my dear friend, if it so be that you are still alive to solace me, send me credit for two hundred pounds on a commercial house at Cadiz. This is the only mode to get me away from here, if it arrives in time." [31]

Evidently this sum did not pass into Miranda's hands. For

---

[30] Add. MSS., 31, 231, f. 208.   [31] *Ibid.*, ff. 257-58.

on May 15 he sent another letter to his faithful friend expressing deep regret that he had not received money at so favorable a juncture. The prisoner lamented as "an unfortunate blow" the death of his old friend Colonel Rutherfurd on whose aid at Gibraltar he had placed dependence.[32] Three months later, Miranda wrote to Vansittart thus: "I do not know whether my letters have reached you, but I well know that I have not received the least news from you." Miranda then declared that he had never swerved from the "honorable and just principles" which had rendered him worthy of Vansittart's esteem. Again he mentioned "the abominable infraction" by Spain of the Treaty of San Mateo. He complained that his timorous gaolers did not even wish him to read the *Gaceta de Madrid.* "Nevertheless," he added, "I have by chance obtained some Latin classics, which enable me to pass the time with utility and pleasure: Horace, Vergil, Cicero, Don Quixote, and Ariosto, as well as the New Testament. * * * But what I absolutely need is a little money." [33]

About this time Miranda addressed pleas for funds to other persons. Anxious to keep his correspondence with the outside world a secret, in the spring of 1816 the state prisoner began to sign his epistles with the pseudonym of J. Amindra. On March 1 he wrote to a firm at Cadiz asking for a sum of money that he declared was on deposit for him. He stated that three hundred pesos were needed "to reëstablish" his fortune: "otherwise I consider myself lost beyond remedy." [34] The memory of former times must have seemed to him like the evening sun upon his soul.

About this time he was attacked by a fever that indubitably interfered with his plans for flight. Scarcely had he recovered when he again began to scheme how he might escape from his island dungeon. One day in March, 1816, the prisoner wrote a letter to an English banking firm at Cadiz declaring that he had recovered from his fever and had arranged to leave next Wednesday or Thursday on a "little journey."

[32] *Ibid.,* f. 269.   [33] *Ibid.,* f. 334.   [34] Rojas, *El general Miranda,* p. 778.

Then he proceeded in a passage that seems purposely vague:

"Everything has been prepared with sufficient care so that we shall arrive happily at Gibraltar. But as the Moors are now our enemies perhaps chance may carry us to a port like Lagos on the Portuguese coast near the strait where it will be necessary to charter a boat or a felucca with the flag of England, or of the United States, or of some other nation that is at peace with them. Because of this possibility, it would be very useful if you would send me directly or through some of your friends at Cadiz a few lines of recommendation for merchants in those ports so that they may aid me in such circumstances to proceed as soon as possible. At the same time, in case I should need more money than I have for this purpose, I ought to carry a draft for two hundred pesos on the house of Turnbull and Company of Gibraltar. It seems to me that in this way I could take with me whatever is necessary for a happy ending without compromising you in any manner." [35]

This information is supplemented by a letter written from Gibraltar by Peter Turnbull to Vansittart on April 7, 1816:

"Since I had last the pleasure of writing you, my Friends at Cadiz have sent me two more letters from our Friend. * * * It is now ten days since I received them—and I feel considerable uneasiness at having in this interval heard nothing further. I earnestly wish that some artful people be not deceiving him, in order to get money from him,—but at any rate it is satisfactory to find that he has means of communication, and that his Health is not bad. From the tenor of the Letters, he seemed on the very point of moving and I shall be all anxiety until I hear something further." [36]

On the following day Peter Turnbull informed a correspondent that he had reason to believe that Miranda would be free "at no distant period." Turnbull stated further that the prisoner had "applied for certain small sums of money for this purpose which I directed to be furnished him. * * * I

---

[35] Rojas, *El general Miranda*, p. 779.   [36] Add. MSS., 31, 232, f. 39.

made the regular Arrangements for his being supplied with whatever he might require—and since that time I have read several letters from him. The last was received about ten days ago—at which time he expressed his intention of proceeding hither in the course of three days." [37] However, some mishap occurred, and the little journey, which Miranda had so hopefully anticipated, had again to be postponed. He then wrote to Peter Turnbull and declared that it had been necessary for him to sacrifice three hundred pesos of the money which he had intended for his journey. "And thus I ask you," implored Miranda, "to send me without delay three hundred pesos by Señora A. in order to replace that loss and to enable me to depart, which I ought to do within three days at the latest; if possible, she should also bring me a letter of recommendation for Portugal." [38]

Miranda's health declined so rapidly, however, that he was not again able to attempt to carry out his plans for escape. During the night of March 25 he was seized with what his faithful attendant, Pedro José Morán, described as an apoplectic fit that threatened to end his life. After he rallied from this he was next attacked by typhus fever. A few days later he was seized by inflammation in the head and a hemorrhage from the mouth which reduced him to the last extremity. About this time the invalid prisoner was removed to the hospital of the arsenal of La Caracca. Four conferences of physicians, said Morán, held out no prospect of recovery. [39] The dying man apparently made no attempt to modify his testament of 1810 or to frame a new one. A priest gave him the holy sacrament of extreme unction. [40]

Early on the morning of July 14, 1816, in the hospital of La Caracca, the chief of the apostles of Spanish-American independence gave up his spirit to the Creator. [41] Pedro Morán who gathered up the papers which his master had carefully

---

[37] To Tayler, *ibid.*, f. 43.   [38] "hoi Jueves" (copy), *ibid.*, f. 40.
[39] Rojas, *El general Miranda*, p. 780.
[40] *Boletín de la academia nacional de la historia*, III, 73; *cf.* Becerra, I, p. cxxii.   [41] Rojas, *op. cit.*, pp. 780-81.

preserved, complained that the friars and priests who were present at Miranda's deathbed would not allow him to perform any funeral rites for his dead master. "In the same condition in which he expired," added his servant, "with matrass, sheets, and other bedclothes they seized hold of him and carried him away for interment; they immediately afterwards came back and took away his clothes and other belongings to burn them." [42] The body of the prisoner of state, whose death certificate declared that his case was still pending and that he was unmarried,[43] was interred in the small cemetery of the district which included La Caracca. There the old soldier began his last bivouac. In view of his tragic imprisonment and death Miranda may not inappropriately be likened to the hero of Haitian independence, Toussaint L'Ouverture, who perished miserably in a French dungeon.

During his long and dismal incarceration at Cadiz the prisoner's friends in London had insistently tried to liberate him. It is clear that they furnished him with considerable money to promote that end. In the inedited papers of Lord Bexley there is a preserved copy of a letter from Mr. C. E. Fleeming from a port in southern Spain, presumably addressed to Peter Turnbull, that helps to interpret this chapter:

"As there seems to be no doubt of General Miranda's death, I beg you will do me the favor to inform me if you are authorized to return me the money I had advanced on his account. Last autumn you informed me you had funds of his in your hands, and I have paid on his account since our conversation on this subject, in September, 1814, Six hundred and fourteen Dollars, and before that period two hundred. You are aware of the difficulty of procuring vouchers in a regular manner, or indeed my being able to make any claim—but I trust to your assistance as well as prudence in taking care the persons employed may not be endangered by any means, for which purpose I take the liberty of recommending you to send any correspondence you may have relative to this transaction

[42] Rojas, *El general Miranda*, p. 781.
[43] *Boletín de la academia nacional de la historia*, III, 73.

by the English Packets, and by no means overland by Post." [44]

As the cemetery of the district including La Caracca was closed a half century later without the ashes of Miranda being removed, the world is today ignorant of his burial place. Although after his death the Captain General of the department of Cadiz transmitted to Madrid the news that Francisco de Miranda had died a natural death, yet strange stories were soon circulated. There was bruited about in his native land a rumor that it was uncertain whether the fallen dictator had died of grief, by poison, or by secret execution. Eventually the melancholy circumstances attending his death, as well as a knowledge of his real services to the cause of Spanish-American independence, caused his compatriots to view Miranda as a martyr.

---

[44] "18 April," Add. MSS., 31, 232, f. 42.

Chapter XXIV

THE MAN AND HIS RôLE IN HISTORY

AFTER THE proscription of September, 1797, Miranda relinquished Paris as a place of residence. Soon he definitely located in London. For a time he occupied rooms in the house of Mrs. Oldham, 33 Great Pultney Street. At one time or another he also lived in Marylebone Road, in Allsop's Buildings, and in Tavistock Street. Ultimately he leased a house at 27 Grafton Street which was adjacent to a bit of meadow called Fitzroy Square. His home was near Tottenham Court Road on the site now occupied by a respectable, three-story brick house with green blinds.

The earliest available document that Miranda composed there bears date of July 18, 1803. On that day he addressed a letter to Nicholas Vansittart to ask that the English Government should be so good as to continue for some time *la gratification extraordinaire que j'ai reçu jusqu'ici.* Only thus, he declared, could he meet the expenses of the house which he had leased in Grafton Street. Within its walls he presumably descanted about art with the pock-marked recluse James Barry, the Irish painter. In its parlor he discoursed with his old friend Melville about literary projects, and gave advice to another littérateur named Thompson. There he entertained his Spanish-American friends as well as certain Englishmen who were interested in the fortunes of the Spanish Indies. In an inner sanctum time and again he pored over revolutionary plans with his secretary who in 1805 was Thomas Molini, perhaps the very bookseller with whom he had had dealings in Paris. An intriguing adventurer named Joseph Pavia, who occasionally borrowed money from Miranda, asserted that he had frequently beheld the arch-conspirator in his residence "in the midst of all sorts of books and numerous charts and maps."

Miranda's residence at 27 Grafton Street comprised nine rooms. Besides a front parlor, a rear parlor, and a dressing room, it included two drawing rooms, two bed rooms, a "Front

Library," and a "Little Library." Though some of the furniture was of mahogany, yet an inventory of Miranda's household goods does not reveal that his home was luxuriously furnished. He had only a modest amount of household silver. Among the pictures that decorated his walls were Apollo, the Lord's Supper, the Ascension, several prints representing Chinese costumes, and some copies of paintings by Raphael. A chart of the world on Mercator's Projection hung, we may be sure, in a prominent place. The front drawing room was adorned with plaster busts of Apollo, Cervantes, and Homer. In the little library there was ordinarily only a desk, a deal table, and one rush-bottomed chair. Upon its walls there probably hung a map of South America. The scale on which the revolutionary was living is shown by the fact that he once expressed his willingness to accept in lieu of the extraordinary grant of funds which covered the rent and running expenses of his house an annual sum of two hundred pounds.[1]

As already indicated, Miranda early displayed a fondness for books. An inventory of his property that was prepared at Habana on February 12, 1783, enumerated about four hundred and fifty volumes. This list contained some works of engineering, history, and mathematics, besides a goodly number of books on politics and literature.[2] Indicative perhaps of special interests are the following classics: Blackstone's *Commentaries on the Laws of England*, Smith's *Wealth of Nations*, and Cæsar's *Commentaries on the Gallic War*. Among French titles were Montecuculi's *Mémoires* and the *Règlemens Prussiens*. During his travels Miranda sent to London from France, Holland, Russia, and Switzerland, boxes crammed with publications concerning the life and history of the countries he had visited. It seems likely that he purchased some of the treatises recommended to him by Dr. Thomas Christie in

---

[1] Miranda to Vansittart, July 18, 1803, Mir. MSS., vol. 48; "Inventory of Furniture," Aug. 2, 1805, *ibid.*, vol. 24. See further *El Cojo Ilustrado*, V, 507-12, where may be found pictures of some of Miranda's personal effects; and Becerra, *Ensayo histórico documentado de la vida de Don Francisco de Miranda*, II, 528, note, where they are mentioned.

[2] "Equipage de la Havana," Mir. MSS., vol. 4.

a list of tomes "such as might be considered to form a tolerably complete Medical Library for a private gentleman who is not of the Profession." [3] In 1802 a shipment of books to Miranda from Paris weighing three tons was detained at an English customhouse pending the payment of duties that aggregated two hundred and fifty pounds.[4]

While browsing in dingy second-hand bookstores in London the Venezuelan made large additions to his library. In truth he became a bibliophile; his collection must have been one of the finest private libraries in the English metropolis. Among the volumes that presumably he possessed when he moved into 27 Grafton Street were the following: Harris, *List of Convent-Garden Ladies;* Rousseau's *Works;* Rollin's *Ancient History;* Tooke's *Life of Catherine II;* Lavater, *Essai sur la physiognomie;* and Alcedo, *Diccionario geográfico-histórico de las Indias Occidentales.*[5] By 1805 he had prepared a catalogue of his collection. It is probable that by this time he had in his possession a "Fine Collection of Spanish Books, particularly relating to North and South America." [6]

On the other hand, in 1807 a barrister estimated that the balance which Miranda owed to London bookstores aggregated some five thousand pounds.[7] Upon being told during his sojourn in Trinidad that a scheme had been formed to place part of his library in the custody of booksellers to whom he was indebted, Miranda's feelings were wounded and he thus appealed to English friends to prevent such a transfer:

"My wishes are that Dulau's bill should be immediately paid, with the Money that may be due me in the Treasury, as nothing could be more disagreeable to me than the removal of a single Book from my House, it really hurts my feelings

---

[3] Undated, Mir. MSS., vol. 22.
[4] White to Miranda, Nov. 2, 1802, *ibid.,* vol. 47.
[5] *Catalogue of the Second and Remaining Portion of the Valuable Library of the Late General Miranda, passim.*
[6] *Catalogue of the Valuable and Extensive Library of the Late General Miranda,* pt. I, title-page.
[7] Kibblewhite to Davison, July 7, 1807, Mir. MSS., vol. 56.

to think of it." [8]

Though Miranda's magnificent collection has long since been dispersed, yet scattered through his manuscripts there still remain rare brochures and obscene squibs which attest his wide interests and suggest his vices. A few illustrations must here suffice. An anonymous pamphlet entitled *Quiesce: Conseils d'un philosophe à Marc-Aurele,* bears Miranda's comment "excellent and wise little treatise." [9] A copy of the *Rules and Articles for the Better Government of the Troops raised, or to be raised, and kept in Pay, by and at the Expence of the United States of America* bears this note in Miranda's handwriting, "presented by Baron Stuben in his retreat near New York in 1784." [10] Among papers concerning France the revolutionary filed away not only the cahier of Auvergne but also a copy of the *Marche des Marseillois, chantée sur differens théatres.* At St. Petersburg he purchased a booklet entitled *État de Russie.* Another rarity is a translation from French into Spanish of Viscardo's *Lettre aux Espagnols-Américains,* which the promoter had prepared for distribution in Spanish America.

Miranda stored his books in the front library of his residence in Grafton Street. They soon overflowed that room. Under his own immediate surveillance he placed the rare papers which he had brought from America as well as diaries, letters, broadsides, and memoranda concerning his travels and negotiations. It appears that when he was not at home his manuscripts were kept under lock and key. To supplement this wonderful collection of data he had various plans and maps which he had gathered during his American and European peregrinations. He also purchased charts from English cartographers. On one occasion William Faden, geographer to the King, dunned Miranda for some sixty pounds for a collection of maps that had been made to order and delivered to his house.[11]

---

[8] Miranda to Turnbull, July 11, 1807, *ibid.,* vol. 53.   [9] *Ibid.,* vol. 35.
[10] Miranda, *Diary,* p. 153.   [11] March 8, 1792, Mir. MSS., vol. 20.

At leisure hours, when he was not importuning publicists, sketching plans, or entertaining fellow conspirators, he spent considerable time in the study of history and politics, the military art, and languages, living or dead. As a result of travel and study, by 1790 he had acquired some knowledge of English, French, and Italian. Subsequently he undertook to master other European tongues. Among the papers concerning his sojourn in France, there is found under date of February 30, 1795, an epitome of the German language which he had begun to study.[12] Whatever progress he may have made in the study of the classics while attending the University of Caracas, after he had attained manhood he frequently displayed an acquaintance with Latin authors. After he had fixed his residence in London, he even undertook to learn the Greek language. In his diary under date of July 19, 1801, Miranda made the following entry: "At home studying my Greek which gave me infinite pleasure." [13]

Yet he was a dilettante scholar. Though his linguistic knowledge was wide, it was not accurate. Among translations of his letters, which he was fond of adorning with citations from classic and modern authors, a clever translator has inserted the following note to a Latin quotation ascribed to "Esop": "Faithfully copied. As several similar blunders occur in Miranda's Latin quotations, there is every reason to suppose that they are *not* attributable to the Transcriber." [14] Nevertheless this criticism should not be taken too seriously; for at various times during his career Miranda employed a secretary whose fine Italian handwriting is not always easily distinguished from his own. Further, among his voluminous papers he was accustomed to file unsigned plans and memorials that had been altogether or in part composed by other persons. He followed this practice without always clearly indicating those portions of the documents that he had helped to pre-

---

[12] "Elemens de la Langue Allemande," Mir. MSS., vol. 43.   [13] *Ibid.*, vol. 77.
[14] F. O., 72/89. A more favorable view of Miranda's linguistic attainments was given in 1815 by Leleux, see Glenbervie, *The Diaries of Sylvester Douglas,* II, 194.

pare. Then, too, as the years passed, Miranda's knowledge of the English language, at least, steadily improved.

As an illustration of Miranda's methods we will print a letter from an Englishman named Jenkins who once acted as his scribe: "Mr. Jenkins presents his Compliments to Col. de Miranda, and assures him that the profoundest regard shall be paid to the secrecy of the Work committed to him— he is sorry to find it extremely defective as to Sense in some places, and very generally as to punctuation, many of the sentences are broken into different paragraphs which cannot be fully remedied without an intire new Copy. Mr. J. however will do all he can to render it complete as possible." [15]

At leisure moments General Miranda renewed his acquaintance with men engaged in literary pursuits. On October 8, 1803, General Melville wrote to him and asked for a loan of a "very valuable work on ancient Printing by Mr. Turnbul." [16] Miranda had also entered into intimate relations with Dr. William Thompson who was busy writing articles concerning the "History of Europe" for the *Annual Register*. As early as December 10, 1798, Thompson had laid before the revolutionary a manuscript concerning the events of 1793 in France with a request for additions and corrections.[17] On September 10, 1799, this author wrote to him again and declared: "I wish it were possible for me to submit to your inspection the subsequent years. * * * Your Sentiments have a Clearness and Force that impresses the Imagination and convince the Understanding." [18] On May 16, 1800, Thompson asked Miranda for information about his imprisonment in Paris; and on September 30 he made inquiry about Miranda's pamphlet of 1795 proposing the reorganization of France.[19] As the result of a conversation that he had had with the general, on February 20, 1804, this industrious scholar submitted to Miranda for correction a sketch of modern military art which

---

[15] "Monday Eveng, Sepr. 26," Mir. MSS., vol. 23.   [16] *Ibid.*, vol. 22.
[17] Thompson to Miranda, Dec. 10, 1798, *ibid.*, vol. 23.
[18] *Ibid.*   [19] *Ibid.*

was based upon a conversation with that general.

Upon transmitting this sketch, Dr. Thompson solicited Miranda's literary advice. He declared that he wished to discuss "sundry points" with the general before he wrote either the dedication or the preface. He asked his mentor to examine the prospectus so that he might clearly understand his design, "which is not so much, or in any direct way, to give a history of the Military Art, as of Battles and Stratagems of War, etc.—I am fully sensible of the facilitation I have received from you, and other Advantages, in the prosecution of my Design—I should be glad to be permitted to acknowledge this, in a public or private manner, and in all possible ways to testify the Gratitude, Esteem, and Attachment with which I have the Honor to be, Dear Sir, your obliged and Obedient servant." [20]

In the first edition of his treatise entitled *Military Memoirs, relating to Campaigns, Battles, and Stratagems of War, Antient and Modern,* Dr. Thompson gratefully mentioned the "private authorities, from which he drew not a little of his information" whose names "would have done credit to the book, had he been at liberty to state them." [21] On November 12, 1805, Thompson wrote to Miranda in part as follows:

"When I spoke to you about publickly acknowledging my great obligations to you in guiding and bridging my Collection of Military Memoirs, you gently dissuaded me—I had a great mind to do it nevertheless. But I did not well know—I hesitated. A 2d. Edition wt. Improvements by Captain James Glenie whom you may have seen at General Melville's—I have introduced your name in an Advertisement prefixed—I have had a great deal of Conversation about all this with Lieutenant Colonel Herbert Taylor, to whom I am greatly indebted on many accounts and whose Name is also introduced —He approved and advised me to bring your Name forward. * * * I will send you a Copy of this new Edition, the very first opportunity. I every day intended to write. I have

---

[20] Mir. MSS., vol. 23.　　　　　[21] Preface, p. xv.

to apologize for not apprizing you. But really I thought it best not to do so." [22]

In the second edition of his treatise Dr. Thompson acknowledged that he had had aid from various persons but that his "great guide and assistant was General Miranda, a man of learning, genius, military talents, experience, and reputation." Thompson did not hesitate to apply to "this distinguished stranger" a characterization which had been made of Scipio Africanus; namely, that there was "no one who spent, with greater elegance, his hours of leisure. He was ever engaged in the improvement of the arts either of war or peace. Addicted wholly to arms or books, he never relaxed either the exercise of his body, in danger, or of his mind, in application to study." [23] In a subsequent letter to his critic the author gratefully wrote: "The *Military Memoirs* have been well received—commended by the Edinburgh Reviewers, that damn most things. For this I am indebted to the General who directed my Attention and gave me a General View of the Vicissitudes and progress of the Art of War." [24]

The private life of Miranda is further revealed by certain steps that he took in regard to the disposal of his property. On August 1, 1805, he wrote to his friends, Chauveau Lagarde and Clérisseau, to direct them that in case of his death they should send his papers and other property in Paris to Turnbull and Vansittart. He instructed the Frenchmen that in such an event they should give one hundred louis d'or to his faithful maid, Française Pelicier. Further, he informed them that his previous testamentary dispositions were cancelled.[25] On the same day, declaring that he was on the point of embarking for America to carry out the plans which had engrossed a large part of his life, Miranda framed a will that contained some curious clauses.

---

[22] Mir. MSS., vol. 56.
[23] Burke, *Additional Reasons for our Immediately Emancipating Spanish America*, p. 65.   [24] Feb. 3, 1808, Mir. MSS., vol. 56.
[25] Robertson, "Miranda's Testamentary Dispositions," in *His. Am. Hist. Rev.*, VII, 283-84.

In that document the testator named Turnbull and Vansittart as his executors and made a list of his property. This inventory included the goods in his home in Grafton Street as well as the bronzes, mosaics, and paintings in the custody of his friends in Paris. It described his private archives that contained documents respecting his ancestry and travels, his correspondence with French generals and ministers, and his papers concerning negotiations with the English Government in regard to Spanish-American emancipation. The will mentioned ten thousand louis d'or as the debt still owing the testator by France because of his military service. In case of death his manuscripts were to be sent to the city of Caracas, provided that Venezuela should become independent or should open her ports freely to other nations.

His household goods were left to one whom Miranda designated as "*mi fiel ama de llaves*, Sarah Andrews," a woman who had for some time been serving as his maid or housekeeper. In case of his death she was to be given whatever remained of six hundred pounds that were deposited with his executors to defray household expenses. His remaining property in London and Paris was to be used for the education of one whom he described as "my natural son Leander whom I especially recommend to my executors and friends; for he is of the tender age of eighteen months, and without any other protection on the part of parents or relatives." [26]

This strange testament is supplemented by a letter of instructions that Miranda framed on August 28, 1805, for Messrs. Turnbull and Vansittart. In this letter he directed them to look after his affairs in London during his absence.

"The house, as well as all the property and furniture which it contains, will be left in the same condition as that in which they actually are at present and in charge of Mrs. Martin who will take all possible care of them. She will receive for this purpose fifty pounds each month in order to pay the rent and the annual taxes, as well as the household and other expenses.

---

[26] Robertson, "Miranda's Testamentary Dispositions," *loc. cit.*, p. 287.

If she has need of anything more it should be advanced to her on my account. The money that Mr. Turnbull has received for this purpose will furnish the necessary sums, as is explained in my letter of the 18th. of this month which Mrs. Martin has in her possession. My testamentary dispositions, which I have left secreted in a drawer, shall be opened if need arises and should be put into execution by your kind services and by virtue of the good friendship for which I am indebted to you. The balance of my accounts with the booksellers Dulau, White, and Evans—the only ones which are not paid up— will be met as soon as I am able. In any case the books that have not been paid for can be returned to those booksellers, according to our agreement." [27]

The private life of Miranda is further illumined by inedited correspondence. In a letter directing John Turnbull to look after his interests in London he declared: "In truth I have said that I desired to have Leander baptized by a priest of the Roman Catholic Church, but it is necessary that this should be done without noise and with the consent of his mother." [28] Excerpts from an epistle sent to Miranda by Sarah Andrews on September 29, 1805, demonstrates that she was actually caring for the child:

"I hope you found all your friends in good Health an happy to see you—my dear leander is everything that a fond Mother can wish, he is everyday more Beautiful, Healthful, an Engaging. His little actions are every moment more endearing—he is my hope an comfort in the absence of my ever dearest friend—God send that we may soon be again under the Protection of the wisest and best of friends—my dear sir I find the loss of you more than ever—I remember with Pain my ingratitude on several occations—and your goodness to forgive me—I will reward you with my Fidelity an conform in everything as I have promis'd—the baptism of my dear Child has not taken place in consequence of not nowing the name you have exprest in your Paper's—an it must be the same. Mr. Turnbull has no relection of anything—the chrisen

---

[27] Mir. MSS., vol. 49.   [28] Miranda to Turnbull, Jan. 4, 1806, *ibid.*, vol. 50.

an family name of the child must be express'd in the Baptism, otherwise it is of no yuse. Mrs. Turnbull advises me to not to Baptise him untill you have the goodness to transmit to me, what shall be done. * * * I am very Pleas'd with the society of Mrs. Molini. I trust I shall soon hear of great news from my dear Genl. One Month has allready Past away since our Departur—I find great Conciliation in my lovely Child. Col. Williamson call'd one eving in a Post Chaise my Leander— so an thought it was you—he was overjoy'd—the Col. appear'd affected with my Child's attencion to him. * * * A thousand Blessings attend you—wright me as offen as you can it will console me." [29]

In a letter dated September 30, 1805, addressed to "Mr. George Martin," John Turnbull wrote that "Leander and Mrs. Martin are very well." He declared that Miranda's wish that Leander "should be christened by a Priest of the Roman Catholic persuasion" would be faithfully carried out.[30]

A clue to the father's sentiments concerning his family is found in a passage from an epistle which he sent to Sarah Andrews from New York on January 4, 1806:

"I long to receive your letters my good Sally—it is from Mr. Turnbull only that I have heard since I quitted England. I have written to you 3 times since my arrival here; I hope all goes well at home, and that your prudence and zeal will be a remedy for the small neglect of others. Take a particular care with the Health and Education of Leander— treat him with mildness and gravity, as to bring his temper to submission without breaking his spirits and liveliness. Let your health be attended to for the sake of us all—I want you as much as anybody else to carry in execution, and terminate with success my schemes. Take advice from Mr. Barry if you want it; don't let your brother come near the house." [31]

Beyond any doubt Leander's mother was Sarah Andrews, an uneducated woman reputed to be of Jewish extraction. Although Ricardo Becerra, a South American littérateur who

---

[29] Mir. MSS., vol. 50. [30] *Ibid.* [31] *Ibid.*

composed a biography of Miranda, asserted that his hero was married to Miss Andrews, yet no certificate of such a marriage has ever been found.[32] On the other hand, there is ample evidence to show that Leander was born out of wedlock. According to a letter from "Sarah Martin" to Miranda the child's birthday was October 9, 1803.[33]

Before the midsummer of 1806, another child was born to Sarah Martin. On June 5 John Turnbull sent this news to Miranda: "Mrs. Martin and your two Boys are very well. She is made happy by the good accounts of your success. Since your departure she has conducted herself with exemplary Prudence and Propriety."[34] On the same day Mrs. Martin wrote to her absent master complaining of the ill conduct of one of his former servants who had remarked that her children were "not lawful."[35] About six months later the doting mother declared that the father had never named her "dear baby," that is to say, the child who became known as Francisco.[36]

In a letter to Miranda dated May 7, 1807, John Rutherfurd mentioned a visit which he had made to 27 Grafton Street. He conveyed his impressions of the children in an interesting fashion: "The eldest boy is a fine, stout, bold little fellow and promises to have Talent and spirit enough to be a general himself.—There is an appearance of frankness and good sense about him that pleases me much." Professing to speak without flattery, Rutherfurd expressed the opinion that with good tutoring he would be a credit to Miranda. "The younger one," continued this correspondent, "appears as if he would be handsomer than the older brother and is extremely good humored but he is too young yet to say more of him than that he is pleasing. The elder one not only resembles you in person, but in one instance when I was there this morning assumed a look in speaking to his mother so much like you that it struck me most forcibly."[37]

The slight extent to which the illicit relations of Miranda

---

[32] Becerra, II, 499.   [33] Oct. 1, 1806, Mir. MSS., vol. 52.   [34] Ibid., vol. 52.
[35] Ibid.   [36] Jan. 6, 1807, ibid., vol. 53.   [37] Ibid.

with Sarah Andrews is stressed in these letters is not because
of any excisions. That lack of emphasis is due to the lax
standards of a profligate age. One has only to glance at the
Diary of Farington the Academician to notice how amazingly
frequent mention is there made of the illicit connections or the
illegitimate offspring of people who were prominent in the
artistic or aristocratic circles of English society.

The resentment expressed by Miranda in a letter to Vansittart about the unsympathetic conduct of Turnbull toward his
family displays a surprising depth of devotion.

"I have written to you about my private affairs at Grafton
Street, and I have since learned more of the blunders and in-
discretion of our friend Mr. Turnbull—I request of you
therefore not to fill out the Power of Attorney with his name
on any account, and if you have done it, to repeal it, for fear
that the man should do me an irreparable mischief before we
can remedy it—My intention is that the House should be kept
until the lease is expired and even for a longer time—Turnbull's want of feeling with that family is beyond conception.
I forgive him, and recommend them to you,—they are objects
too near my own heart, not to trouble my best friends with
their protection. I tremble when I consider that the imprudent behavior of Turnbull might have occasioned the death
of that Mother and left the children unprotected in the Streets.
This is enough, I won't trouble you any more on this disagreeable subject." [38]

On his departure for Venezuela Miranda did not much
alter the will that he had framed in 1805. On the second page
of his testament he inserted a clause concerning the disposal
of his manuscripts, and by a footnote to the following page
he acknowledged Francisco as his natural son. He added a
codicil dated October 5, 1810, which stated that he ratified and
confirmed this testamentary disposition and asked that his
friend and executor, Nicholas Vansittart, should carry it out.

---

[38] Jan. 6, 1807, Mir. MSS., vol. 53. Brief mention of Miranda's family is
found in Farington, *Diary*, IV, 30.

In the provisions of the court for the administration of the estate, the testator was described as a bachelor.[39] Instead of the mother of Miranda's children being an English noblewoman of illustrious lineage, the precursor's own papers clearly demonstrate that she was an untutored domestic whose rough hand was not even adorned by the wedding ring. Thus another Mirandian tradition long cherished by admiring South Americans is demolished by the iconoclastic blows of Time.[40]

To an extent Miranda's morality was that of his age and environment. A fondness for good, red wine had not left him when he entered the French military service. His ideals of behaviour were far below those of his gifted fellow countryman, Antonio José de Sucre, the Chevalier Bayard of Spanish America. From a moral point of view Miranda may rather be likened to Miguel Hidalgo, the daring and unconventional priest who has been styled the "Father of Mexican Independence." In truth, some pages in the history of the Venezuelan patriot reflect the low standard of social conduct that prevailed in certain circles during the latter part of the eighteenth century. During his early career a code of sexual morality no higher than that which was occasionally followed by contemporary courtiers of the Continent was Miranda's. A diligent and unrestricted search through his papers would reveal material for a spicy article on his amorous adventures.

To the writer this has been emphatically demonstrated by the perusal of a large mass of inedited manuscripts concern-

---

[39] Robertson, "Miranda's Testamentary Dispositions," in *His. Am. Hist. Rev.*, VII, 292.

[40] An entertaining story that Francisco de Miranda, Jr., was the son of Lady Hester Stanhope was told by a Colombian littérateur named Medardo Rivas in a bit of historical fiction entitled "Los dos hermanos," published in his *Obras*. In that sketch (pp. 466-67) Rivas prints an alleged letter of Leander de Miranda that mentions a fortune left to himself and his brother by Lady Hester. This epistle was evidently concocted; for by that Lady's will drawn in 1807 she bequeathed her property to her brothers, see Hamel, *Lady Hester Stanhope*, Appendix A. See further *supra*, II, 225-28, where it is clearly shown that Francisco and Leander were sons of General Miranda by Sarah Andrews born years before he met Lady Hester. The legend that these children of Miranda were sons of that noblewoman has been kept alive by South Americans.

ing his travels. Portions of the diary of Francisco de Miranda describing his tour of Europe are unprintable because of their gross immorality. In fact certain squibs and memoranda which the writer found preserved in his papers might appropriately be consigned to a pornographic collection. On the other hand, such patent evidence of Miranda's acquaintance with the wanton manners of the demimonde has not been found in the material concerning his later life. Neither has there been found in his papers any evidence of illicit relations with women who belonged to the higher strata of society.

A story has been handed down by Venezuelans that, after Francisco de Miranda had perished, the English Government bestowed an allowance upon the mother of his children. The writer has found no confirmation of this, however, in the archives of England. In early manhood the sons of General Miranda proceeded separately to the land of their father. In an epistle to Leander de Miranda in 1827 Simón Bolívar confessed that a picture of Leander which he had seen had suggested "ideas that were both glorious and melancholy," for it recalled the physiognomy of his illustrious father.[41] Francisco de Miranda became attached to the train of the Liberator of northern South America. As the result of an acrimonious dispute over a love affair, the martyr's namesake shot the Dutch consul general in the first duel fought in Colombia.[42] In April, 1831, immediately after the battle of Cerinza, the unfortunate Francisco was executed,—a victim of the politico-military dissensions that began to devastate that country. Leander, who seems to have retained his British citizenship, eventually returned to Europe. He died in Paris in 1883.[43] Lineal descendants of the first Dictator of Venezuela still live in Italy as well as in South America.

Contemporary judgments upon Miranda's personality

---

[41] Bolívar, *Papeles*, p. 155. On Leander see further O'Leary, *Memorias*, XXXI, 453; Gutiérrez Ponce, *Vida de Don Ignacio Vergara*, I, 286.

[42] Boussingault, *Mémoires*, III, 188-90. On Francisco see further Posada, "Apostillas," in *Boletín de historia y antigüedades*, XIII, 90-94.

[43] O'Kelly de Galway, *Les généraux de la révolution*, p. 72.

vary widely. Estimates of his character were not infrequently distorted by prejudice. For these warped views he was himself in part responsible. His intimate friend Dr. Guthrie warned him that at St. Petersburg his frank manner of expressing his opinions on all subjects "without paying attention to a number of little formalities and considerations" that were observed at the Russian court had probably won him "as many enemies as admirers." [44] To a casual acquaintance Miranda could appear jovial and cordial, yet to statesmen and publicists he ordinarily presented a dignified demeanor. This hauteur veiled an analytical mind which not infrequently detected hidden motives. Throughout life he was an ardent and discriminating student of men.

During his mature years, however, Miranda displayed a large amount of personal vanity. Fond of praise, despite his critical spirit, at times he was inclined to lend too willing an ear to flatterers and to mistake adulation for genuine appreciation. Miranda's good qualities were alloyed with a mixture of bad. As has been indicated in this biography, when discussing his own life or plans, Miranda sometimes left the strait path of truth. He frequently capitalized at too high a value such reports as he received about the discontent of his compatriots with Spanish rule. In certain cases he misrepresented the facts; notably, as when, in addition to altering the order of his baptismal names, he designedly decreased his age. Among his manuscripts there still reposes an authenticated copy of his baptismal certificate that he altered by inserting a phrase which made his birthday four years later than the actual date.[45]

The religious ideas of Miranda were in part the result of his diverse experiences. Though he was by training a Roman

---

[44] Guthrie to Miranda, letter dated Oct. 28, 1789, Mir. MSS., vol. 18.

[45] *Ibid.*, 1; *cf. Boletín de la academia nacional de la historia*, XI, 22, where the baptismal certificate preserved in copy in the Mir. MSS. is printed but where the inserted phrase, "y quatro" is neither printed nor mentioned. A facsimile of the original certificate which the author obtained in 1924 from A. C., libro de bautizos de blancos, vol. 13, f. 196, is found in Miranda, *Diary*, p. 12.

Catholic, and though he received the sacrament of confirmation in the Catholic church, yet before he left the Spanish service he was denounced to the Inquisition because he entertained beliefs that were not orthodox.[46] During his travels in the United States he derided peculiar religious practices: adult baptism, public confession of sin, a puritanical Sabbath. Profoundly was he impressed by the toleration that prevailed in the Middle Colonies. Of New Jersey he wrote in his *Diary*: "Each person praises God in the language and manner dictated by his own conscience. There is no dominant religion or sect,—all are good and equal." [47] Yet the influence of his Catholic training was shown in his unfavorable reaction to the emergence of Unitarian beliefs in Boston. After visiting King's Chapel he recorded in his *Diary*: "A few days ago that fool Freeman dared to preach in the Anglican Church that the mystery of the Trinity was absurd, and that the Athanasian Creed was apocryphal. In another country the people would have burned him but here they only smiled, and he remained the preacher in his pulpit." [48]

Neither was he pleased with narrow sectarianism. "Damnation Murray," a Presbyterian pastor who prayed God to extirpate all other Christian sects, "in such a manner that in a moment he excluded all the Universe, except his own flock, from the divine protection," Miranda stigmatized as a "barbarian" and an "ignoramus." [49] Another interesting viewpoint is furnished by the fact that in New Hampshire he was displeased to see ecclesiastics exerting an influence in the legislature. He objected to the constitutional requirement in that state that a member of the legislature should profess Christianity.[50] To Samuel Adams the critical visitor pointed out an inconsistency between the theory and the practice of the Massachusetts constitution. "The contradiction," said Miranda, "which I noticed, was on the one hand, between admitting as

---

[46] Medina, *Historia del tribunal del santo oficio de la inquisición de Cartagena de las Indias,* p. 362, note 1.
[47] Miranda, *Diary,* p. 50.   [48] *Ibid.,* p. 120.   [49] *Ibid.,* p. 136.   [50] *Ibid.,* p. 134.

one of the rights of humanity the worship of the Supreme Being in the manner that seemed best to each individual without according by law predominance to any sect, and, on the other hand, the exclusion from legislative or representative office of any person who did not profess the Christian religion." [51] It would accordingly seem that his American travels induced Miranda to believe in religious toleration, while they did not necessarily destroy his faith in Catholic doctrines. Most significant of all perhaps is the fact that his journal reveals him as opposed to any sectarian influence in politics.

Although Miranda wished to have his child Leander baptized by a Catholic priest, yet there is nothing which demonstrates that at this epoch of his career his religious sentiments were particularly devout. One of his followers in the expedition of 1806 was so shocked at the attitude of indifference that Miranda took toward Protestant services which were held on board the *Leander* that he wondered whether his chief had any religious faith at all. "If, as a philosopher, he deems religion false," wrote Biggs, "as a politician, he should allow it to be useful." [52] However, the revolutionary had a high opinion of the influence exerted by Jesuit missionaries in the Indies. "The Jesuits have done more good to South America," he maintained, "than any other set of Men or Religious Order that ever went to that Continent. The civilized portion of the Community received *gratis* the best system of education and Literature they ever had—and the savage Indians the most rational Christian Civil and moral institutions that ever were applied since the conquest, for their benefit and happiness." [53] Perhaps the fairest judgment upon the religious doctrines of Miranda would be that he tended to drift from Roman Catholicism to Deism. Yet it seems possible that in his last mournful years he found consolation in the doctrines of the Church of St. Peter.

[51] *Ibid.*, p. 118.
[52] Biggs, *History of Don Francisco de Miranda's Attempt to effect a Revolution in South America*, p. 91.
[53] Miranda to Thompson, July 16, 1808, Mir. MSS., vol. 58.

The military ideals of Miranda were the result of study and experience. He was doubtless influenced by his service under the flags of France and Spain. Yet his leanings were generally toward the academic side rather than the practical. In particular, he studied such classic authorities as Montecuculi, Turenne, and Frederick the Great. Not without significance perhaps is the fact that among his memoranda is preserved an analysis drawn from Montecuculi of the circumstances when a commander should avoid giving battle. This authority maintained that an encounter should be avoided when it is apparent that the enemy will defeat himself; when a commander's forces are inferior to those of his enemy; when a commander expects aid; when the enemy occupies a strategic position; and when there is more to be lost than to be gained.[54]

Champagneux, who discussed military affairs with Miranda in La Force, declared that he was acquainted with all the authors who had ever written on the military art whether historians or theorists. That Frenchman expressed the opinion that for Miranda to excel in the art of war it would be necessary for him to add more experience to the large amount of theory with which he was acquainted. This critic added that his fellow prisoner was so imbued with the principles of military art that he would not willingly have consented to capture a town against its rules.[55] In 1806, when describing to his followers the dangers of a military career, Miranda sometimes ended his anecdotes by mentioning the honor acquired by those soldiers who endured privations with fortitude. After discussing the hairbreadth escapes which soldiers often experienced, he frequently descanted upon his own exploits and sufferings in military service. One of the unfavorable judgments of an American upon Miranda was due to his predilection for those persons who liked to hear him speak in that vainglorious fashion. "I believe," opined Biggs, "that vanity

---

[54] "Raisons d' eviter Batailles," Mir. MSS., vol. 29.
[55] Champagneux, *Oeuvres de J. M. Ph. Roland,* II, 409-16.

and egotism, which are qualities destitute of any recommendation whatever, are generally associated with other traits that
have no claim to approbation." [56] Upon his return to Venezuela the revolutionist apparently formed a low opinion of
the military ability of his compatriots. Tradition has it that
in a disgusted mood he once said that they ought to learn how
to handle a musket before fastening epaulets on their own
shoulders.[57]

An inquiry as to the source of the economic and political
ideals of Miranda furnishes an interesting problem. Allusions
and citations scattered throughout his papers show that he
had read more or less widely in such writers as Jovellanos, Vattel, Montesquieu, John Locke, and Jean Jacques Rousseau.
In 1809, after perusing a report of the Spanish publicist
Jovellanos respecting a project of an agrarian law, Miranda
wrote an appreciative note that may be rendered as follows:

"This is a work dictated by the purest patriotism. It em-
bodies profound and philosophic views concerning the bad
administration of Spain, particularly about the two important
activities of agriculture and commerce. It would do honor even
to Turgot, Adam Smith, or Montesquieu. This treatise is probably the cause of the infamous persecution that thrust Jovellanos into the dungeons of Palma in the island of Majorca
where he was detained for seven years." [58]

The academic attitude of Miranda toward the doctrine of
the separation of governmental powers was possibly due to
Montesquieu. Another philosophic writer who perhaps influenced the Venezuelan doctrinaire directly or indirectly was
Jean Jacques Rousseau; for his philosophy of the social compact seems to underlie some of Miranda's reasoning about political rights. In his arguments regarding the rights of Spain
over her colonies the Venezuelan was undoubtedly influenced
by the views of the Swiss writer, Emmerichs de Vattel, whom

---

[56] Biggs, p. 27.
[57] Gil Fortoul, *Historia constitucional de Venezuela*, I, 194-95.
[58] "Nota Bene," April 8, 1809, Mir. MSS., vol. 60.

he styled "the wisest and most celebrated of modern publicists." In a proclamation prepared in 1801 for distribution
among his compatriots Miranda cited Vattel's *Droit des Gens*
in support of his contention that Spain did not have a valid
title to the Indies. As an illustration of the mode in which the
doctrinaire leaned upon this jurist we will quote from that
part of the manifesto which followed a terrible indictment of
the Spanish conquistadors:

"Confounded and reduced to silence upon this important
matter, the sinister advocates of the court of Spain take
refuge in their inmost intrenchments. As a last argument they
ask 'how can you displace the government of His Catholic
Majesty when a proscription of three hundred years has given
it legitimate rights over you and your property?' But Vattel
and the consensus of opinion before him have thus responded
to these miserable defenders of usurpation and tyranny: 'The
Sovereign who pretends to be the absolute master of a people
reduced to slavery brings to pass a state of war between the
subjugated people and himself.' Have not the people inhabit-
ing the Hispanic-American colonies groaned for more than
three centuries under foreign oppression?"

The manner in which Miranda's reasoning about the re-
version of political rights to the people was based upon a free
use of the classic apologist for the English Revolution of 1788
may be illustrated by the same proclamation. He argued that
it was time to overthrow the frightful tyranny in the Indies
and to let "the real proprietors re-occupy their usurped do-
mains. Let the reins of public authority return to the hands
of the ancient inhabitants and natives of the country from
whom a foreign force has torn them. 'It is manifest,' said Locke,
'that the government of such a conqueror is most illegitimate,
is most contrary to the law of Nature, and that one cannot
overthrow it too quickly.' " [59]

The promoter of revolutions also drew inspiration for his
attack on Spanish colonial policy from a prominent French

---

[59] "(C) Proclamation," Mir. MSS., vol. 47.

economist and statesman. In a memoir dated August, 1798, Miranda thus quoted doctrines that he attributed to Anne Robert Jacques Turgot:

"Wise and happy will be that nation which first learns to adapt her policy to new circumstances, which will see in her colonies only allied provinces! Wise and happy will be that nation which first becomes convinced that her policy in regard to commerce consists in employing all her land in the mode most advantageous for the landed proprietor and in employing all her labor in the mode most useful for the individual who works! That is to say the policy of using land and labor in the manner in which each person guided by his own instinct would use them. If one would allow *laissez faire:* —all the rest is simply illusion and vanity. When the total separation of America from Europe forces all the world to recognize this truth and purges European nations of commercial jealousy, then a great cause of war will disappear from among men. It is very difficult not to pine for an event that should prove to mankind a good augury." [60]

So far as his ideas about the commercial policy to be followed by liberated Spanish America are concerned, Miranda had caught the spirit of *laissez faire*. Though he did not wish to establish free trade, yet he did advocate a considerable reduction on the duties levied upon goods imported into the emancipated Spanish colonies. In this particular he was a disciple of Turgot and Adam Smith.

Although Miranda's philosophy about the right of revolution was presumably influenced by the writings of Thomas Paine, yet some of his political ideas were in sharp contrast with those of that expatriated Englishman. Upon severing the political bonds which had so long united the Spanish colonies with the metropolis Miranda did not wish to establish a democracy but rather to form an imperial republic. During his travels in North America he was occasionally startled at the extremes to which he thought the spirit of democracy had

---

[60] "Plan Militar formado en Londres en Agosto, 1798," Mir. MSS., vol. 46.

carried the people of the emancipated English colonies. Although in a sense a democrat, yet he had monarchical leanings. Strange though it may appear, the Spanish officer who had fought against English redcoats during the American Revolution, was guided in his main governmental conceptions not so much by the example of the United States as by that of England. The *Diary* of his American tour demonstrates that even before he landed in London he had become a passionate admirer of English political institutions.[61] When Miranda made his remarkable tour of Europe he was no admirer of French doctrines, and although he became for a time a champion of French liberty, yet he later revolted against the ultrademocratic principles of the French Revolution. It is not misleading to say that Francisco de Miranda was an aristocratic democrat.

One of the most striking features about the mentality of Miranda is the catholicity of his interests. During his youth and early manhood, at least, his appetite for knowledge was insatiable. More than one well-informed person who came into contact with him during his remarkable travels commented upon the accuracy and the universality of his knowledge. In 1788 Professor Pictet of Geneva wrote to a friend of Miranda: "He is the most extraordinary man whom I have ever met because of the extent of his travels in the four quarters of the world, because of the information that he has thus imbibed, because of the richness of his conversation, because of his knowledge of history, literature, fine arts,—in a word because of a universality of which I had no idea and of which I had never beheld an example." [62] In a more critical spirit some years later Miss Williams thus described the general: "Miranda had a very lofty spirit, much general information, and a keen taste for literature. Further, he spoke several languages. My admiration for his character was so strong that I almost pardoned him for the boastfullness with which he

---

[61] *Diary*, p. 22.   [62] Pictet to Bordier, Sept. 30, 1788, Mir. MSS., vol. 15.

always talked about great principles." [63]

Scattered through Miranda's papers are numerous proofs of the variety of his emotional and intellectual interests. He collected maps of the Old World and the New and saved pictures of such diverse characters as Cagigal, Montesquieu, and Catherine the Great. Among recipes that he carefully filed away was one for the manufacture of mineral water. A jealously guarded prescription was one designed to prevent venereal contagion. He preserved memoranda on divers subjects: a description of the royal gardens at San Illdefonso; Hamilton's reports on the finances of the United States; the number of invalids in Greenwich Hospital; the revenues of Bengal; a comparison of the inscriptions on the theatre of Potsdam with those on the Haymarket Theatre; an enormous elm tree in Hyde Park twenty-two feet in circumference; and "Directions for to fight Cocks, Jamaica, 1781." [64] On the margin of a handbill describing certain museum exhibits Miranda wrote of an enormous rattlesnake that it was "a most beautiful animal possessed of an incredible audacity and ferocity!"[65] His critical spirit is illustrated by a diarial entry to the effect that upon visiting a so-called Roman bath he found it to be an English bathtub which had been chiselled out of a Roman sarcophagus.

One of the most comprehensive views of Miranda's mental traits, making allowance for time and circumstance, was that presented to the Revolutionary Tribunal by Chauveau Lagarde. When he spoke of his client's reputation the French advocate argued that if the witnesses had "differed among themselves in their more or less honorable terms of praise, they were in unanimous agreement concerning Miranda's great republican virtues. * * * You have seen that in disdain of rank, honor, and fortune, and to the hatred of the oppression and despotism that had persecuted him, he had consecrated himself almost completely to the study of science, art, and philos-

---

[63] *Souvenirs de la révolution française*, p. 98.
[64] Mir. MSS., vol. 3.   [65] *Ibid.*, vol. 24.

ophy, and to the study, the spread, and the glory of his idol, liberty, without which he believed that people could not attain true happiness." [66] The eloquent pleader likened Miranda to Socrates.

An interesting estimate of Miranda's personality is furnished by one of his followers in the Caribbean cruise. An officer named James Biggs declared that his chief occasionally acted like a teacher of ethics. This officer stated that Miranda professed to abhor vice and meanness in every degree and shape and avowed himself to be an enthusiastic lover of virtue. "To use his own language, he 'abominates tyranny; hates fools; abhors flatterers; detests pride; and laments the diabolical corruptness of modern days. He loves freedom; admires candor; esteems wise men; respects humility; and delights in that noble and beautiful integrity and good faith which distinguished the golden times of antiquity.' " [67] Yet a careful study of his career shows that although this promoter of revolutions was fond of inculcating lofty ideals, yet he often fell short of living up to them in practice. Like other men who have lived less romantic lives, Miranda was a poseur.

Here and there in this biography contemporary descriptions of Miranda's character and personality have been presented. Our image of his personal traits at maturity gains color from a picture drawn by the observant Captain Biggs. That officer declared that when seated General Miranda was "never perfectly still; his foot or hand must be moving to keep time with his mind which is always in exercise." A fine exemplar of temperance, Miranda always slept "a few moments after dinner," and then walked "till bed time, which with him is about midnight." He never complained about a poor meal, and used "no ardent spirits; seldom any wine." Dignified and graceful in his movements, the revolutionist could artfully dissimulate his feelings, except when he was angry. Captain Biggs, who was no blind admirer of his filibustering chieftain, thus depicts his personal appearance:

---

[66] *Plaidoyer pour le général Miranda*, p. 45.   [67] Biggs, pp. 100-1.

"He is about five feet ten inches high. His limbs are well proportioned; his whole frame is stout and active. His complexion is dark, florid, and healthy. His eyes are hazel coloured, but not of the darkest hue. They are piercing, quick and intelligent, expressing more of the severe than the mild feelings. He has good teeth, which he takes much care to keep clean. His nose is large and handsome, rather of the English than Roman cast. His chest is square and prominent. His hair is gray, and he wears it tied long behind with powder. He has strong grey whiskers growing on the outer edges of his ears, as large as most Spaniards have on their cheeks. In the contour of his visage you plainly perceive an expression of pertinaciousness and suspicion. Upon the whole without saying he is an elegant, we may pronounce him a handsome man." [68]

As already indicated, the revolutionary had gathered a splendid collection of books. A lawyer estimated in 1807 that they were worth almost nine thousand pounds.[69] In the autumn of 1810 this library was left at 27 Grafton Street in care of Sarah Andrews. In the last copy of his will Miranda stated that his books numbered some six thousand volumes.[70] In May, 1817, through an official of the English Government who tore the document out of a bound volume of Miranda's archives, Molini obtained the manuscript catalogue of his master's library.[71] In July, 1828, a well-known auctioneer of London named Evans placed a part of that collection on sale. Among the interesting items which attest the deceased owner's wide interests were the *Correio Braziliense*, Barry's *Works*, Buffon's *Histoire Naturelle*, and Milton's *Poetical and Prose Works*. A rare item was the *Biblia Sacra Polyglotta*. To make his copy of that learned work more perfect, Miranda had added to it the improved text of Montanus's edition of the Bible and the Apocryphal Books.[72] The auctioneer's note on

---

[68] Biggs, pp. 288-89.
[69] Kibblewhite to Davison, Aug. 17, 1807, Mir. MSS., vol. 57.
[70] Robertson, "Miranda's Testamentary Dispositions," *loc. cit.*, p. 290.
[71] Memorandum of G. Mayer, May 9, 1817, Mir. MSS., vol. 53.
[72] *Catalogue of the Valuable and Extensive Library of the Late General Miranda*, p. 11.

this part of the sale shows that some five hundred items brought almost three hundred and fifty pounds.[73]

Another portion of Miranda's library was sold by Evans in April, 1833. Among rare works which it contained were *Théâtre de l'Hermitage de Catherine la Seconde,* Quatremère de Quincy, *De l' Architecture Egyptienne,* and *Vocabularia linguarum totius orbis comparativa,* a work that had been undertaken at the order of Empress Catherine. Miranda's interests had even extended to manuscripts, for the auctioneer also placed on sale "the Correspondence of the Celebrated Marshal Keith with Lord J. Drummond, and Lord E. Drummond." [74] An auctioneer's note on the second part of the sale shows that it brought almost eight hundred pounds.[75] In accordance with the provisions of Miranda's will, one hundred and sixty-six classical volumes belonging to his collection were transferred by his administrator to the University of Caracas where they formed the nucleus of its library.[76]

Miranda was an assiduous reader. While in the Spanish military service he perused volumes concerning the art of war in ancient and modern times. At intervals during his first visit to the United States he read books about the history and customs of the American people. After reading Cotton Mather's *Magnalia Christi Americana,* he wrote in his *Diary* that it was "one of the most curious and authentic documents of fanaticism which one could imagine." [77] Throughout life he was particularly fond of reading about the history and literature of Spain and the Spanish Indies. His critical comments on certain works furnish clues for the interpretation of his mentality. With regard to Raynal's history of the Indies, which we now know was mosaic in its workmanship, he wrote on April 2, 1784, that he had perused the seventh volume of Abbé Raynal. "I find much Declamation, Argument, and Philosophical Re-

[73] *Catalogue of the Valuable and Extensive Library of the Late General Miranda* (British Museum), Appendix, p. 23.
[74] *Catalogue of the Second and Remaining Portion of the Valuable Library of the Late General Miranda,* p. 43.   [75] *Ibid.* (British Museum), p. 44.
[76] Landaeta Rosales, "El General Francisco de Miranda," in *El Universal,* Sept. 26, 1919.   [77] *Diary,* p. 95.

flection; but little Information, few Facts, and what is most unpardonable, these are seldom true, as I could show almost in every page. I wish he may be better informed concerning South America and the East Indies, but I own I am very doubtful." [78]

In the creole's fertile brain more than one literary project was formed that he never executed. In March, 1787, he wrote the following entry in his journal. "I presented Prince Potemkin with the *Historia de México* by Clavijero which I bought in Rome in order that it might be translated in England." [79] In a diarial passage dated May 9, 1788, Miranda wrote that he had reached his hotel in Utrecht, feeling very tired, at eight in the evening. "I went to bed," he said, "and lay there reading *Gil Blas* which certainly appeared incomparable to me." On the following Sunday he recorded this judgment: "To me *Gil Blas* appears to be an excellent composition; the book gives an exact picture of the life of a courtesan and of false appearances in this world. Certainly it is passing strange," he soliloquized, "that I have not earlier perused this precious book." [80] After reading Rousseau's *Confessions*, under date of May 17, 1788, his judgment was that although not well written, yet it was "original and contributed not a little to a knowledge of the interior of the human heart." Then he asked why he had not "read this book earlier?" [81] After spending the next day reading "with pleasure and profit" Miranda inscribed this sentiment in his journal: "Oh, my beloved books, what an inexhaustible solace they are for the alleviation of human life!" [82]

Other sources illustrating what may be termed Miranda's philosophy of life are found among his papers. On the flyleaf of a volume of his manuscripts that were presumably bound shortly before he left England in 1810 there are inscribed some stanzas which evidently pleased his fancy, whoever was their author: [83]

---

[78] *Diario,* Mir. MSS., vol. 5.   [79] *Ibid.,* vol. 10.   [80] *Ibid.,* vol. 13.
[81] *Ibid.*   [82] *Ibid.*   [83] *Ibid.,* vol. 1.

Saber poner en practica el Amor,
  que á Dios, y al hombre debes profesar,
  á Dios como á tu fin ultimo amár,
  y al hombre como imagen de su Autór.

Proceder con lisura y con Candór,
  á todos complacér sin adulár;
  sabér el propio genio dominár,
  y seguir á los otros el humór.

Con gusto el bien ageno promovér,
  como propio el ageno mál sentir;
  sabér negar, sabér condescender.

Saber disimulár, y no fingir;
  todo esto con prudencia has de exercér,
  para acertar la Ciencia de vivir.

In another volume of Miranda's manuscripts there is written on the flyleaf a passage from a favorite author which may be thus done into English: "Few matters are conquered by impetuosity; some are solved by force; many by suffering; and almost all by reason and interest." Another motto inscribed on the same page reads as follows: "Perseverance will carry out labors that have been commenced: do not lift your hand from them until they have been crowned with a fortunate result." [84] On the flyleaf of another tome of his manuscripts Miranda copied a quotation from Cervantes that runs in this wise: "There are no better soldiers than those men who forsake the study for the battle field. No scholar becomes a soldier who does not become a fighter of the best type; for whenever force is joined to ingenuity and ingenuity to force there is formed a miraculous combination in which Mars rejoices, which supports Peace, and which causes the Republic to advance." On the same page, ascribed to himself, is this moral maxim: "Cities are made neither by imperishable stones nor robust timbers nor artful walls. But wherever there are men who know how to defend themselves by their own

---

[84] Mir. MSS., vol. 45.

strength,—there are fortifications, there are illustrious cities!" [85]

An outstanding trait of Miranda was his persistence. It is not easy to find in the chronicles of filibusters or revolutionists a perseverance excelling that possessed by this Venezuelan patriot. To find a good parallel in the history of North America one must go to the adventurous annals of exploration. Miranda's perseverance was not unlike that of the indefatigable Frenchman, Cavalier de la Salle, who amidst innumerable, unknown perils with undaunted front explored the mysterious basin of the majestic Mississippi. To aid him to maintain a buoyant spirit in the midst of the frequent trials and bitter disappointments of his career Miranda was possessed of a vast fund of energy. His mind, if not his body, seemed always in motion. Another aid in the pursuit of means to accomplish his designs was a large degree of personal ambition. It appears that by September, 1810, he considered himself the leader who was destined to achieve the overthrow of Spanish rule in his native land.

Endowed with a visionary and doctrinaire type of mind, Miranda was much less successful in executing certain tasks that were intrusted to him than in plotting splendid schemes on paper. There is probably no better way to suggest this trait of his character than to notice briefly the comments of ex-President John Adams concerning Miranda's elaborate plan of 1798 for a tripartite alliance of England, the United States, and Spanish America. Adams likened the revolutionary promoter's project to "a Quixotic attack of a windmill," and said that Miranda was "either an Achilles, hurt by some personal injury, real or imaginary, * * * or he is a knight errant, as delirious as his immortal countryman, the ancient hero of La Mancha." The ex-President declared that it would have been about as plausible for a group of North American patriots to have proposed to the Duke de Choiseul in 1773 a triple alliance of France, Spain, and the United States against

---

[85] *Ibid.*, vol. 27.

England. He imagined that the Duke would have responded
by requesting those patriots to present their full powers, and
that when they failed to produce them he would declare: "You
have no powers; you represent nobody." [86]

With respect to the attitude of the English cabinet, Adams
asked if it were possible that Miranda should be such a con-
jurer as to bewitch Mr. Pitt and his colleagues into a serious
belief that South America was "to be revolutionized so easily
by Miranda and his two Jesuits?" [87] Somewhat too dogmat-
ically asserting that Miranda and his associates had no authority except their *ipsi dixerunt*, Adams argued that it was extremely improbable that a plan like Miranda's for a confederation of free governments could have been carried out in the
Spanish Indies. To him such a project seemed as chimerical
as "similar plans would be to establish democracies among the
birds, beasts, and fishes." [88]

Diverse judgments have been passed upon the career of
Francisco de Miranda. It would seem that in his public activities he was not always consistent but changed his ground to
suit the exigencies of the occasion. A clever opportunist, in
some particulars his attitude toward nations, as well as toward
society, may be compared with the attitude taken in the nadir
of his life by Aaron Burr. It should be admitted that Miranda
would not have fancied this comparision,—quite otherwise;
for he once said that Burr's ideas and character were as opposite to his "as two extremes can be." [89] In another letter to an
American friend in 1809 he deprecated the association of his
name with that of Burr: "You know I never had any connection with this strange Being, and much less compatibility of
Ideas or sentiments." [90] Though Miranda may not have realized it, a point of resemblance is that Burr evidently conspired
to separate a portion of the Spanish dominions from the
metropolis. Like Aaron Burr, Miranda was apt to become
disgusted with men and with nations when they laid aside his

---

[86] Adams, *Works*, X, 143-44.   [87] *Ibid.*, p. 141.   [88] *Ibid.*, p. 145.
[89] Miranda to Loudon, Nov. 2, 1809, Mir. MSS., vol. 61.
[90] Miranda to Ogden, Nov. 2, 1809, *ibid.*

schemes or postponed their execution. Thus it was that, after his disappointment at the outcome of the Nootka Sound Controversy, he turned eagerly to France in the hope that in their revolutionary enthusiasm her aspiring leaders might be induced to hearken to his schemes for the emancipation of the Spanish Indies. In the case of Miranda we are certain that he disavowed allegiance to the flag under which he had been born in order to promote the consummation of his designs.

Disappointed at the turn which events had taken in France, in 1798 Miranda again viewed England as the nation that was destined to carry out his designs. But when he felt that English ministers were holding him too long in the leash against Spain, his thoughts turned to France where Napoleon had become first consul, and then to the United States where he sanguinely expected to receive aid or coöperation. In view of his ruling passion, it is accordingly only just to Miranda to say that in reality he was not inconsistent. What he aimed to accomplish was the liberation of his native land: as an opportunist who wished above all else to promote this end, he was prepared to seek succor or encouragement from whatever nation held the best prospect of success. In this respect he resembles Christopher Columbus; for, like the great Genoese, Francisco de Miranda traveled from court to court offering, though he knew it not, a New World to European nations for conquest.

The rôle of Miranda may also be considered from the viewpoint of his actual conduct in military campaigns. Peculiar though it may seem, he was singularly unsuccessful in crucial operations in which he became engaged. Three events in his career, the battle of Neerwinden, the engagement with the Spanish coast guards on the Venezuelan shores in 1806, and the fateful Capitulation at San Mateo six years later,—all lent color, if not support, to the accusations of certain contemporaries that there was in Miranda a streak of cowardice. As already shown, because of his conduct at Neerwinden he was accused of treason toward the government that he was serving. His unanimous acquittal by the jury in a memorable trial before the Revolutionary Tribunal leaves no doubt that he had been unjustly accused. In that case the blame for his inglorious failure seems to lie rather with the weak morale and lax discipline of his untrained volunteers than with his defects as a general. The mildest judgment upon his attack on Venezuela in 1806 is that it was indeed quixotic; his flight from the Spaniards who attacked the unarmed schooners was more prudent than chivalrous.

For the fateful surrender at San Mateo the generalissimo was denounced and betrayed by his own compatriots. Nevertheless a careful study of this event in the light of his personal experiences with agents of the Spanish Government discredits the view that he was a traitor to the cause of Venezuelan independence. The fairest interpretation of his actions which can be made is that he wished to evade his implacable enemies and later to resume the struggle for independence. His faith in the movement for Spanish-American independence was unwavering. He was constant to his mistress,—Liberty.

The story of Francisco de Miranda's life is not simply a biographical sketch. He symbolizes a type: he had forerunners who seem destined to remain comparatively unknown; he had associates like Nariño and O'Higgins; and he had successors like Simón Bolívar, José de San Martín, and Antonio José de Sucre. A Venezuelan poet has aptly said that Miranda was more than a man,—he was an idea. A herald of independence, Miranda incarnates the idea which at one time or another animated many Spanish Americans of the early revolutionary era, namely, that they could not successfully revolt against their Spanish masters without foreign aid. He was a leading representative of those South Americans who suffered incarceration in Spanish dungeons because of their liberal principles or who pleaded to European cabinets for succor in the Lernæan task of emancipating their native continent from the domination of the Spaniards. Though Spanish Americans occasionally looked to France or to the United States, yet the power that they generally viewed as their most probable coadjutor was England. By a clever appeal to commercial and

Antonio José de Sucre. Portrait by Martín Tovar y Tovar. Palacio Federal, Caracas. Reproduced by courtesy of Señor Vicente Lecuna.

political motives Miranda often directed the thoughts of European or American publicists and students to the future of the Spanish Indies.

The epic of Miranda amply shows that during the period of the French Revolution and Empire the Spanish Indies was frequently viewed by England as a domain that should be separated from the Motherland in order to prevent France from revolutionizing it. The story of Miranda's life is a portion of the history of the attitude of world powers toward the disintegrating empire of Spain as well as a part of the narrative of the protracted struggles for the independence of Spanish America. Imperfectly known though it has been, the romantic career of this knight-errant of Venezuela has fired the imagination of filibusters and revolutionists. A unique filibuster, the chief apostle of Spanish-American independence, and a founder of the Venezuelan Republic, Francisco de Miranda will live long in the song and story of two hemispheres.

Another viewpoint from which the activities of Miranda can be judged is that of his self-imposed task as a drafter of constitutions. The fundamental laws that he undertook to frame for the emancipated Spanish Indies from 1790 to 1808 were based to some extent upon a study of the governmental systems then existing in America and Europe. To a degree which cannot easily be measured Miranda's governmental projects were affected by the political and constitutional notions of his foreign friends. Perhaps the most distinctive feature of those plans was that they provided for the establishment of a constitutional monarchy or of constitutional monarchies in the liberated regions.

Miranda's proposal for the establishment of a dictatorship in critical times was perhaps an indication that he perceived the need of the Spanish Americans for a strongly centralized government after the Roman model. Though certain features of his constitutional plans were patterned after specific provisions of the Constitution of the United States, yet in many essentials his model was the English Government. In that particular, as well as in respect to the notion of providing a censorship over morals, Miranda furnished precedents for the political ideals of Simón Bolívar. A study of the governmental plans entertained by the Liberator in 1819 and 1826 indicates that in certain constitutional matters he had presumably been influenced by Miranda's ideas.

In his mature constitutional projects Miranda made considerable allowance for the utilization of Amerindian institutions, such as the cacique, the *curaca*, and the Inca. He also planned to concede larger functions to the *cabildos*. Gil Fortoul, the accomplished student of Venezuelan constitutional history, has expressed the opinion, however, that in 1808 the creoles of Venezuela, who were intrenched in the town councils, would have strenuously objected to some of Miranda's constitutional proposals,—especially to his project to reënforce the *cabildos* by persons selected from the aborigines and the colored people of the country.[91] As has been indicated, in 1811 the Venezuelan patriots would not accept Miranda's constitutional views; for they fondly dreamed that Spanish Americans could organize and operate a government fashioned after the most liberal republican type. In general, they failed to realize that people who had never assembled in local legislatures like the inhabitants of the Thirteen Colonies, who had never sent delegates to inter-colonial congresses, and who had not yet organized such a political entity as a state, were scarcely ready for a régime like that of the United States. There is a possibility that if Miranda's constitutional plans had been accepted in South America, they might in certain respects have been shown to be better adapted to the genius of the people than the federal and republican types ordinarily adopted there in the era of emancipation.

The discovery of the lost papers of Miranda now makes it possible to consider his financial affairs with considerable exactness. As has been already shown, the expenses of his trip to Spain and the cost of his captaincy in the Spanish service

---

[91] Gil Fortoul, "El primer fracaso de Miranda," in *El Cojo Ilustrado*, XV, 328.

were met by his father. Although on more than one occasion Miranda alluded to his estates in South America and also stated that he had received financial aid from his relatives there, yet there is no proof that he regularly received an income from that quarter. In view of the vigilant watch that the Spaniards kept on his movements and of the small amount of communication which he was able to carry on with his native land, it seems improbable that any considerable sum of money reached Miranda from his relatives after 1790. It is clear that the itinerant colonel borrowed money from North American friends to help defray the cost of his peregrinations in the United States and Europe.

During his sojourn in Russia, Empress Catherine II conceded to Miranda a purse of gold. Her munificent present indeed enabled him to pay off debts which he had incurred during his extensive travels.[92] There is no evidence to show, however, that the French Government ever fully paid the general for his military services to the Republic. The spirit in which he tried to settle one of the debts that he had incurred in France may be illustrated by an extract from a letter of Stone to Miss Williams in which the former said of Miranda: "He will be so kind as to inform you, since you are his correspondent, whether assignats lent in the spring of 1793 can be repaid by the same number of assignats in 1796, or if a sum which cost me upwards of £120 sterling can be balanced by 20 shillings?"[93]

During the major portion of his career as a revolutionary promoter Miranda was dependent upon English sources of revenue. On certain occasions when he was much in need of money his friends Davison and Melville loaned him funds. His mercantile friend John Turnbull advanced him large sums on credit. Though the extant records of the English Government do not disclose that Miranda's name was ever inscribed on its

[92] A. H. Sutherland's Account of "Count François de Miranda," June 16, 1789, shows that by virtue of a letter of credit from St. Petersburg, which was sent by order of the Empress, Sutherland disbursed on Miranda's account at London from Oct. 30, 1787, to June 16, 1789, sums that aggregated £886-10-5, Mir. MSS., vol. 21.   [93] June 3, 1786, *ibid.*, vol. 43.

list of regular pensioners, yet during his sojourn in England he was either conceded lump sums by English ministers or was paid a stipulated allowance of hundreds of pounds per annum. He was indubitably granted money by Pitt in 1791; in the autumn of 1799 he was given a stipend of three hundred pounds per year; he was paid a substantial annual allowance by the Addington ministry from 1801 to 1805; and when the decision was reached to dispatch an expedition under Sir Arthur Wellesley to Spain instead of to South America, an arrangement was again made that he should be paid regular sums from the English treasury.

When the Venezuelan left London for his native land, in addition to a financial grant that had been made to his secretary, he was enjoying an annual allowance of seven hundred pounds. Though no adjustment was made by English ministers on his departure, yet that government ceased making payments to the promoter. At least there is no evidence available to show that it ever paid him a single penny after October, 1810. During his early career Miranda undoubtedly formed expensive habits; and later his finances were sometimes embarrassed because he generously advanced money to needy fellow countrymen who were interested in the fortunes of Spanish America. On certain occasions he was reduced to solicit money from quondam acquaintances or intimate friends. At other times, when rubles or francs or pounds were readily at hand, he lived in relative financial ease. It is indeed remarkable that a man who after 1783 did not regularly earn a salary or enjoy an inherited income was able to live in a comfortable or even a luxurious manner. Undoubtedly this is one reason why his life was marred by many acrimonious disputes about monetary matters.

Incidents in the career of a man who might not inappropriately be styled a chronic revolutionist indeed raise the inquiry as to whether or not he was engaged in an attempt to emancipate the Spanish Indies for selfish gain. Two different conceptions of Miranda's character may be entertained: one that he was a patriot; and the other that he was a mercenary.

The view may be held that Miranda was nothing more than an avaricious soldier who disposed of his services to the nation which remunerated him most generously. A Spanish writer has interpreted the rôle of Miranda in Venezuela in 1812 as being simply that of a shifty adventurer who betrayed the liberty of his native land in return for gold. That conception would place him on a lower level than a mediaeval soldier of fortune. On the other hand, the view may be held that Miranda was a pure-minded patriot. Dominated by this conception, certain Spanish-American literati have formed exaggerated estimates of Miranda's services to the cause of Spanish-American independence. Such writers have forgotten, however, that the persistent attempt to incite rebellions in Spanish America was with Miranda not only a ruling purpose,—it was an obsession. In fact, it became his profession. Miranda was a promoter of revolutions. The writer cannot agree with that Spanish-American author who extravagantly declared that in the task of the redemption of the world the Venezuelan revolutionist was "the Nazarene." [94] Indeed it is to be doubted whether, if that author had beheld the evidence that is preserved in Miranda's inedited papers, he could have retained his exalted opinion of the St. John the Baptist of Spanish-American redemption.

Bolívar is the Spanish-American leader with whom Miranda may most aptly be compared. Each of these leaders got his initial impulse from a sojourn in strange lands. In early manhood both men dedicated themselves to the task of Spanish-American liberation. In mature life both became convinced that among world powers England was destined to establish the most significant relations with Spanish America. Unlike Miranda, however, Bolívar made no sustained effort to accomplish the emancipation of South America through the aid and support of foreign nations. Yet when the epoch of Spanish-American independence actually dawned, Bolívar had a great advantage over his aged compatriot, for he had re-

---

[94] Rojas, *El general Miranda*, p. xi.

mained in close touch with his fellow countrymen; besides, his wide family connections gave him added influence and prestige. Though Miranda had dreamed of liberating the widely-scattered sections of South America, of establishing there a new family of states, and of giving them autonomous constitutions, yet the personage who did most toward the accomplishment of that ideal was Bolívar. It was indeed fortunate that fate intrusted this task to Bolívar's hands; for the Colombian Liberator had the rare persistence, the youthful magnetism, and the unresting energy essential to that Herculean enterprise.

As the narrative of his life has clearly shown, there were occasions when our Venezuelan hero must have been animated by mixed motives,—resentment against Spanish bureaucrats mingled with love for the land which gave him birth. Francisco de Miranda was both filibuster and patriot. Neither in his public nor private morals does he rise in our estimation when compared with the white-souled Argentine hero, José de San Martín, who was without fear and almost without reproach. To an extent Miranda's change from a faithful officer to a revolutionary plotter resembles the transformation of the Mexican Liberator, Agustín de Iturbide, from a royalist colonel to a rebel commander.

Miranda must be ranked as inferior to Bolívar with respect to lasting military and political achievements. The mantle of the unfortunate revolutionary indeed fell upon the shoulders of Bolívar, who after a bloody and protracted struggle became celebrated as "The Liberator." In truth, by virtue of genius, persistence, and good fortune the Liberator at last succeeded in consummating some of the designs that Miranda had sincerely cherished. Simón Bolívar became the uncrowned king of northern South America.

Still, among the founders of the Venezuelan Republic the great precursor of independence, Francisco de Miranda, occupies a niche which is not the least distinguished. As a promoter of revolutions, General Miranda holds a place in the history of Spanish America which is unique. In certain re-

Bolívar the Liberator. Portrait by an unknown artist. In the Suárez-Costa-Miranda Collection, Villa Selva e Guasto, Florence, Italy. Reproduced by courtesy of Signor Diego Suárez Costa y Miranda.

spects he may not inappropriately be compared with the puritan revolutionist Samuel Adams who has been styled "the man of the town-meeting." In other respects Miranda may be likened to that prophet of democracy, Thomas Paine. Indeed the martyred Venezuelan may appropriately be styled the morning star of the Spanish-American Revolution.

Miranda's international rôle was important. During an age signalized by transformations in the political order in both the Old World and the New, this Venezuelan was one of the first students of politics to discern the significant relation of the Spanish Indies to the bitter struggle that was being waged between the two great powers of Europe. His insistent activity stimulated the interest of both France and England in the future of Spanish America. It is to be supposed that his labors as a propagandist were not without influence upon the practical policy which English statesmen eventually formed in regard to the commercial and political future of Mexico and South America.

The achievements of Miranda have been commemorated in both America and Europe. In two hemispheres medals have been minted in his honor. He has been praised by historians and publicists, by poets and statesmen. Let it suffice to mention here two of the most signal of these tributes. Long after he had ceased to importune Napoleon, the notable services of the creole general to the French Republic were accorded signal recognition. By order of the French Minister of the Interior, in 1836 the name of Francisco de Miranda was carved on the *Arc de Triomphe* at Paris amidst the names of distinguished generals of the French Revolutionary and Napoleonic Era. The most fitting recognition by Venezuela of the services of Miranda was the unveiling in her national pantheon on July 5, 1896, of a memorial cenotaph erected at the right of Tenerani's stately monument to the Liberator. Under that cenotaph a marble tomb still awaits Miranda's ashes.

BIBLIOGRAPHY

NOTE

SOME SECONDARY accounts contain source material. On Miranda's career as a revolutionary promoter useful sources are quoted in Robertson, W. S., *Francisco de Miranda and the Revolutionizing of Spanish America, American Historical Association Report,* 1907, vol. I, pp. 491-510, Washington, 1909 (abbreviated in the footnotes of the present work as Robertson, *Miranda*). The abbreviations used for manuscript sources in the footnotes of the present work are given below.

A. SOURCES

a. *MANUSCRIPTS*

Adams MSS.	General Correspondence of John Adams, Massachusetts Historical Society, Boston.
Add. MSS.	Additional MSS., British Museum, London.
Am. MSS.	American MSS., Royal Institution of Great Britain, London.
A. A. E.	Archives du ministère des affaires étrangères, correspondance politique, Paris.
A. C.	Archivo de la catedral, Caracas, Venezuela.
A. G.	Archives du ministère de la guerre, Paris.
A. G. I.	Archivo general de Indias, Seville, Spain.
A. G. N.	Archivo general de la nación, city of Mexico.
A. G. S.	Archivo general de Simancas, Simancas, Spain.
A. H. N.	Archivo histórico nacional, Madrid, Spain.
A. N.	Archives nationales, Paris.
A. U.	Archivo de la universidad central, Caracas.
Ch. MSS.	Chatham MSS., Public Record Office, London.
Cub. MSS.	Cuban MSS., Library of Congress, Washington.
Eg. MSS.	Egerton MSS., British Museum, London.
Ham. MSS.	Hamilton MSS., Library of Congress.
	Henry Adams' Transcripts, Library of Congress.
I. & A.	Bureau of Indexes and Archives, Department of State, Washington.
Jeff. MSS.	Jefferson MSS., Library of Congress.
Knox MSS.	Knox MSS., New England Historic Genealogical Society, Boston.
	Lavater Collection of Portraits, National Bibliotek, Vienna.

Mad. MSS.   Madison MSS., Library of Congress.

Mel. MSS.   Melville MSS., Papers of Earl Bathurst, Pinbury Park.

Mir. MSS.   Miranda MSS., Academia nacional de la historia, Caracas. 63 volumes here cited as a continuous series in the order listed in the *Indice del archivo del general Miranda.*

Mon. MSS.   Monroe MSS., Library of Congress.

Pick. MSS.   Pickering MSS., Massachusetts Historical Society.

Prerogative Court of Canterbury Records. In the Principal Registry of the Probate, Divorce, and Admiralty Division of the High Court of Justice, Somerset House, London.

PUBLIC RECORD OFFICE, LONDON:

Ad. R.   Admiralty Records,

A. M.   Admiralty Musters,

A. O.   Auditor's Office,

C. O.   Colonial Office,

F. O.   Foreign Office,

S. L.   Ships' Logs,

T.   Treasury Records,

W. O.   War Office.

Sp. MSS.   Sparks MSS., Widener Memorial Library, Cambridge, Mass.

Stiles' MS.   Stiles' MS. Diary, Library of Yale University, New Haven, Conn.

b. *PUBLISHED MATERIAL*

I. BOOKS AND PAMPHLETS

Abrantès, Duchesse d', Mémoires de Madame la Duchesse d'Abrantès, vol. I. Paris, 1831.

Adams, J., The Works of John Adams, Second President of the United States, edited by C. F. Adams, vols. I, VIII, and X. Boston, 1856.

American State Papers; Foreign Relations, vol. III. Washington, 1832.

Annals of the Congress of the United States, ninth, tenth, and eleventh congresses. Washington, 1852-53.

Annual Report of the American Historical Association, 1896, vol. I. Washington, 1897.

Antepara, J. M. [and Miranda, F. de], editors. South American Emancipation: Documents Historical and Explanatory, shewing the designs which have been in progress, and the exertions made by General Miranda for the attainment of that object during the last twenty-five years. London, 1810.

Aulard, F. A., La société des Jacobins: recueil de documents pour l'histoire du club des Jacobins de Paris, vol. V. Paris, 1895.

Austria, J. de, Bosquejo de la historia militar de Venezuela en la guerra de su independencia. Caracas, 1855.

Baggsen, J., Timoleon und Immanuel. Documente einer Freundschaft, edited by J. C. Baggsen. Leipzig, 1910.

Barras, P. F. J. N. de, Mémoires de Barras, membre du directoire, edited by G. Drury, vol. II. Paris, 1895.

Bartenev, P. I., editor. Archiv knjaza Voroncova, vols. IX, XXX. Moscow, 1876, 1884.

Bentham, J., The Works of Jeremy Bentham, edited by J. Bowring, vol. X. Edinburgh, 1843.

[Biggs, J.], The History of Don Francisco de Miranda's Attempt to effect a Revolution in South America, in a series of letters. Boston, 1808.

Biographical Anecdotes of the Founders of the French Republic, and of Other Eminent Characters who have distinguished themselves during the Progress of the Revolution, vol. I. London, 1799.

Blanco, J. F. (and Azpurúa, R.), editors. Documentos para la historia de la vida pública del libertador de Colombia, Perú y Bolivia, 14 vols. Caracas, 1873-77.

Bolívar, S., Cartas de Bolívar, 1799 á 1822, edited by R. Blanco-Fombona. Paris (1912).

Bolívar, S., Papeles de Bolívar publicados por Vicente Lecuna. Caracas, 1917.

Boussingault, J. B. J. D., Mémoires de J. B. Boussingault, vol. III. Paris, 1900.

Brissot, J. P. . . . . Correspondance et papiers, edited by C. Perroud. Paris, 1911.

British and Foreign State Papers, vol. I, pt. II. London, 1841.

Browning, O., editor. England and Napoleon in 1803, being the Despatches of Lord Whitworth and Others. London, 1887.

Bulletin du tribunal criminel révolutionnaire, nos. 30-37, and suppléments. Paris, 1793.

Burke, W., Additional Reasons for our Immediately Emancipating Spanish America. London, 1808.

———Derechos de la América del Sur y México. Caracas, 1811.

———South American Independence, or the Emancipation of South America, the Glory and Interest of England. London, 1807.

Burr, A., The Private Journal of Aaron Burr, during his residence of four years in Europe, edited by M. L. Davis, 2 vols. New York, 1838.

Cartel entre las yslas de Cuba y Jamaica, 1781 [Kingston, 1781].

Casas, P. de las, and Others, Defensa documentada de la conducta del comandante de La Guaira, Sr. Manuel María de las Casas, en la prison del general Miranda y entrega de aquella plaza á los Españoles en 1812. Caracas, 1843.

Castlereagh, Viscount, Memoirs and Correspondence of Viscount Castlereagh, edited by C. Vane, vols. VI, VII, and VIII. London, 1851.

Catalogue of the Valuable and Extensive Library of the late General Miranda; Part the First. London, 1828.

Catalogue of the Second and Remaining Portion of the Valuable Library of the late General Miranda. London, 1833.

...Causas de infidencia: documentos inéditos relativos á la revolución de la independencia, edited by L. Valenilla Lanz. Caracas, 1916.

Champagneux, L. A., editor. Oeuvres de J. M. Ph. Roland, vol. II. Paris, 1799.

Chauveau Lagarde, C. F., Chauveau à ses concitoyens. (Paris, 1793).

————Plaidoyer pour le général Miranda, accusé de haute traison et de complicité avec le général en chef Dumouriez. Paris (1793).

Cochelet, A. P. B., Rapport fait au comité militaire de la convention nationale. Paris (1793).

Codazzi, A., Atlas físico é político de la república de Venezuela. Caracas, 1840.

————Resumen de la geografía de Venezuela. Paris, 1841.

Colchester, Charles Abbot, The Diary and Correspondence of Charles Abbot, Lord Colchester, edited by Charles, Lord Colchester, vol. II. London, 1861.

Colección de los decretos y órdenes que han expedido las cortes generales y extraordinarias desde su instalación en 24 de setiembre de 1810 hasta igual fecha de 1811, 2 vols. Madrid, 1813.

Custine, D. de, Delphine de Custine, belle amie de Miranda. Lettres inédites ... edited by C. Parra-Pérez. Paris, 1927.

Diario de las discusiones y actas de las cortes, vol. XV. Cadiz, 1812.

Diario de las operaciones de la expedición contra la plaza de Panzacola concluida por las armas de S. M. Católica baxo las órdenes del mariscal del campo D. Bernardo de Gálvez. Habana, 1781.

Díaz, J. D., Recuerdos sobre la rebelión de Caracas. Madrid, 1829.

...Documentos históricos sobre la vida del generalísimo Miranda. Maracaibo, 1896.

Documentos interesantes relativos á Caracas: Interesting Documents relating to Caracas. London, 1812.

Documentos relativos á los antecedentes de la independencia de la República Argentina. Buenos Aires, 1912.

Dumouriez (C. F. D.), Correspondance du général Dumourier avec Pache, ministre de la guerre. Paris, 1793.

——La vie du général Dumouriez, 3 vols. Hamburg, 1795.

——La vie et les mémoires du général Dumouriez, 4 vols. Paris, 1822-23.

Estados Unidos de Venezuela; acta de la independencia, MDCCCXI (Caracas, 1911).

Eustace, J. S., Le citoyen des États-Unis d'Amérique ... à ses freres d'armes. Paris, 1793.

——Official and Private Correspondence of Major-General J. S. Eustace. Paris, 1796.

Extrait du procès-verbaux des délibérations du comité de la guerre. ...Interrogatoire du général Miranda. Paris, 1793.

Farington, J., The Farington Diary, vols. I-VII. London, 1923-27.

Flinter, G. D., A History of the Revolution of Caracas. London, 1819.

García de Sena, M., translator. La independencia de la Costa Firme justificada por Thomas Paine treinta años ha. Philadelphia, 1811.

Glenbervie, Sylvester Douglas, The Diaries of Sylvester Douglas (Lord Glenbervie), edited by F. Bickley, vol. II. London, 1928.

Hamilton, A., The Works of Alexander Hamilton, edited by H. C. Lodge, 9 vols. New York, 1885-86.

Hansard, T. C., The Parliamentary Debates, vols. I-XI. London, 1812.

Hereida, J. F., Memorias sobre las revoluciones de Venezuela. Paris, 1885.

Junius (pseudonym, ascribed to G. Dulac, as well as to Miranda), À Jean Skei Eustace, se disant citoyen des États-Unis d'Amérique, et général de brigade des armées françoises (Paris, 1793).

——Reponse à une affiche signée le Baron; pour le général Labourdonnaye (Paris, 1793).

Kerner, J., Das Bilderbuch aus meiner Knabenzeit, Errinnerungen aus den Jahren 1786 bis 1804. Stuttgart, 1886.

King, R., The Life and Correspondence of Rufus King, edited by C. R. King, 6 vols. New York, 1894-1900.

Lavater, J. K., À mes amis (Zurich), n.d.

Lettres des généraux Miranda, d'Arçon et Valence au ministre de la guerre, imprimées par ordre de la convention nationale (Paris, 1793).

El libro nacional de los Venezolanos, actas del congreso constituyente de Venezuela en 1811. Caracas, 1911.

...Libro 4° de actas del supremo congreso de Venezuela en 1812. Origenes de la república. Caracas, 1926.

Louvet de Couvrai, J. B., Mémoires (in Bibliothèque des mémoires relatifs à l'histoire de France pendant le 18ème siècle, vol XII), edited by F. Barrière. Paris, 1848.

Machado, J. E., editor. Centón Lírico. Caracas, 1920.

Madison, J., Letters and Other Writings of James Madison, Fourth President of the United States, vol. II. Philadelphia, 1865.

————The Writings of James Madison, edited by G. Hunt, vol. VII. New York, 1908.

Mallet du Pan (J.F.), Correspondance inédite de Mallet du Pan avec la cour de Vienne (1794-1798), edited by A. Michel, 2 vols. Paris, 1884.

Manning, W. R., editor. Diplomatic Correspondence of the United States concerning the Independence of the Latin-American Nations, vols. I, II. New York, 1925.

Manuscripts of J. B. Fortescue, Esq., preserved at Dropmore, Historical Manuscripts Commission, thirteenth report, appendix, part III; fourteenth report appendix, part V; Report on the Manuscripts of J. B. Fortescue, Esq., preserved at Dropmore, vol. VI; Report on the Manuscripts of J. B. Fortescue, Esq., preserved at Dropmore, vol. VIII; Report on the Manuscripts of J. B. Fortescue, Esq., preserved at Dropmore, vol. IX. London, 1892-1915.

Minutes of a Court Martial, holden on board His Majesty's ship *Gladiator* in Portsmouth Harbor, on Friday, the 6th day of March, 1807, ... of Capt. Sir Home Popham. London, 1807.

Miranda, F. de, Copie de la lettre du général Miranda aux commissaires députés dans la Belgique (Paris, 1793).

————Correspondance du général Miranda avec le général Dumouriez, les ministres de la guerre, Pache et Beurnonville. Paris (1793).

————The Diary of Francisco de Miranda; Tour of the United States, 1783-1784, the Spanish Text, edited by W. S. Robertson *(Hispanic Society of America)*. New York, 1928.

————Discours que le général Miranda se proposait de prononcer à la convention nationale, le 29 mars dernier, le lendemain de son arrivée à Paris (Paris, 1793).

————Le général Miranda à la representation nationale. Paris, (1795).

————Indice del archivo del General Miranda. Caracas, 1927.

———Lettre de Miranda au président de la convention nationale, Paris, le 4 avril, 1793, l'an 2 e. de la République (Paris, 1793).

———Miranda à ses concitoyens. Discours que je me proposais de prononcer à la convention nationale, le 29 mars dernier (Paris, 1793).

———Opinion du général Miranda sur la situation actuelle de la France, et sur les remèdes convenables à ses maux. Paris, 1795.

Money, J., The History of the Campaign of 1792 between the Armies of France under Generals Dumourier, Valence, &c., and the Allies under the Duke of Brunswick. London, 1794.

Moore, J. B., A Digest of International Law, vol. I. Washington, 1906.

Morris, G., The Diary and Letters of Gouverneur Morris, vol. II. New York, 1888.

Mosquera, T. C. de, Memorias sobre la vida del libertador Simón Bolívar. New York, 1853.

O'Higgins, B., Epistolario de D. Bernardo O'Higgins, edited by Ernesto de la Cruz, vol. I. Santiago de Chile, 1916.

O'Leary, D. F., Memorias del general O'Leary, publicados por su hijo Simón B. O'Leary, vols. IX, XIII, XXVII, XXXI. Caracas, 1880-87.

[Palacio Fajardo, M.], Outline of the Revolution in Spanish America. London, 1817.

Pétion de Villeneuve, J., Réponse très succincte . . . au long libelle de Maximilien Robespierre. Paris, 1793.

Pons, F. de, Travels in South America, . . . translated from the French, 2 vols. London, 1807.

Poudenx, H., and Mayer, F., Mémoire pour servir à l'histoire de la révolution de la capitainerie générale de Caracas. Paris, 1815.

Pownall, T., A Memorial, Most Humbly Addressed to the Sovereigns of Europe. London, 1780.

El precursor, documentos sobre la vida pública y privada del general Antonio Nariño (Biblioteca de historia nacional, vol. II), edited by E. Posada and P. M. Ibáñez. Bogotá, 1903.

The Proceedings of a General Court Martial, held at Chelsea Hospital on Thursday, January 28, 1808, . . . for the Trial of Lieut. Gen. Whitelocke, 2 vols. London, 1808.

Quatremère de Quincy, A. C., Lettres sur le préjudice qu'occasionneroient aux arts et à la science le déplacement des monumens de l'art del' Italie, le démembrement de ses écoles, et la spoliation de ses collections, galeries, musées. Paris, 1796.

———Lettres sur l'enlèvement des ouvrages de l'art antique à Athenes et à Rome ècrites les unes au célebre Canova, les autres au général Miranda. Paris, 1836.

———Précis pour Miranda (Paris, n. d.).

Report on Canadian Archives, 1889, 1890, by D. Brymner. Ottawa, 1889, 1890.

Report on the Petition of A. Scott, House Report No. 72, 20th Congress, 2d Session. Washington, 1829.

Rickman, T. C., The Life of Thomas Paine. London, 1819.

Rojas, A., editor. Miranda dans la révolution française. Caracas, 1889.

———Miranda en la revolución francesca. Caracas, 1889.

Rojas, Marqués de, editor. El general Miranda, Paris, 1884.

Ségur, Comte de, Mémoires, souvenirs et anecdotes, vol. II. Paris, 1859.

Semple, R., Sketch of the Present State of Caracas, including a Journey from Caracas through La Victoria and Valencia to Puerto Cabello. London, 1812.

[Servan, J. M. A.], Notes sur les mémoires du général Dumouriez, 2 vols. [Paris, n. d.].

[Sherman, J. H.], A general Account of Miranda's Expedition, including the trial and execution of ten of his officers. New York, 1808.

Smith, M., History of the Adventures and Sufferings of Moses Smith, during five years of his Life. Brooklyn, 1812.

Smith Papers, Historical Manuscripts Commission, twelfth report, appendix, part IX. London, 1891.

Sparks, J., editor. Diplomatic Correspondence of the United States of America, 7 vols. Washington, 1834.

Stiles, E., The Literary Diary of Ezra Stiles, edited by F. B. Dexter, vol. III. New York, 1901.

Thiébault, Baron, The Memoirs of Baron Thiébault. Translated and Condensed by A. J. Butler, vol. I. London, 1896.

Thompson, W., Military Memoirs, relating to Campaigns, Battles, and Stratagems of War, Antient and Modern. London, 1804.

Torres Lanzas, P., editor. Independencia de América, fuentes para su estudio, primera serie, vols. I-III. Madrid, 1912; segunda serie, vol. I. Seville, 1924.

The Trials of William S. Smith and Samuel G. Ogden, ... in July, 1806. New York, 1807.

Universidad de Caracas, La, La intolerancia político-religiosa vindicada, Mexico, 1826.

Urquinaona y Pardo, P. de, Memorias de Urquinaona (comisionado de la regencia española para la pacificación del Nuevo Reino de Granada). Madrid, 1917.

————Resumen de las causas principales que preparon y dieron impulso á la emancipación de la América Española. Madrid, 1835.

Urrutia, F. J., editor. Páginas de historia diplomática (Biblioteca de historia nacional, vol. XX). Bogotá, 1917.

Vejarano, J. R., editor. Origenes de la independencia sur-americana. Bogotá, 1925.

(Viscardo y Guzmán, J. P.), Carta derijida á los Españoles Americanos. Por uno de sus compatriotas. London, 1801.

————Lettre aux Espagnols-Américains. Par un de leurs compatriotes. Philadelphia, 1799.

[Walker, A. A., and Miranda, L. de], Colombia, being a Geographical, Agricultural, Commercial, and Political Account of that Country. London, 1822.

Walton, W., An Exposé on the Dissentions of Spanish America. London, 1814.

————Present State of Spanish Colonies; including a particular report of Hispaniola, 2 vols. London, 1810.

Wellington, Duke of, Supplementary Despatches, Correspondence, and Memoranda of Field Marshal, Arthur, Duke of Wellington, vol. VI. London, 1860.

Williams, H. M., Letters containing a Sketch of the Politics of of France, 3 vols. London, 1795.

————Souvenirs de la révolution française. Translated by C. C [oquerel]. Paris, 1827.

II. Newspapers, Periodicals, and Publications of Learned Societies

I. *Newspapers*

The Aurora, Philadelphia, 1805-7.
The Baltimore American, Baltimore, 1810.
The Baltimore Evening Post, Baltimore, 1810.
The Barbadoes Mercury and Bridgetown Gazette, Bridgetown, 1806.
The Connecticut Journal, New Haven, 1806-8.
Chronique de Paris, Paris, 1793.
The Columbian Centinel, Boston, 1806.
The Courier, London, 1808-10.
Courrier Universal, Paris, 1795.
The Evening Post, London, 1806.
The Examiner, London, 1808-10.
The Federal Gazette and Baltimore Daily Advertiser, Baltimore, 1806-8.

Journal de l'Empire, Paris, 1810-13.

Journal de Paris, Paris, 1796.

The London Packet, London, 1810-12.

Le Messager du Soir, Paris, 1797.

Le Moniteur, Paris, 1792-98 (réimpression).

The Morning Chronicle, London, 1810.

The Morning Post, London, 1800-10.

The National Intelligencer, Washington, 1806, 1810-12.

Poulson's American Daily Advertiser, Philadelphia, 1811-12.

El Publicista de Venezuela, Caracas, 1811.

Le Publiciste de la République Française, Paris, 1793.

Le Rédacteur, Paris, 1796.

El Redactor General, Cadiz, 1814.

Relf's Philadelphia Gazette, Philadelphia, 1811.

The Richmond Enquirer, Richmond, 1806.

The Statesman, London, 1808-10.

The Times, London, 1808-10.

The Western World, Frankfort, 1806, 1807.

The United States' Gazette, Philadelphia, 1806-8.

2. *Periodicals; Publications of Learned Societies.*

The American Historical Review, III, 674-702, "Diary and Letters of Henry Ingersoll, Prisoner at Carthagena, 1806-1809." New York, 1908.

———VII, 706-35, "English Policy toward America in 1790-1791." New York, 1902.

———VI, 508-30, "Miranda and the British Admiralty, 1804-1806." New York, 1901.

... Anales de la universidad central de Venezuela, vol. I. Caracas, 1900.

The Annual Register, 1790, 1806-10, vols. XXXII, XLVIII—L. London, 1802, 1808-10.

Aurora de Chile, 1812-1813. Santiago de Chile, 1903.

Boletín de la academia nacional de la historia, XI, 21-28, "Archivo del general Miranda." Caracas, 1928.

———IV, 421-60; V, 687 ff.; VI, 977 ff., "Cronica suscinta del primer congreso de Venezuela en 1811," by E. A. Yanes. Caracas, 1921-23.

———III, 81-82, "Documento inédito del general Francisco de Miranda." Caracas, 1914.

———III, 73, "Documento que informa del paradero de los restos del general Miranda." Caracas, 1914.

———IX, 66 ff.; X, 42 ff., "Documentos relativos á las actividades revolucionarias de Miranda." Caracas, 1926-28.

———IV, 460-99, "Relación de Domingo de Monteverde al ministro de la guerra." Caracas, 1921.

El Cojo Ilustrado, nos. 109, 440, 469. Caracas, 1896, 1910, 1911.

El Colombiano. London, 1810.

Correio Braziliense ou armazem literario, vols. I-IX. London, 1808-1812.

The Edinburgh Annual Register, 1808-11, vols. I-IV. Edinburgh, 1810-13.

The Edinburgh Review, or Critical Journal, XIII, 277-311, "Emancipation of Spanish America." Edinburgh, 1809.

El Español por J. Blanco White, 8 vols. London, 1810-14.

Gaceta de Buenos Aires, 1810. Buenos Aires, 1910.

Gaceta de Caracas (Gazeta de Caracas) scattered numbers. Caracas, 1808-10.

The London Chronicle, 1785, 1786, 1806-8.

The London Gazette, 1808-13.

The Monthly Magazine, or British Register, vol. XXVII. London, 1809.

The Monthly Review, or Literary Journal, 1807, 1808, vols. LVII-LVIII. London, 1808-9.

The Political Herald and Review; or A Survey of Domestic and Foreign Politics, vol. I. London, 1785.

Sbornik Imperatorskago Russkago Istoricheskago Obschestvo, vol. XXVI. St. Petersburg, 1879.

The Weekly Register (edited by H. Niles), vols. I-IV. Baltimore, 1811-13.

B.   SECONDARY ACCOUNTS

a.   *BOOKS AND PAMPHLETS*

Academia nacional de la historia; prólogo á los anales de Venezuela. Caracas, 1903.

Alboise (M.M.), and Maquet (A.), Les prisons de l' Europe. Paris, 1845.

Amunátegui, M. L., Vida de Don Andrés Bello. Santiago de Chile, 1882.

Arcaya, P. M., Influencia del elemento venezolano en la independencia de la América Latina. Caracas, 1916.

Azpurúa, F. de, Breves observaciones á los recuerdos que sobre la rebelión de Caracas acaba de publicar en esta corte el Señor Don José Domingo Díaz. Madrid, 1829.

Azpurúa, R., Biografías de hombres notables de Hispano-América,

4 vols. Caracas, 1877.

Baralt (R. M.), and Díaz (R), Resumen de la historia de Venezuela desde el año de 1797 hasta el de 1830, 2 vols. Paris, 1841.

Barbé-Marbois (F. de), Histoire de la Louisiane. Paris, 1829.

Becerra, R., Ensayo histórico documentado de la vida de Don Francisco de Miranda, 2 vols. Caracas, 1896.

Bemis, S. F., Jay's Treaty, A study in Diplomacy and Commerce. New York, 1923.

Blanco, E., Venezuela heroica. Paris, n.d.

Chandler, C. L., Inter-American Acquaintances. Sewanee, Tenn., 1917.

Chisholm, A. S. M., The Independence of Chile. Boston, 1911.

Chuquet, A., La traison de Dumouriez. Paris, 1891.

Conway, M. D., The Life of Thomas Paine, vol. II. New York, 1908.

Copinger, W. A., On the Authorship of the First Hundred Numbers of the "Edinburgh Review." Manchester, 1895.

Coquelle, P., Napoléon et l'Angleterre, 1803-1813. Paris, 1904.

Damiron, A., Compendio de la historia de Venezuela. Caracas, 1840.

Danvila y Collado, M., Reinado de Carlos III, 6 vols. Madrid, 1890-1891.

Dauban, C. A., Les prisons de Paris sous la révolution. Paris, 1870.

Dávila, V., Diccionario biográfico de ilustres próceres de la independencia suramericana, 2 vols. Caracas, 1924-26.

————Investigaciones históricas, 2 vols. Caracas, 1923-27.

Drake, F., The Life of Major-General Henry Knox, Memorials of the Society of the Cincinnati of Massachusetts, vol. I. Boston, 1873.

Ducoudray-Holstein, H. L. V., Memoirs of Simón Bolívar, President Liberator of the Republic of Colombia. Boston, 1829.

Fernández de Béthencourt, F., Historia genealógica y heráldica de la monarquía española, casa real y grandes de España, vol. III. Madrid, 1901.

Figueroa, P. P., Diccionario biográfico de Chile, vol. II. Santiago de Chile, 1897.

Fish, C. R., American Diplomacy. New York, 1923.

Gayangos, P. de, Catalogue of the Manuscripts in the Spanish Language in the British Museum, 2 vols. London, 1875-77.

Les généraux de la révolution, le général Miranda. Paris, 1890.

Gil Fortoul, J., Discursos y palabras (1910-1915). Caracas, 1915.

————Centenario de la independencia; sesión solemne del congreso nacional, 5 de Julio de 1911. Caracas, 1911.

————Historia constitucional de Venezuela, vol. I. Berlin, 1907.

Goetz-Bernstein, H. A., La diplomatie de la Gironde; Jacques

Pierre Brissot. Paris, 1912.

González, E. G., Al margen de la epopeya. Caracas, 1906.

González, J. V., ... Biografía de José Félix Ribas. Paris, n.d.

González Guinán, F., Hallazgo del acta solemne de independencia de Venezuela y otras actas del congreso constituyente de 1811. Valencia, 1908.

———Historia contemporánea de Venezuela, vol. I. Caracas, 1909.

Grisanti, A., Miranda y la Emperatriz Catalina la Grande. Caracas, 1928.

Gutiérrez Ponce, I., Vida de Don Ignacio Gutiérrez Vergara y episodios históricos de su tiempo (1806-77), vol. I. London, 1900.

Hamel, F., Lady Hester Lucy Stanhope: A New Light on her Life and Love Affairs. London, 1914.

Hasbrouck, A., Foreign Legionaries in the Liberation of Spanish South America (Columbia University Studies in History, Economics, and Public Law, no. 303). New York, 1928.

Hernández, M., Sinopsis de historia de Venezuela. Maracaibo, 1914.

Historia de la vida y reinado de Fernando VII de España, vol. I. Madrid, 1842.

Humbert, J., Histoire de la Colombie et du Vénézuéla des origines jusqu'à nos jours. Paris, 1921.

Jiminez Arraiz, F., Panegírico del generalísimo Francisco de Miranda. Caracas, 1916.

Jomini (A. H. de), Histoire critique et militaire des guerres de la révolution, vols. I-III. Paris, 1820.

Landaeta Rosales, M., La casa histórica de la esquina de las Gradillas en Caracas. Caracas, 1916.

———Gobiernos de Venezuela desde 1810 hasta 1905. Caracas, 1905.

———Maracay (1697 á 1915). Caracas, 1916.

———El panteón nacional. Caracas, 1911.

———Riqueza circulante en Venezuela. Caracas, 1893.

Larrazábal, F., The Life of Simón Bolívar, vol. I. New York, 1866.

———Vida y correspondencia general del libertador Simón Bolívar, vol. I. New York, 1901.

Latané, J. H., The United States and Latin America. Garden City, 1920.

Lemly, H. R., Bolívar, Liberator of Venezuela, Colombia, Ecuador, Peru, and Bolivia. Boston, 1923.

Levene, R., Ensayo histórico sobre la revolución de Mayo y Mariano Moreno (Estudios editados por la facultad de derecho y ciencias sociales de Buenos Aires, vols. VIII and IX), 2 vols.

Buenos Aires, 1920.

Lockey, J. B., Pan-Americanism: Its Beginnings. New York, 1920.

Loo, H. Van, Voor Oud en Jong. Een edel Driemanshap. Amsterdam, 1888.

Machado, J. E., Rasgos biográficos sobre el general Francisco Miranda. Caracas, 1916.

Mancini, J., Bolívar et l'émancipation des colonies espagnoles des origines à 1815. Paris, 1912.

Manning, W. R., The Nootka Sound Controversy, *American Historical Association Report*, 1904, pp. 279-478. Washington, 1905.

Marshall, J., Royal Naval Biography; or the Memoirs of the Services ... , vol. X. London, 1835.

Martin, F. X., The History of North Carolina, vol. II. New Orleans, 1829.

Martínez, C., El hijo del generalísimo, episodio histórico. Caracas, 1878.

Maugras, G., Delphine de Sabran, Marquise de Custine. Paris, 1912.

Medina, J. T., Historia y bibliografía de la imprenta en Buenos-Aires (1780-1810), in *Anales del museo de la Plata, sección de historia americana*, vol. III. La Plata, 1892.

———Historia del tribunal del santo oficio de la inquisición de Cartagena de las Indias. Santiago de Chile, 1899.

———La imprenta en Caracas (1808-1821), notas bibliográficas. Santiago de Chile, 1904.

Mehegan, J. J., O'Higgins of Chile. London, 1913.

Mitre, B., Historia de Belgrano y de la independencia argentina, 3 vols. Buenos Aires, 1887.

———Historia de San Martín y de la emancipación sud-americana, 3 vols. Buenos Aires, 1887-88.

Moses, B., The Intellectual Background of the Revolution in South America, 1810-1824 *(Hispanic Society of America)*. New York, 1926.

Moses, B., Spain's Declining Power in South America, 1730-1806. Berkeley, 1919.

Navarro y Lamarca, C., Compendio de la historia general de América, vol. II. Buenos Aires, 1913.

Ofrenda á la memoria del general Carlos Soublette en su centenario. Caracas, 1890.

Ô'Kelly de Galway, A., Les généraux de la révolution: Francisco de Miranda..... biographie et iconographie. Paris, 1913.

Parra-Pérez, C., Miranda et la révolution française. Paris, 1925.

Paxson, F. L., The Independence of the South American Republics. Philadelphia, 1916.

Pereyra, C., El general Sucre. Madrid, n.d.

Petre, F. L., Simón Bolívar, "El Libertador." London, 1909.

Pezuela, J. de la, Diccionario geográfico, estadístico, histórico de la isla de Cuba, vol. I. Madrid, 1865.

Picón-Febres, G., La literatura venezolana en el siglo diez y nueve. Caracas, 1906.

Piferer, F., Nobiliario de los reinos y señoríos de España, vol. II. Madrid, 1858.

Ponte, A. F., La revolución de Caracas y sus próceres. Caracas, 1918.

————Bolívar y otros ensayos. Caracas, 1919.

Posada, E., Apostillas á la historia colombiana. Madrid, 1918.

Pownall, C. A. W., Thomas Pownall, M. P., F. R. S., Governor of Massachusetts Bay. London, 1908.

Procès-verbal. Paris, 1800.

Rafter, M., Memoirs of Gregor M' Gregor. London, 1820.

Randall, H. S., The Life of Thomas Jefferson, vol. III. New York, 1858.

Report on the Manuscripts of Earl Bathurst preserved at Cirencester Park, Historical Manuscripts Commission, no. 76. London, 1923.

Restrepo, J. M., Historia de la revolución de la república de Colombia, vol. III. Paris, 1827.

Rippy, J. F., Latin America in World Politics. New York, 1928.

Rivas, A. C., . . . Ensayos de historia política y diplomática. Madrid, n.d.

Rivas, M., Obras de Medardo Rivas, parte primera. Bogotá, 1883.

Rivas Vicuña, F., Las guerras de Bolívar, primera guerra, 1812-1814. Caracas (1921).

Robertson, W. S., "The Beginnings of Spanish-American Diplomacy," in the Turner Essays in American History, pp. 231-87. New York, 1910.

————Francisco de Miranda and the Revolutionizing of Spanish America, American Historical Association Report, 1907, I, 189-540. Washington, 1909.

————Hispanic-American Relations with the United States. New York, 1923.

————Rise of the Spanish-American Republics as Told in the Lives of Their Liberators. New York, 1918.

Rojas, Marqués de, Simón Bolívar. Paris, 1883.

————Tiempo perdido: colección de escritos sobre literatura y hacienda pública. Paris, 1905.

Rojas, A., Estudios históricos. Caracas, 1926.

————Historia patria, estudios históricos, origenes venezolanos, vol.

———I. Caracas, 1891.

———Leyendas históricas de Venezuela, 2 vols. Caracas, 1890-91.

———Los hombres de la revolución, 1810-26: el canónigo José Cortés Madariaga, el general Emparán. Caracas, 1878.

———Origenes de la revolución venezolana. Caracas, 1883.

Roof, K. M., Colonel William Smith and Lady. Boston, 1929.

Rose, J. H., William Pitt and National Revival. London, 1912.

Rubio, J. M., La infanta Carlota Joaquina y la política de España en América (1808-12). Madrid, 1920.

Salas, C. I., Bibliografía del general Don José de San Martín y de la emancipación sudamericana, 5 vols. Buenos Aires, 1910.

Sánchez, M. S., Bibliografía venezolanista. Caracas, 1914.

———El publicista de Venezuela. Caracas, 1920.

Scarpetta, M. L., and Vergara, S., Diccionario biográfico de los campeones de la libertad de Nueva Granada, Venezuela, Ecuador i Perú. Bogotá, 1879.

Schryver, S. de, Esquisse de la vie de Bolívar. Brussels, 1899.

Shepherd, W. R., The Hispanic Nations of the New World (*The Chronicles of America*, vol. L). New Haven, 1919.

Sherwell, G. A., Antonio José de Sucre (Gran mariscal de Ayacucho). Washington, 1924.

———Simón Bolívar (El Libertador). Washington, 1921.

Smyth, W. H., The Life and Services of Captain Philip Beaver. London, 1829.

Sorel, A., L'Europe et la révolution française, vols. I-III. Paris, 1893-97.

Soto Hall, M., Venezuela; ensayo de papel-moneda en 1811. New York, 1921.

Stanhope, P. H., Notes of Conversations with the Duke of Wellington, 1831-1851. New York, 1888.

Sucre, L. A., Gobernadores y capitanes generales de Venezuela. Caracas, 1928.

Tejera, M., Vida del general Francisco Miranda. Caracas, 1877.

———Venezuela pintoresca e ilustrada, vol. I. Paris, 1875.

Tejera, P., Manual de historia de Venezuela. Caracas, 1913.

Tooke, H., Life of Catherine II, Empress of Russia, 3 vols. London, 1800.

Torrente, M., Historia de la revolución hispano-americana, vol. I. Madrid, 1829.

Vaucaire, M., Bolívar the Liberator, translated from the French by Margaret Reed. Boston, 1929.

Viarz, M. de (pseudonym of Roergas de Serviez), L'aide de camp ou l'auteur inconnu, souvenirs des Deux Mondes. Paris, 1832.

Vicuña Mackenna, B., El ostracismo del jeneral D. Bernardo O'Higgins escrito sobre documentos inéditos i noticias auténticas. Valparaiso, 1860.

——La corona del héroe, recopilación de datos i documentos para perpetuar la memoria del jeneral Don Bernardo O'Higgins. Santiago de Chile, 1872.

——Vida del capitán general de Chile Don Bernardo O'Higgins, Brigadier de la República Argentina i gran mariscal del Perú. Santiago de Chile, 1882.

Villamayor, F., El general Don Francisco de Miranda. Buenos Aires, 1910.

Villanueva, C. A., Historia de la república argentina, vol. I. Paris, 1914.

——Historia y diplomacia: Napoléon y la independencia de América. Paris, 1911.

——La monarquía en América: Bolívar y el general San Martín. Paris (1911).

——Paris. Paris, 1897.

Villanueva, L., Vida de Don Antonio José de Sucre, gran mariscal de Ayacucho. Paris, n. d.

Wallon, H., Histoire du tribunal révolutionnaire de Paris avec le journal des ses actes, vol. I. Paris, 1880.

Ward, A. W., and Gooch, G. P., The Cambridge History of British Foreign Policy, vol. I. New York, 1922.

Washington, G., ... Calendar of the Correspondence of George Washington, commander in chief of the Continental Army, with the Officers, vol. III. Washington, 1915.

Wilberforce, R. I., and S., The Life of William Wilberforce, vol. III. London, 1838.

Winsor, J., Narrative and Critical History of America, vol. VIII. Boston, 1889.

Wright, T., The Works of James Gillray the Caricaturist with the History of his Life and Times. London (1873).

Zuñiga, A. R., La logia "lautaro" y la independencia de América. Buenos Aires, 1922.

b. ARTICLES IN NEWSPAPERS AND PERIODICALS

Acosta de Samper, S., "Traición y Castigo," *El Cojo Ilustrado,* I, 30-51. Caracas, 1892.

Aguilar, J. M., "Aportaciones á la biografía del precursor de la independencia sur-americana, D. Francisco de Miranda," *Boletín del centro de estudios americanistas de Sevilla,* año V, no. 19, pp. 3-25; no. 20, pp. 1-26. Seville, 1918.

Alemán, T., "Aus der Vorgeschichte der Mai-Revolution," *Die Kette,* IV (no. 13), 17-24. Buenos Aires, 1925.

Arismendi, P., "La muerte de Miranda; versos escritos en el proposito de concurrir á un certamen." *El Cojo Ilustrado,* V, 452. Caracas, 1896.

Artigas, P., "Nobiliario de Soria: la casa de los Mirandas," *Boletín de la real academia de la historia,* LXXX, 514-22. Madrid, 1922.

Clavery, E., "L' anniversaire de Valmy: une lettre de Pétion à Miranda," *Journal des Débats.* Paris, September 21, 1928.

Clavery, E., "Les archives de Miranda à Caracas," *Revue de L' Amérique Latine,* XVII, 113-19. Paris, 1929.

———and Parra-Pérez, C., À propos de Miranda," *Journal des Débats.* Paris, September 29, 1928.

Correa, L., "Miranda," *El Cojo Ilustrado,* XIX, 247. Caracas, 1910.

Domínguez, R., "Miranda en la Universidad," *El Universal.* Caracas, December 2, 1925.

"Entre los planes del general Miranda estaba la libertad completa du Nueva España," *Excelsior.* Mexico, September 16, 1928.

Figueredo, C. D., "Para pagar la cabeza del 'Traidor Miranda,' " *El Cojo Ilustrado,* XX, 654-57. Caracas, 1911.

"Gazeta de Caracas," *Boletín de la biblioteca nacional,* IV (no. 17), 513-14. Caracas, 1927.

Gil Fortoul, J., "Los movimientos precursores del 19 de Abril," *El Cojo Ilustrado,* XIX, 219-20. Caracas, 1910.

———"El primer fracaso de Miranda (con documentos inéditos)," *El Cojo Ilustrado,* XV, 324-28. Caracas, 1906.

González, E. G., "Tras la pista de Leleux," *Boletín de la academia nacional de la historia,* X, 196-98. Caracas, 1927.

González, J. V., "Los hombres del 5 de Julio," *El Cojo Ilustrado,* XX, 362-63. Caracas, 1911.

(Green, Harriet E.), "Historical Index to the Pickering Papers," in *Collections of the Massachusetts Historical Society,* 6th series, vol. VIII. Boston, 1896.

Hall, H., "Pitt and General Miranda," *Athenæum,* no. 3886, pp. 498-99. London, 1902.

Hemenway, H. B., "The Relationship of Masonry to the Liberation of Spanish America," the *Builder,* I, 259-64. Anamosa, 1915.

Key-Ayala, S., "Apuntes sobre el terremoto de 1812," *El Cojo Ilustrado,* XXI, 158-61. Caracas, 1912.

Landaeta Rosales, M., "La casa donde nacio en Caracas el generalísimo Francisco de Miranda," *La Nación.* Caracas, October 28, 1910.

———"El general Francisco de Miranda," *El Universal.* Caracas,

September 26, 1919.

———"Historia patria: las casas donde nacieron en Caracas los generales Francisco Miranda, Narciso López y Antonio Guzmán Blanco," *El Tiempo.* Caracas, July 20, 1899.

"Les papiers de Miranda," *Annales historiques de la révolution française,* IV, 412-16; V, 597. Reims, 1927, 1928.

Martínez, J., "Miranda," *El Cojo Ilustrado,* V, 508-9. Caracas, 1896.

Mendoza, C. L., "Á los manes del patriota martir, Don Francisco de Miranda," *El Cojo Ilustrado,* V, 510-12. Caracas, 1896.

Mendoza Solar, E., "Escudos de armas de Caracas, Miranda, Nueva Granada, la Gran Colombia y Venezuela, desde la conquista hasta el año 1911," *El Cojo Ilustrado,* XXI, 327. Caracas, 1912.

Ortiz, P. P., "El jeneral Miranda y Hamilton," in *La Revista de Buenos Aires,* VI, 74-87. Buenos Aires, 1865.

Parra-Pérez, C., "El testamento de Miranda," *El Nuevo Diario.* Caracas, May 14, 1924.

Pérez Díaz, Lucilia L. de, "Miranda, Precursor of Feminism," *Bulletin of the Pan American Union,* LXII, 1105-10. Washington, 1928.

Posada, E., "Apostillas," *Boletín de historia y antigüedades,* XIII, 90-94. Bogotá, 1920.

Rangel Báez, C., "La expedición de Miranda," *Cultura Venezolana,* no. 57, pp. 136-46; and no. 58, pp. 35-44. Caracas, 1924.

Robertson, W. S., "The Juntas of 1808 and the Spanish Colonies," *English Historical Review,* XXXI, 573-85. London, 1916.

———"The Lost Archives of Miranda," *Hispanic American Historical Review,* VII, 229-32. Durham, 1927.

———"Miranda's Testamentary Dispositions," *Hispanic American Historical Review,* VII, 279-98. Durham, 1927.

———"Viaje de Miranda por América y Europa." Translated by S. Key Ayala. *El Cojo Ilustrado,* XX, no. 476, pp. 398-400. Caracas, 1911.

Rojas, A., "Miranda," *El Cojo Ilustrado,* I, 344-46; 361-64; 384-86. Caracas, 1892.

Sánchez, M. S., "Miranda como filósofo y erudito," in supplement to no. 16 of *Cultura Venezolana.* Caracas, 1920.

———"Origenes de la imprenta en Venezuela," *El Universal.* Caracas, October 24, 1917.

Selva, S. de la, "On the Character of Francisco de Miranda," *Bulletin of the Pan American Union,* LI, 567-75. Washington, 1920.

[Sheldon, F.,] "General Miranda's Expedition," *Atlantic Monthly,* V, 589-602. Boston, 1860.

Tejera, F., "Ultimo sueño de Miranda," *El Cojo Ilustrado,* V, 509-510. Caracas, 1896.

Turner, F. J., "The Origin of Genet's Projected Attack on Louisiana and the Floridas," *American Historical Review,* III, 650-71. New York, 1898.

———"The Policy of France toward the Mississippi Valley in the Period of Washington and Adams," *American Historical Review,* X, 249-79. New York, 1905.

Valenilla Lanz, L., "De un libro inédito, segunda parte, democracia, capítulo I, la evolución democrática," *El Cojo Ilustrado,* XIV, 666-72. Caracas, 1905.

"Venezuela Acquires the Precious Miranda Archives," *Bulletin of the Pan American Union,* LXI, 216-18. Washington, 1927.

Villanueva, C. A., "Páginas históricas, Bonaparte y el general Miranda," *Mundial Magazine,* III, 231-39. Paris, 1912.

Yanes, E. A., "Semblanzas de próceres civiles; cuadros históricos; Doctor Juan Germán Roscio," *El Cojo Ilustrado,* I, 406-8; II, 15-16, 30-32, 50-52, 72-73. Caracas, 1893.

INDEX